A POLITICAL
HISTORY OF UGANDA

A POLITICAL HISTORY OF UGANDA

SAMWIRI RUBARAZA KARUGIRE

Formerly Executive Director of Makerere Institute of Social Research and Head of the Department of History, University of Zambia

HEINEMANN EDUCATIONAL BOOKS
NAIROBI LONDON

Published by
Heinemann Educational Books
P.O. Box 45314, Nairobi, Kenya
22 Bedford Square, London WCIB 3HH
4 Front Street, Exeter, New Hampshire 03833, U.S.A.

EDINBURGH MELBOURNE AUCKLAND
HONG KONG SINGAPORE KUALA LUMPUR NEW DELHI
KINGSTON PORT OF SPAIN

ISBN 0   435 94524 6   (cased)
      0   435 94525 4   (paper)

Dedicated to all those Ugandans, men and women, old and young,
whose efforts were, are and will continue to be geared towards
making Uganda a happy country for everyone to live in.

Printed by
Kenya Litho Limited,
P.O. Box 40775, NAIROBI.

CONTENTS

A POLITICAL HISTORY OF UGANDA

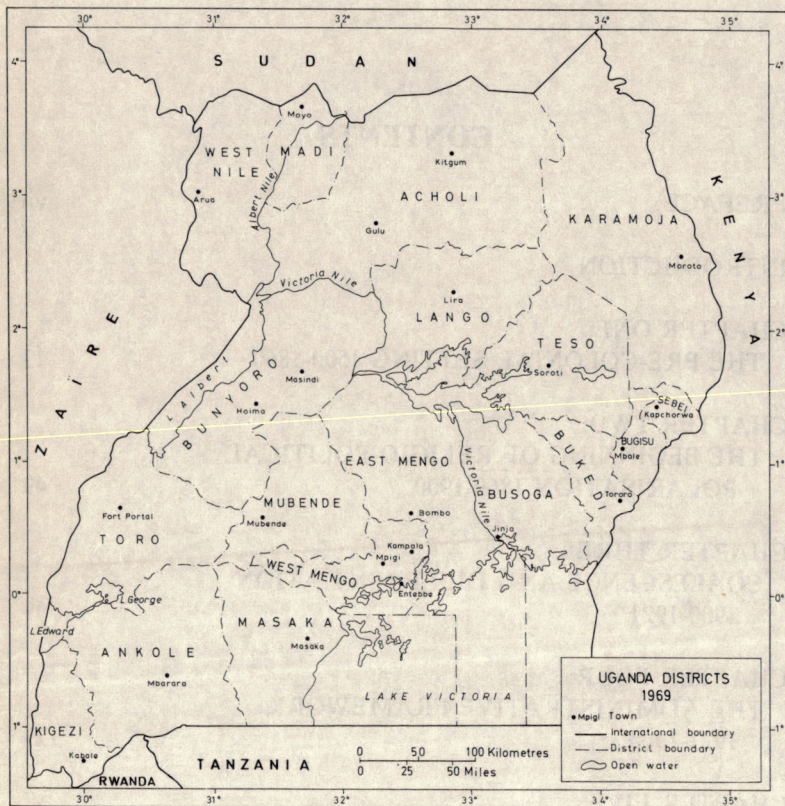

UGANDA DISTRICTS
1969

• Mpigi Town
―――― International boundary
------ District boundary
〜〜〜 Open water

PREFACE

In undertaking this piece of work I was mindful of the fact that this was an ambitious project and one that could not be fulfilled satisfactorily owing to circumstances beyond my, or any one's, control. It will become immediately obvious that the second part of the Introduction is incomplete in regard to the content of information that it gives about Ugandan societies in pre-colonial times and so also is Chapter One in this respect. This is due to two major factors. The first is that our researches on the various communities of Uganda is far from complete so that for some societies we know almost next to nothing of their history. Secondly, even where some research has been done, some of the conclusions reached are still tentative as will become evident when we use Seminar Papers as source material. Some of these researchers were, and in some cases are, carrying out further researches in order to polish up their findings and bring them up to what could be regarded as finished products. It was obviously not possible to keep track of all these researchers or to know the degree of completeness that their endeavours had achieved. To this extent therefore I admit that it is a questionable procedure to use provisional conclusions as material in a work of this nature. But this could not be helped as our aim is to get at least a rough picture of Ugandan societies using, as we must, the information that is available to us.

To undertake to write a history of a country whose societies are so different, almost in all respects, is a task that imposes its own limitations. This means that the historian has to choose what aspects of history appear to be important and this judgement is inevitably arbitrary in many ways. But then any interpretation of history involves attaching different degrees of importance to *historical facts* and such degrees are established by historians and not by the facts themselves. To say this is not to say that historians make history, because they do not; it only means that, given a number of facts, different historians will give them different interpretations and this should surprise no one since interpretation also involves personal judgement. History would indeed be a dreary subject if this were not so.

I make no pretence at being a "detached" recorder of the events that are narrated in the following pages as this work is not an "academic" exercise, particularly the last two chapters. This is because most of this work is about a country which is my home and people who are my countrymen and for this reason I cannot be a detached observer of their successes and failures because, in a fundamental way, these are also my successes and failures. To say this, however, is not to say that one should distort the happenings that one finds disagreeable or magnify those that are not. This would be a task of a political activist and not that of a historian. To quote one of the world's greatest minds that this century has produced:

> "Since I do not believe that a person without a bias exists, I think the best that can be done with a large scale history is to admit one's bias and for the dissatisfied readers to look for other writers to express an opposite bias. Which bias is nearer to the truth must be left to posterity."*

Bertrand Russell was referring to his *History of Western Philosophy* the excellence and magnitude of which the following pages do not even pretend to approximate, but the underlying principle is the same. I merely admit the obvious fact that my interpretation of such events as I narrate in these pages bears my own ideas and personality, neither of which are as absolutely objective in the same sense as the answers which issue out of computers.

The first drafts of this work were read by Mr. Lwanga-Lunyiigo, M.A. (Legon) and I am deeply indebted to him for his discerning criticisms from which I have benefited greatly.

---

*The Autobiography of Bertrand Russell, Vol. II, 1914–1944 (London, 1968) p. 223–4.

INTRODUCTION

In an undertaking of this nature, the first problem one has to resolve is to establish a starting point which has got some logical significance for the body of the whole work. One could, for instance, start as far back in history as the Stone Age and work forwards. I did not consider that the labour involved in making this my starting point would be justified by the returns, for this part of our history is not strictly essential to the theme of the present work. I decided to start at a point when the present Ugandan Societies began to take their modern shape and for this reason the date around 1500 AD was chosen as the starting point for reasons that are explained below.

Some questions might be asked about the legitimacy of writing a history of Uganda extending back into the 16th century or so when in fact the country of that name came into existence only at the turn of the 19th century and even then as a result of European intrusion. By the logic of this argument the history of Uganda begins from about 1900 onwards. But this would be to accord more importance to the form rather than to the substance of the subject. Governments as well as nations come into being just because there are people who form them. By the time the territory known as Uganda was given definite geographical boundaries, the people who live there, or more accurately their ancestors, were living there. So the people existed before the legal and other colonial formulations which gave definite limits to the country we now know as Uganda. This is almost axiomatic. It is true that the geographical limits of Uganda were imposed on Ugandans by the British: that is the form. But the substance—the people—were already there and not through the agency of any colonial policy but on their own initiative and at the behest of factors that have brought different peoples into different territories the world over and throughout history. There is a comic irony in beginning the history of Uganda from the arrival of Jackson, Lugard and others just because their interpreters mispronounced the name of the kingdom of Buganda as a result of which the whole country obtained its name.

There is yet another fundamental justification for this line of argument. For centuries before the coming of colonial rule many Ugandan communities shared common experiences and influenced each other in various ways as we shall attempt to show in the subsequent pages. Thus for Ugandans, as for most peoples of Africa and elsewhere, the history of their people predates the creation of the single state in which they came to live. For that reason this study, which is much more about the people's history rather than about the history of the boundaries of their country, is justified. It is also possible to say that the pre-colonial history of Uganda is best understood or studied as different histories of the different communities that were to be brought under a single administration by the British. There is a large measure of truth in this. But since these societies had so much to do with each other, whether in war or in peace time, it is still valid to group them together on account of their shared historical experience.

For the history of Uganda there is a major event which, either at the end of the 15th or the beginning of the 16th century, was of paramount importance in relation to the settlement of the different parts of Uganda by its modern inhabitants and to the formation of social and political institutions there. We refer to the migration of the Luo-speaking peoples from the southern provinces of the republic of the Sudan into north western Uganda during that period.[1] According to the available sources, the original homeland of these people was the grassland plains of the present Equatoria and the eastern parts of Bahr-el-Ghazal provinces of the Sudan although even this has not yet met with unanimous agreement of the historians.[2] Then towards the end of the 15th century some of these Luo-speaking people started on their southward migration towards the areas around Juba and Nimule. The cause of this migration is not known but it was part of the wider and gradual social process of the movement of peoples from the north southwards. Just as the same period saw the emergence of the states of Luba, Lunda and Kuba in Central Africa, this migration was part of the transformation that came about as a result of internal developments within these societies and regions of the continent. Several factors have been postulated as possible causes of this migration. Thus overpopulation, overstocking and soil erosion, social or political disagreements, and so on, have been suggested as possible causes of this event, that is, either any one of them, a combination of some of them or all of them. It is so far not possible to pin down the precise causes of this migration and it probably will never be possible to do so.

What seems to be certain is that the main party of these immigrants continued to move southwards along the Nile and to have further divided at Pubungu (an area usually identified with Pakwach of modern northern Uganda). As a result of this division one group spread out to colonise lands occupied by Sudanic-speaking peoples: the Lendu, Okebo and Madi groups and over these peoples the immigrants proceeded to establish limited forms of chiefships in the present West Nile district of Uganda. Another group continued to travel southwards, crossed the Albert Nile, and invaded Bunyoro and the Babito dynasty founded. The third group stayed at the dispersal centre at Pakwach for some period and eventually moved inland through eastern Uganda and finally most of them arrived in eastern Kenya. Each of these three movements is important for the history of Uganda not only because they contributed to the peopling of the country by its modern inhabitants but also because they had a profound effect on the social and political organization of the societies that were to evolve. For the sake of clarity and at the risk of the contingent danger of seeming to oversimplify a fundamentally complex subject, we shall briefly outline what these effects were by taking each movement in turn.

For our purpose, the major importance of those of the migrants who stayed on in northern Uganda lies in the great impact they had in spreading the Luo language and in the expansion which led to the effective occupation of Acholi, Lango and West Nile where their impact was most felt. The coalescence of the different elements that form most of the modern societies of northern Uganda owes a great deal to this group of immigrants. These societies, moreover, assumed their permanent identities after the arrival of the Luo speakers into the area.

The group that migrated to Bunyoro can reasonably be divided into two sub-groups: the party that actually set up the ruling house of Bunyoro—better known to history as the Babito—and the other party that settled in the northern part of that kingdom, the area known as Chope in Bantu speech or Pawir among the Luo speakers. The primary reason for this division is that those who founded the kingdom of Bunyoro lost their language and their way of life and were thus culturally absorbed by the Bantu speakers over whom they established their rule whereas those who stayed in Pawir (Chope) kept their culture more or less intact. Furthermore their migration out of Bunyoro sometime towards the end of the 17th century had important consequences on the subsequent developments in northern and eastern Uganda.

To take the question of the Babito first, we are faced with the problem of determining whether their advent in Bunyoro was an invasion or just a peaceful settlement. But before an attempt can be made to estimate—and we can do no more than this, given the present state of our knowledge—the nature of the Babito's advent into the area, it is best to examine the circumstances obtaining in the region prior to their arrival.

In the area covered by the present Ugandan districts of Bunyoro, Toro, Ankole and Mubende there exists a strong tradition about the "semi-legendary" Bacwezi rulers of the distant past who ruled the area as an empire before the Luo speakers arrived into the area. These rulers are referred to as "semi-legendary" not because they did not exist but because of what the traditions say about these rulers themselves and, in particular, because of the superhuman achievements believed to have been accomplished by them and, finally, because subsequent to their departure these rulers were deified and worshipped right into the colonial period. It is now generally accepted by historians that the Bacwezi did in fact exist and had a loose empire in this region although the precise extent of this empire is not, and perhaps shall never be, known. All these traditions are united in identifying the capital of that empire to have been Bigo bya Mugyenyi[3] and the Ntutsi area and these sites have since the 1950's been proved authentic by archaeological excavations and have been found to be consistent with a pastoral culture such as the Bacwezi are said to have possessed. It would seem that this empire was extremely loose in an administrative and military sense and this too seems to be in accord with a non-expanding state whose primary occupation was the preservation of the cattle within their borders such as the Bacwezi state appears to have been. The fact that these rulers were compelled to construct defensive forts—and these are what the Bigo were—indicates that external threats had made such measures necessary. But whereas such forts could have afforded the defenders a last line of defence against a determined onslaught, they could hardly be effective in keeping the empire's integrity unless they were backed by an effective military organisation which the Bacwezi do not seem to have developed. Thus it would seem that towards the end of the 15th century the Bacwezi ruled over a loose empire whose centre was the grazing lands of Bwera (now in western Buganda) and that this centre was the area where they exercised immediate and effective influence whereas in the rest of the empire, their rule was more formal or nominal than actual.

Against this background we can estimate the impact of the Luo upon this loose empire. There are two ways of looking at the advent of these immigrants into the empire of the Bacwezi. One way is to say that the empire of the Bacwezi had disintegrated on its own prior to the arrival of the Luo-speaking immigrants so that these latter had nothing to do with the process of disintegration and that perhaps this disintegration facilitated the peaceful settlement of the new arrivals. This view presupposes that the causes of disintegration were internal or, that if they were external, their source is unknown but unrelated to the migration in question. Another way of looking at this question is to say that the advent of the Luo was an invasion which was the cause of the disintegration of the Bacwezi empire. I confine this interpretation to two alternatives because I believe that the third—that the arrival of the Luo was the occasion rather than the cause of the break up of the Bacwezi empire—would be very convenient but specious and difficult to sustain even remotely with any kind of evidence.

In order to adopt the first proposition with any degree of certainty, it would be necessary to adduce from these traditions some evidence of internal strains that led to the disintegration of the Bacwezi state or to gauge some external factors, in the period preceding the advent of the Babito, that could have led to the break up of the empire. We do not find such evidence in these traditions and we have therefore to look at the second alternative for a possible answer. This of course is not to suggest that the absence of such evidence is in itself conclusive proof that the Bacwezi empire could not have broken up owing to either an internal or external stimulus. After all, the nature of oral evidence is such that one cannot dismiss these possibilities out of hand. But this is not the point. The point is that one can adduce from these traditions evidence that seems to support the conquest theory to the exclusion of the peaceful settlement alternative.

In order to get a proper perspective it is necessary to examine the second alternative by reference to what the traditions say about the end of the Bacwezi rule. According to Nyakatura and Katate and Kamugungunu—and these are the earliest and most copious recorders of this period of this area's history—the Bacwezi simply left their empire and "disappeared" in disgust because their subjects had become disobedient and openly contemptuous of their authority and also because the stream of fortune-tellers which was consulted by the Bacwezi rulers in rapid succession foretold misfortunes that were about to befall the dynasty. This is the essence of the traditions which "explain" the end of the Bacwezi rule in this region. The suggestion that the Bacwezi "left" their kingdom because their subjects had rebelled against them seems to be inconsistent with the fact that they were to be worshipped soon after their departure and by the same "rebellious" subjects. Additionally, this is a region that has almost no tradition or precedent of mass rebellion against the rulers who succeeded the Bacwezi and one can therefore reasonably infer that even during the rule of the Bacwezi no such rebellion took place. It is perhaps not without significance that, according to these traditions, many of the fortune-tellers who foretold the doom that was about to befall the Bacwezi were procured from the north of Lake Kyoga, from which direction the Luo invaders were to come. Moreover, it is significant that both Bunyoro and Ankole traditions also claim that their new rulers (after the Bacwezi) were of "Bukiri" parentage. Thus Mpuga-Rukidi (the founder of the Babito dynasty in Bunyoro) who is said to have been born of a Nilotic (Mukiri) mother and Ndahura, from whom Ankole traces the descent of their rulers, is said to have had several children in "Bukiri' and by Nilotic women. It is perhaps necessary to observe that "Bukiri" (the country) and "Bakiri" (the people) in Bunyoro and Ankole referred to the whole of the northern province of Uganda and to Teso and Bukedi districts of eastern Uganda and this is the general area through which the Luo speakers passed before they arrived in Bunyoro.

One may also refer to the concerted effort of this region's traditions to forge a genetic link between the Bacwezi and the dynasties which replaced them. It is fair to say that the manner in which this genetic link is said to exist is comparatively easy to break down but the point is that this attempt was made at all. It seems that this effort was made in order to establish the legitimacy of the new rulers. It is most unlikely that this was done without official encouragement and this was sound politics because after the initial conquest it would have been necessary for the Babito to win the acceptance of the people by linking themselves genetically to the rulers they had just supplanted.

Finally, one may also refer to a historical fact. This is the fact that to the south of what became the kingdom of Bunyoro, there simultaneously developed several kingdoms—Ankole, Buganda, Burundi, Rwanda, Karagwe, Kyamutwara, Ihangiro, etc. The point is that if the advent of the Luo speakers in Bunyoro had been a peaceful one, one would have to find an explanation for the sudden desire of all these societies to organise themselves in more coherent and larger political units at the same time as the Luo arrived to the north of their lands. It is contended that these states were set up as defensive units against the invaders and that they succeeded in arresting the Luo drive southwards. To explain away the development of these kingdoms as merely a coincidence would be an unjustifiable oversimplification. All these considerations taken together suggest that the region's traditions tend to conceal the reason that made the Bacwezi lose their power by oblique and mystical explanations.

It would seem therefore that the Luo immigrants who made their way to what came to be known as Bunyoro were a conquering people and that their advent in that area had the repercussion of sending other groups farther south—the groups which fled because, for a variety of reasons, they could not live under the new rulers—and that the result of these movements was the formation of these other states. To explain away the defeat of the displaced rulers whom the population may have liked–probably by default since the incidence of their rule seems to have been very light and of not too long a duration—their subjects could be forgiven for saying that they had "disappeared."

The Babito themselves, as the rulers of Bunyoro came to be known in their new linguistic context, established themselves in Bunyoro and one of the families among the people who moved southwards in their wake founded the kingdom of Ankole as well as other kingdoms of north–western Tanzania (mainland). Then, during the same momentous period, the same family that had established its rule in Bunyoro founded the kingdom of Buganda. It is perhaps necessary to note that whereas the traditions of Buganda and Bunyoro are in agreement about how and by whom the kingdom of Buganda was founded, modern Baganda historians have come out against these traditions for reasons that seem to be more emotional than historical and which, in any event, are unconvincing.[4] To this subject we shall return later in more detail.

We now take up the thread of the immigrants we left in the north of Uganda in order to keep some vestiges of continuity in the hope that the composite picture which emerges will be less confusing. The original wave of the Luo migration, a branch of which had gone as far south as Bunyoro, had left settler families all over northern Uganda, especially in Acholi and West Nile. Some of the more spirited immigrants had struck farther south-eastwards reaching modern Bukedi district and spilling over into the Nyanza province of Kenya and, eventually, into north Mara and Musoma districts of Tanzania. At about the same time there occurred another movement of people—the Ateker—from their main settlement in Karamoja. This movement, unlike that of the Luo of the same period which was from the north-west towards the south-east, was from the north-east towards the south-west. The Ateker people, of whom the Iteso of Uganda and Kenya are a very important branch, do not seem to have moved as a result of any particular disagreement or natural calamity. As these movements proceeded apace, there was a fusion of the Luo and Ateker cultures at major contact points. The major result of such fusions was the creation of new peoples, notably the Langi and the Kumam. Other communities became bilingual as a result of these new experiences. For example, the Jo Abwor not only have a language of their own but they understand the Acholi language (Luo) and Jie (Ateker). Thus the Jo Abwor have had their culture influenced both from the north-west and north-east.

The importance of the Ateker migration is not limited to their fusion with the Luo to bring new communities into existence. It is also important for the settlement of Teso and of some of the counties of Bukedi district in which the Iteso are numerically predominant even today (especially in Tororo and Pallisa). As the colonisation of Teso by the Ateker proceeded, new environmental factors changed the style of life of the new immigrants and this started the process which ultimately made the Karimojong (those who stayed behind in Karamoja) and the Iteso (the pioneer settlers of Teso) into distinct peoples. One of the major factors augmenting this process was that Teso was far more suitable for settled agriculture than Karamoja owing to generally more fertile soil and dependable rainfall. Periodic epidemics and famines gradually made the Iteso more dependent on agriculture although they did not abandon cattle keeping altogether. Thus, in time, the Iteso became primarily an agricultural community which supplemented agricultural produce with cattle products. The Karimojong, however, in their drier plains stuck to their cattle and cultivation remained a peripatetic occupation of women in the few arable river beds at the same time as the Iteso were becoming more skilful agriculturalists. It was thus inevitable that significant changes should have occurred between the two societies—changes in their styles of life which in turn influenced the development of their political and social institutions—sufficiently for the Karimojong and the Iteso to regard themselves as different peoples. Soon a major event was to occur which accentuated this feeling of separateness. The event was the Iworopom war of around 1830 which has been described so graphically by Webster.[5]

The Iworopom, who were an agricultural community, seem to have been attacked as a result of a famine and a cattle epidemic which struck the Karimojong around this period. The Iworopom were overwhelmed by the Karimojong who drove them southwards and the majority of these fleeing refugees found shelter among the Iteso, many of them settling in the Amuria county of Teso from where they mounted a series of raids against the Karimojong. As a result of the influence of the new settlers among the Iteso society, the raids that these mounted against the Karimojong in vengeance and the fact that the Iteso had sheltered a people the Karimojong had come to regard as their enemies, the rapture between the Karimojong and the Iteso was complete. It was complete in the sense that the two no longer regarded themselves as one people as had been the case before and during the colonization of Teso.

During this period and over the whole of northern Uganda there was intense activity of cultural transformation and social construction. The region's major linquistic groups—the Sudanic, Luo and Ateker— began to establish rudimentary forms of government, the primary nucleus of which was the clan. In this system of political and social organisation, each clan managed its own affairs, settled disputes between its members and recognised no other authority beyond this unit. Then around 1680 there occurred a significant migration of the Luo-speaking peoples who had settled in northern Bunyoro and who came to be known as the Palwo. It has already been pointed out that although these had lived in and formed part of the state system of Bunyoro, they had remained Luo in speech and culture. The date of this migration seems to suggest that the Palwo migrated partly, if not largely, because of the political upheavals which took place in Bunyoro during this period. The king of Bunyoro, Chwa I, had invaded Ankole and had gone farther and invaded Rwanda where he seems to have been overwhelmed and killed. In the meantime a woman regent (Masamba) had assumed the control of Bunyoro kingdom (the only woman remembered to have achieved this feat in this region), but the important chiefs of the kingdom had not been happy with being ruled by a woman. She was soon murdered and succeeded by Chwa's young son who took the title of Kyebambe I. It would seem, therefore, that these political changes, which were accomplished by violence, must have at least been instrumental in causing the Palwo to move and seek calmer political climates.

This new wave took the Palwo through Acholi and Karamoja. Some settled in Kaberamaido (Teso) for some period before moving on the Bukedi and Western Kenya—following in the footsteps of the earlier immigrants. In Bukedi the Palwo joined the pioneers of the earlier migrations and began the systematic colonisation of Budama. These were the people who came to be known as the Padhola (or Jopadhola) of modern Bukedi district. Ogot tells us that the colonisation of west Budama was aided by the fact that the Padhola found the area virtually empty so that they did not engage in conflicts to displace the indigenous people as their brothers who had struck farther east into western Kenya were to do until the advent of colonial rule.[6] Bukedi itself, lying on one of the major corridors of migration, was to receive a heterogeneous collection of ethnic groupings and its population still reflects this. As the Padhola of the later migration were arriving, migration from Busoga eastwards into western Kenya was in progress. The result of this criss-crossing was that Bukedi had among its population Bantu ethnic groups (the Banyore, Bagwere, Bagwe and Samia), Nilotic Padhola, Nilo-Hamitic Iteso and the Bakenyi, who are a mixed people and who do not belong exactly and exclusively to any of these other groups. This diversity of ethnic groups in an area so small reflects the different migrations at different periods of peoples whose paths crossed here.

From Bunyoro the Palwo brought with them new concepts of government into Acholi and into northern Busoga. It is to be borne in mind that in these areas rudimentary forms of government were already in existence so that the Palwo brought new concepts of kingship as an institution and also sought to enlarge the scale of political organization. The new concepts in particular were the idea of hereditary kingship which was associated with the idea of the possession of a royal drum. This latter aspect of regal power (the drum being a prerequisite of exercising authority) seems not to have existed in Acholi prior to the arrival of the Palwo who, in turn, seemed to have copied the association from Bunyoro. Additionally, certain items of regalia—royal spears, stools, etc.—were also introduced into the Acholi states which were formed after the arrival of the Palwo. It should be noted in passing that not all of the sixty or so kingdoms that were formed in Acholi by the 19th century were formed by the Palwo. On the contrary the more common pattern was that the pre-existing kinship groups in Acholi copied the new concepts of the Palwo and then applied them to their own states; this is how the states of Patiko, Payera and Atyak (in West Acholi) and Ajali, Patongo and Adilang (in East Acholi) were formed, to mention only a few.

The states of Acholi remained essentially small—the average population being roughly between 2,000 and 15,000 people per state. In this respect the Acholi states also resembled the political entities that had been set up among the Alur of West Nile district. There are several factors which account for the small scale of political organization among the communities of northern Uganda. In the first instance the formation of political entities that embraces several clans each was itself a major departure from the traditions of the Luo speakers and must have come about, at least in part, as a result of the conditions under which they lived. The need for mustering more effective means of defence than that which the clan could offer must have played a considerable part in inducing this development. This, in turn, had other benefits that were extraneous to such political associations—for example the formulation of more certain and formal means of arbitration and the expansion of the areas of economic activity and security, and so on. Sometimes the enlargement of such political units was augmented by specific natural events which brought all these attributes of wider political association into sharper focus. For example, the great famine which swept this area towards the end of the 18th century and as a result of which the Langi raided deep into Acholi made the smaller entities very insecure and hastened them into joining the larger existing ones.

Secondly, one has to consider what appears to have been a general attitude among the Luo speakers—the tendency not to solve family disputes by force. Along the migration routes, the chief causes of separations were disagreements among the family for a variety of reasons. After the establishment of these states, we find that some of them broke up into even smaller units as a result of disputed succession.

The contending candidates did not take up arms to decide the issue: the dissatisfied aspirant merely moved off and set up his own state and in this way some of these states were broken up into smaller units. Often, moreover, this fissiparous tendency was aided by natural factors. In some areas frequent famines led to the break-up of communities which were not reconstituted on the same scale even after the famines had subsided. This was particularly the case in East Acholi during the 18th and 19th centuries. This factor largely accounts for the development of comparatively larger states in West Acholi where rainfall was heavier and more regular than in East Acholi.

But perhaps more important than all these considerations was the fact that the formation of these states did not lead to the abandonment of the fundamental philosophy upon which the Luo political organization rested: the belief and practice that all important decisions affecting the community could only be arrived at, not by a single person, but by the consensus of the elders representing the different clans constituting the particular community. Thus even when the kingdoms were formed, the king, or *rwot*, reigned rather than ruled. He acted as a spokesman for the elders among whom he was *primus inter pares*—he himself being a clan head of his own clan and hence its spokesman. Hence it follows that, as in the ancient city states of Greece, in a political community in which decisions have to be arrived at by almost unanimous consent of the groups forming that community, the scale or size of that community had by definition to be small. The era of representative or non-representative "democracy" had not dawned upon these societies. Thus it can be stated that the type of political organization that developed in Acholi and among the Alur represented a compromise between completely segmentary societies such as the Langi and the Bakiga and the more bureaucratic state systems that were developed in such kingdoms as Buganda and Bunyoro. It is from this fundamental belief and practice that one has to look for an explanation as to why these societies did not develop bureaucratic state systems rather than in the lack of "civilization" and in "barbarism" as some of their latter day detractors were to say during and after the colonial period because in many ways these societies were often more humanely governed than their more "sophisticated" neighbours in the southern parts of Uganda.

The process by which the different communities which comprise modern Uganda developed their respective identities and political institutions was a long and gradual one and, in each case, owed a lot to environmental conditions and a multiplicity of other factors which dictated the terms upon which these ethnic groups, with different historical experiences, came together to order their lives towards common goals. It is perhaps a truism to state that any given group of individual persons—and the number of such individuals is immaterial in this context—can only live together under rules and regulations or under a system that gives them more advantages than separate existence could afford such individuals. I am not here trying in any way to introduce the theory of the contract between the rulers and the ruled so beloved of the capitalist political theoreticians of the 18th and 19th century Europe. In the context of pre-colonial Ugandan societies, John Locke's contract was as irrelevant as European classical feudalism. The fact of the matter is that nowhere in pre-colonial Ugandan societies, whether in kingdoms or segmentary societies, would one find the ruled tied to a specific piece of land or obliged to stay under a political system that was inimical to him and to his family interests. Their relationships were not conceived in terms of mechanical abstractions but in personal relationships. This is why there is no word in Uganda languages which meant *government* in a European sense—whatever words that came to be used during the colonial period were approximations and they denoted, among other things, an element of remoteness and hostility.

The foregoing statement is as valid for the Bakiga whose segmentary existence afforded them ample scope to develop in their mountain home as it is for the Baganda whose kings developed the most efficient bureaucracy in pre-colonial Uganda. In the case of the former and of those whose political and social institutions were similar or identical, it is true to say that they lived a collective life, the basic unit of which was the clan. Within this unit the interests of each of the component parts were also general interests of the whole and any dissatisfied member or group could opt out of the unit and establish a more satisfactory mode of existence. But because this association was based on blood kinship—and whether or not such relationship was real or imagined is of no consequence since the point is that it was believed to be real—it was in the interests of the whole group to keep together than to separate. The overriding concern of the clan unit was the protection of the whole unit's integrity and economic welfare in the most satisfactory way possible. When it became necessary to co-operate with other clans, it was because there was a common objective to be achieved or a common danger to be averted but such objective or danger had to be of equal concern to such clans and their co-operation would be based on nothing more than this understanding. Within this system some individuals were more wealthy than others just as some were poorer than others. The wealthy never lost sight of their obligations to the kinship group just as the poor members of such a group were never slow in claiming their due from them. The point is that nobody could become wealthy without reference to his kinship group for this must have helped him in numerous ways although his personal merits may contribute towards his success. In such societies there had never been room for individualism or impersonal governorships requiring equally impersonal regulations to service them.

In kingdoms, too, the clan was of paramount importance and this is best illustrated by reference to two examples. In Buganda one of the means by which the ruling house secured the loyalty of its subjects was by the rulers marrying from as many clans of their subjects as possible. This was even improved further by introducing a social practice by which all the kings belonged to the clans of their mother so that there was no royal clan in Buganda since every clan was free to—and most if not all of them did—offer wives to the kings. The political importance of this practice comes into sharper focus when one realises that the rest of the Baganda—that is all Baganda except their ruling house—had rules of patrilineal succession and that every Muganda, again with the same exception, took the clan of his father. It then becomes clear that the convention of the kings taking the clans of their mother was political and not primarily a social one—in fact in a purely social context it would have made no sense at all. And, as Kiwanuka illustrates in his *A History of Buganda*, it was not until the height of Buganda's expansion that the rulers felt confident enough to begin encroaching upon the powers of the clan leaders and even then this was achieved by means of gaining the support of a set of clans by means of patronage before some unfortunate clans would be disgraced. By the beginning of the 19th century, Buganda had developed the efficient bureaucracy that the British found and admired when colonial rule arrived but even up to then the clans were still of paramount importance in the whole structure and if any proof of this is needed, Kiwanuka's account of how Mutesa I came to the throne against everyone's prediction should be sufficient.

Additionally the fact that the Kabaka assumed the title of "Sabataka" or literally "the Father of clan leaders" or "leader of all clan leaders" is itself indicative of the paramount importance of the clan as the basic unit of social and political organization. The point to emphasise here is that even in Buganda—the most bureaucratic of all of Uganda's pre-colonial state systems—blood kinship was the basis of political association. And within this system the Kabaka had managed, for a variety of reasons, to acquire sufficient power to control the clans, but even so none of the kings ever became strong enough to offend all or most of the clans at the same time and none tried. At this level the clans which happened to command the most influence at court (and hence wealth and power) at any given period—which means some clans all the time—were under the same obligation to look after the welfare of their members as was the case in segmentary societies which did not develop this type of political system. This is why when a clan fell out of royal favour, its members never questioned the rightness of all of them taking the consequences for an offence that may have been committed by one or a few of their number; the rebellion against Kabaka Kagulu in mid-18th century and the subsequent persecution of his maternal clan is one of several instances in Buganda history catalogued by Kagwa and Kiwanuka.

We may take the second example from Ankole—or Nkore as it was known in pre-colonial times. This was a kingdom that was basically decentralised. The state did not depend on the kind of bureaucracy that was developed in Buganda and clans did not, as in Buganda, develop clan institutions such as clan leaders or clan lands, etc. This did not happen because land did not acquire the kind of importance it did in Buganda. The king had therefore to rely on developing common interests between himself and his subjects within the framework of a cattle–oriented economy and government. In a nutshell this took the form of the kings recruiting their administrative agents from among the cattle owning class. This is not the place to go into the details of how this system embraced the cattle owners as well as the agriculturalists since this has been explained elsewhere[7] and since it is not immediately relevant to the point we are pursuing. For our purpose it is sufficient to note that even here the clans were of paramount importance, not only because the rulers themselves came from a specific clan—the Bahinda clan—but also because no one could hope to attain any position of prominence without the support of his clan; having attained that position, he could never hope to maintain it without meeting the corresponding obligations of looking after the welfare of his clansmen. Here, too, and throughout the history of the kingdom, members of any given clan accepted as a matter of course any punishment, no matter how severe, for wrongs done by any of their members and no one could have questioned the justice of such a punishment. Equally the *Omugabe* (king) never dared frame his policies in such a way that they could offend a substantial number of numerically powerful clans at any one time. Even in order to punish a powerful clan justification had to exist and to be seen to exist by the other clans. Here as elsewhere in Uganda political association was based on blood kinship and the basic unit in this structure was the clan.

Against this background we can make some general observations about the fundamental principles underlying the types of political systems that were developed in Uganda. The first is that whether or not a given community could expand the size of its political scale was largely determined by its environment, especially by how much of their energies could be devoted to conquering such environment in order to establish a satisfactory way of life, socially and materially. It was upon this foundation that these political systems were built. But—and this is the argument of this discourse—whether we speak of a kingdom or of a segmentary society, there was no individualism and up to the coming of colonial rule, the clan continued to be the most effective unit of political and economic association. This is the situation in which it would make no sense to speak of a rich Kabaka in the same way as one could speak of Prime Minister X of this or that European country or of King Y of European middle ages. The Kabaka was rich only in the sense that he was conceived, by his subjects, to "own" everything every Muganda possessed. In a sense his wealth was the collective wealth of Buganda. Again one may quote an Alur example:

> "The chiefship, as so often in African societies, was economically based very largely on a reciprocity of goods and services in which the chief was the main centre of exchange. He was a very genuine risk-bearer in staking his position on his ability to balance receipts hospitality unfailingly required of him help to the needy and rewards for the faithful, as well as in his ultimate guarantee to vanquish drought and famine."[8]

This is a fair summary of what a leader—be it a king or head of a clan—was supposed to do and did or else he would have lost his position. What these leaders received by way of what came to be misleadingly termed "tribute"—land produce (beer, foodstuffs and livestock)—was not meant for their exclusive use. The particular king or clan head's family could not want because this did not have a separate existence from his person and office so that so long as his subjects or clansmen did not want so also could his family not want. There were hardly any exploitative landlords or oppressed landless peasants—this dubious bounty was bestowed upon us by "civilisation" and "progress"—i.e. individualism. The existence of any scale of political organisation was conditional upon this sense of social responsibility right from the family unit to the largest kingdom. Because the political objectives these political associations were fashioned to achieve were limited, their structures were necessarily unsophisticated. Consequently, these structures rested upon personal relationships and not upon abstract legal formulae. Thus the clanhead knew his clansmen and he was related to them. The king relied on a range of administrative appointees to govern his kingdom and these were known to him personally for it was to this knowledge that they owed their appointment in the first instance. To some of them, moreover, he was related either by marriage or by some special exchange of gifts. At no point in the structure would one find an impersonal link–hence the irrelevance of abstract theories as models to explain their functioning.

The second general observation that one can make is that the political systems that we have outlined did not find it necessary to devise institutional restraints against the abuse of political power—restraints such as the British House of Lords for example or the American Senate—because this was unnecessary. This is not to argue that given sufficient time the forces that gave rise to the necessity of formulating these or similar devices could not have arisen. It is merely to point out that such a stage of development had not been reached and that these societies and their organs had not assumed the complex shape that necessitate such safeguards. We must now examine the relationship that had developed between the different communities in Uganda before the advent of colonial rule. It is then that we can get a proper perspective of the organic developments that were taking place without external stimulus.

1. This section relies on: B. A. Ogot: *A History of the Southern Luo*, Vol. I (E.A.P.H., 1967). J. B. Webster: in *Tarikh* Vol. 3/2/1970 and to some extent on the researches of Dr. Shiroya (among the Lugbara), Dr. Herring (among the Labwor) and Prof. J. B. Webster (among the Acholi).

2. B. A. Ogot: *op. cit.* p. 42.

3. For a narrative of these traditions see: J. W. Nyakatura: *Abakama ba Bunyoro-Kitara* (Canada, 1947), p. 6–65. A. Katate and L. Kamugungunu: *Abagabe b'Ankole* (Kampala, 1955), p. 1–31.

4. See B. A. Ogot's review of M. S. M. Kiwanuka's *The Empire of Bunyoro-Kitara: Myth or reality?* in *East African Journal:* October 1969, p. 46–7.

5. J. B. Webster: in *Tarikh* Vol. 3/2/1970.

6. B. A. Ogot: *op. cit.* p. 85–6.

7. S. R. Karugire: in *Tarikh* Vol. 3/2/1970.

8. A. W. Southall: *Alur Society* (London, 1956), p. 80.

CHAPTER ONE

THE PRE-COLONIAL SETTING (1500-1860)

In this section it is intended to examine the major forms of contact or relations between the different communities of Uganda prior to the advent of British rule. It is perhaps just as well to start by making the general observation that contacts between communities that lived far from each other were severely circumscribed by a host of factors, the chief of which was the lack of satisfactory means of communication. These factors therefore limited the frequency with which such communities got into contact with each other and, usually, such infrequent contacts as were possible were necessitated by the need to obtain some essential commodity which while abundant in one area was scarce or non-existent in another. But before we can examine these contacts it is necessary to get the context, in an outline form, in which they took place and this brings us to the examination of the actual mechanisms by which these communities ordered their everyday life. For this purpose, we shall take a few examples which have the major characteristics by which we can illustrate the whole in order, it is hoped, that we can get a good picture of the overall developments in the whole country. An exhaustive treatment of each of the Uganda's pre-colonial communities, apart from being an enormous task, is not possible as our present lack of knowledge does not permit it. And even if we had all the knowledge we needed, it would still be a thankless task—it might conceivably make the reader throw away the whole thing because of exhaustion or worse.

In the previous section a rough indication was made of the major patterns of settlement and of the different political systems that were evolving. In the areas that remained segmentary in political organisation, it was indicated that the societies concerned found common identity in the common culture and language which they evolved over a period of time. In the case of Uganda this primarily refers to the Langi, Lugbara and Karimojong of northern province, the Bakiga of western Uganda, and the Iteso, Bagishu, Sebei and the various Bantu and Padhola groups of Bukedi in the eastern province. For these societies, once the territory of settlement had been occupied, there were comparatively fewer internal conflicts and compromises to be made than among the Kingdom areas, primarily because these societies were not developing new forms of political organisation on a scale wider than the kinship unit, but rather they were improving upon those which existed, and with which they were familiar, in order to meet the changing circumstances. Where interactions with neighbours occurred—as with the Iteso and the Bagishu for instance—such interactions were conducted within the same framework of nuclear independence. In this set-up the whole community was brought together by some cultural foci—such as the biannual circumcision ceremonies of the Bagishu or they united to repel invaders or mount an offensive against a common enemy or rival such as the Bakiga frequently did. Outside such events which were of concern to the whole community, the clans managed their daily concerns independently and whenever it was necessary to resolve differences between two neighbouring clans, their respective leaders met and hammered out such differences, as was the practice among the Lugbara for instance. In these communities the idea of decentralised democracy prevailed so that authoritarian leadership did not evolve. Perhaps one can also observe that in this type of organisation it was the elders who managed the affairs of their various clans because the young men had comparatively little say in the management of public affairs.

The story of the development of the kingdoms was radically different because not only did one have new families trying to establish political control over different peoples, but also there were many concepts of authority to be made acceptable. For these reasons it was initially necessary to carry out certain political bargains and compromises in order to make the new political order acceptable. It has already been indicated that the first area to feel the political impact of the Luo invaders was Bunyoro where the Babito established a new dynasty. The major compromise that the Babito seem to have made in their new kingdom was that they adopted the religious practices and customs of the people they ruled over and this seems to have minimised possible internal conflict in their new domain. This appears to be so because they subsequently lost all traits of their original culture including their language and became absorbed into the Bantu society over whom they ruled. It is reasonable to suggest that this compromise was necessary because the Babito do not seem to have been numerically strong so that although they may have found it relatively easy to defeat their Bacwezi predecessors, who were themselves ill-equipped to defend their ill-administered kingdom, their numerical inferiority militated against crowning their military conquest with cultural conquest. To change the basic form of social behaviour may have aroused widespread resentment which they may very well not have been able to contain. It is this numerical weakness, moreover, that seems to have confined this conquest to Bunyoro which was only a small part of the Bacwezi kingdom.

In these circumstances, therefore, the Babito found it necessary to appease the indigenous population, whose leaders they must have relied upon to administer the country. In Bunyoro, as elsewhere when the kingdoms were in the process of being formed and institutionalised, the new rulers made extensive use of marriage alliances with the local clans in order to forge blood kinship and enhance the loyalty of such clans to their dynasties. All the Palwo rulers who founded the small states of Busoga such as Bukooli, Kigulu and Luuka I–II—to name a few—are said to have done this extensively in the process of building up their states. These, in the early stages, were necessary political decisions to take and implement. In Bunyoro too, as in Nkore, the new rulers also claimed a genetic relationship to the Bacwezi rulers they had just supplanted. This claim also seems to have been aimed at legitimisation of their rule since rule based on force alone, and when the rulers were a minority, lacks permanence—a consideration that was apparently known to these state builders. That they succeeded in making their subjects believe in the "fact" of their regal descent is borne out by the fact that the traditions of these areas still state this relationship as a fact of history to the present day. What this belief did for the rulers of Bunyoro and Nkore was to supplement other measures which were being taken simultaneously to consolidate the authority of the new rulers.

From the traditions of this region, the kingdom of Bunyoro was much larger than it was to become when the British finally signed an "agreement" with her rulers in 1933. We know this to be the case by tracing Buganda's stages of expansion which was largely at the expense of Bunyoro and also by noting that Toro, which became an independent kingdom during the 19th century, had been part of Bunyoro. Additionally, towards the end of the 19th century, British officials excised parts of Bunyoro territory and ceded them to Buganda —this being part of the punishment meted out to Bunyoro as a result of her resistance to the establishment of foreign rule. These considerations taken together show that Bunyoro was an extensive territory. But then the rulers of Bunyoro do not appear to have developed the necessary administrative machinery to consolidate their hold over this vast territory and this brings us to the examination of Bunyoro's system of government and also to the consideration of one of the major problems of the historiography of Uganda.

Considerable literature exists from which we may gather the structure of the government of Bunyoro and of this literature we shall cite three sources which are sufficiently representative. J. Roscoe: *The Bakitara or Banyoro* (Cambridge, 1923) A. R. Dunbar: *History of Bunyoro-Kitara* (Nairobi, 1965) and G. N. Uzoigwe: *Revolution and Revolt in Bunyoro-Kitara* (Makerere History Papers No. 5). Of the authors themselves the first was a missionary, the second an agricultural officer in the colonial civil service and the third is a professional historian. According to Roscoe, Bunyoro's government was headed by a king who was "an absolute despot" and had the power of life and death over his subjects. Below the king there was a group of powerful chiefs he terms "The Sacred Guild" who advised the king on all matters of state and who ruled the country during the interval between the death of one king and the installation of the next one. He then describes a host of other grades of chiefs. Roscoe's account contains at least one basic contradiction and this is that in a system of government where the king is an absolute despot, there could not be a formal council of chiefs which could be described as "powerful". Moreover, the impression one gets from Roscoe's account is that of a tightly administered country with a rigid hierarchy of chiefs and this, too, seems to be contradicted by Bunyoro's history as will become apparent as our story unfolds.

Dunbar's rendering of Bunyoro's internal administration differs from that of Roscoe in very important particulars. He tells us that the king ruled indirectly through grades of chiefs—county, sub–county and parish chiefs—who respectively administered these divisions into which the kingdom was divided. He then describes a group of special counsellors, who appear to be the equivalent of Roscoe's "Sacred Guild" but who do not appear to have had any specific judicial or administrative functions. Then for good measure, and in addition to all these, we are told of the existence of a cabinet and a parliament, Perhaps it is not necessary to belabour the point that in the circumstances then obtaining in Uganda such a structure of government would have been a guaranteed prescription for chaos. The kind of governmental structure ascribed to Bunyoro by Dunbar is quite simply too modern and too western to have been known in Bunyoro in pre-colonial times.

Uzoigwe's account represents the more recent and scholarly treatment of this kingdom's history and it seems to be in accord with other historical developments within Bunyoro since a structure of government could hardly evolve in a vacuum or in a violent disagreement with other aspects of social organisation of the same society. He tells us that the king ruled through a group of regional chiefs who were the administrative heads of the various regions into which the kingdom was divided. Below these were a variety of smaller functionaries. But, and this is the major difference between Uzoigwe and other writers on Bunyoro, he tells us:

"Kitara chiefs wielded much independent authority, unlike in Buganda where all authority flowed from the Kabaka."

Uzoigwe observes that this often led to insurbodination and insurrection as occasionally happened when chiefs could conspire and invade another province of the kingdom without reference to the king. We are bound to accept this analysis because it agrees with other aspects of the development of states in this region—it explains, for example, why by the 19th century Buganda had overtaken Bunyoro as the most powerful kingdom in the inter-lacustrine region. What in fact Uzoigwe does not say but what is nevertheless a logical extension of his analysis is that a system of government in which provincial governors had the ability to defy the king and attack each other with impunity had all the elements of institutionalised chaos. In these circumstances the territorial integrity of Bunyoro was nearly impossible to maintain and defend because such an extensive territory needed a centrally controlled administrative and military machinery. It is in Bunyoro's system of government that we have to look for an explanation of her diminishing influence and to this subject we shall return later. In retrospect what is surprising is not that Bunyoro lost her outlying provinces but that she survived as a kingdom at all.

Immediately to the south–east of Bunyoro was the kingdom of Buganda. It has already been indicated that this kingdom, like the neighbouring kingdoms in the lake regions, came into being around 1500 and that the ruling house of Buganda was related to that of Bunyoro according to the traditions of both Buganda and Bunyoro although this is denied by some historians. In disputing these traditions, for example, Kiwanuka advances the curious argument that if the kingdoms of Buganda and Bunyoro had been founded by the same family of the Babito as the traditions say, then these kingdoms would not have become rivals as undoutedly they became. This argument is curious because it is historically illogical since often national consider-ations were of more importance than common ancestry. One would be hard put, for example, to explain the rivalries and frequent wars between Busoga states, which rivalries even Kiwanuka narrates, and yet these rulers openly acknowledged their Babito origins. Kiwanuka, moreover, dismisses the customs that were common between Baganda and Banyoro royal families such as the preservation of the jawbone shrines and the fact that the Baganda kings were forbidden to marry in the bush buck clan (which is a clan of the Babito) facts that were adduced by Oliver and Gray respectively by saying that jawbones were preserved before Kimera and that there is no evidence to show that Baganda and Banyoro were not incestuous.[1] His overriding concern to show that Buganda's ruling house was not of Babito origin would probably have been better served had he contended that in fact in Buganda and Bunyoro incest was acceptable and this would have been plain nonsense since both in Buganda and Bunyoro the rules of endogamy and exogamy were strictly observed.

In the beginning Buganda was much smaller than Bunyoro in extent and, as Kiwanuka describes it,[2] her administrative system evolved around the royal household. Even at this early stage of her history and in the formative years of her administration, Buganda's rulers had a flair for hierarchical organization since even the royal household and its immediate environs were administered by a hierarchy of chiefs of varying degrees of importance. At this early period, too, the political system seems to have those elements which made it so competitive by the 19th century that pursuit of position could be so absorbing and achievement so satisfying and dangerous. The administrative system did not acquire its permanent features until Buganda's period of greatest territorial expansion which was during the 17th and 18th centuries. During this period a succession of imaginative kings ascended the throne of Buganda and as this kingdom expanded, its rulers worked out and implemented a machinery of administrative control which was to impress the British officials so much at the turn of the 19th century that much of its features were made the model by which to govern the whole of Uganda protectorate. From the foundation of the kingdom to mid 18th century the kings of Buganda steadily gained most of the political power from the traditional centres of power—especially the clan heads whose social importance was underscored by the fact that every Muganda belonged to some clan. The leaders of clans had a variety of functions within their respective clans some of which were ritual but some of which were also political so that within Buganda of the pre-expansion period the clanheads wielded a great deal of power and influence.

The basic unit of administration was the county or *saza* and some of these had been held on a hereditary basis within some important clans. It would appear that this arrangement may not have been entirely unrelated to the political weight of such clans at the beginning of the kingdom's existence. In the course of the new dynasty's establishment, it might well have been necessary to accord certain privileges to some important clans in return for recognition and support. As expansion proceeded apace, new units of administration—the Bitongole which have been approximated to modern subcounty divisions—were developed and these assumed great importance as tools of administrative control. The acquisition of new territories gave the kings great leverage of power since these new areas were the ones in which no clans had any traditional claims so that the kings had ample rewards to give to the faithful, the brave and the favourite without the necessity of transgressing upon any claims of the established clans of Buganda. Moreover, wars brought more material rewards—cattle, women and other prizes of war. The distribution of all these was in the hands of the kings and, in time, even the clanheads were reduced to competing for the king's favours and patronage like everyone else. Eventually—and especially by and during the reign of Kabaka Mawanda around the middle of the 18th century—the kings felt strong enough to dismiss traditional chiefs and to replace them with their own appointees on consideration of meritorious service rather than traditional claims to those positions. By this period the kings' power to appoint and dismiss had acquired two edges to it: in the new territories he could appoint anyone he fancied without arousing any clan's hostility since no clan had any claim in these territories. Secondly, he could dismiss a clan chief and replace him with a member of the same clan thereby neutralising any possible resentment because, at any given time, the number of clansmen aspiring to such elevation was considerable. Thus, by the beginning of the 19th century, the king of Buganda was the source of power and wealth and every functionary of the state held office at the king's pleasure. The development of this centralised bureaucracy saved Buganda the kind of territorial problems that beset Bunyoro because the administrative system was cohesive enough to maintain the integrity of the kingdom in its expanded form.

In Buganda, as elsewhere in Uganda, there were no standing armies so that armies were drummed up as and when they were needed for defensive or offensive purposes. In this system every adult male was liable for military service and this is why the chief was not merely an administrative functionary but also a military leader of the region under his jurisdiction. This was as true of Buganda as it was of Bunyoro. But Buganda, unlike Bunyoro, had a sedentary agricultural population and her political system was fashioned and developed around this fact. Agriculture was the mainstay of the national economy and landholding and usage was intimately linked to the holding of political office. Thus a chief—such as a county chief for instance—was not merely an office holder in the sense of exercising jurisdiction over the county for along with that went also the control of land under his jurisidiction, usufruct right over the produce of that land and so on. The Kabaka's powers were similarly conceived in these terms. In this way economic interest and political authority were harmonised in the social system thereby giving the society political and social cohesion.

In contradistinction Bunyoro rulers do not seem to have been particularly concerned with the type of economy upon which their rule was to be based—that is to say that Bunyoro's economy was neither predominantly agricultural nor predominantly pastoral. This may well be explained in terms of ecological factors but this cannot explain the problem that this caused the Bunyoro state and the importance of this can hardly be overemphasised. Often the rulers themselves seemed not to be decided whether they prized cattle more than agriculture— witness their frequent costly raids for cattle, the most spectacular of which was that mounted against Nkore and Rwanda, in one sweep, towards the end of the 17th century and during which the king of the day was killed. Perhaps the importance of the absence of a mono-culture–based economy in unsophisticated administrative systems— unsophisticated in the sense of having a limited range of objectives to achieve—will become clear if we refer to another example.

In Nkore, Bunyoro's southern neighbour, the system of administration was loose or decentralised and there existed no institutional adjuncts such as the clanheads of Buganda for example. But the main occupation of the rulers and the yardstick of the society's wealth was cattle. In time this became the mainstay of the national economy and the administrative system was built around this. Because the acquisition and rearing of cattle did not require an elaborate machinery of administration, the rulers of Nkore developed none. But these rulers took particular care to make sure that their administrative agents, who were also military leaders, had a stake in this kind of economy and this is how it came about that no one could hope to occupy a public office of any consequence if such a person possessed no cattle.[3] Thus the society's conception of wealth was welded to the exercise of authority in such a way that social cohesion was achieved. It is thus not clear whether the lack of such developments in Bunyoro was the cause of the administrative system we have described or the other way round. But what seems certain is that this was a source of weakness in the Bunyoro state system.

We can usefully conclude this outline by reference to a different political order that seems to have successfully married the two methods of political organizations which prevailed in pre-colonial Uganda—that is the segmentary and the kingship systems. We have already indicated that the Palwo who had settled in northern Bunyoro started moving out around 1680 and started forming small kingdoms in Acholi. We shall take one of these kingdoms as an example—the kingdom of Paimol. The founder of this kingdom was Omol.[4] The major groups that Omol found in what came to be Paimol were the Tea Gule and the Atura. Both of these were predominantly pastoral communities whereas Omol and his followers were predominantly agriculturalists. Thus the economic activities of the newcomers and of the indigenous people were complementary. In return for accepting Omol's political leadership, the leader of the Tea Gule became Omol's Jago (king's representative in a region) and to the leader of the Atura was assigned the duty of performing certain rituals pertaining to kingship. By these measures or compromises the rudiments of state machinery were set up in Paimol. As new clans joined Paimol each leader of the incoming clans was assigned some special function and all the leaders of clans sat in the Lukwena (or what might be termed a council of state). In time, too, Luo became the official language although the Luo were the smallest of the ethnic groups constituting Paimol. But by the 19th century it became difficult to incorporate more clans by expanding the Lukwena to accommodate the representatives of the new arrivals. Thereupon a new institution was devised—the Twon Lok or Military Council. This body dealt with matters of war and peace and, in time, it also acquired responsibilities in judicial matters thereby almost excelling the Lukwena in prestige. Members of this council were chosen on personal merit so that the new clans could also be represented there and they were. But the ruler did not sit either in the Lukwena or the Twon Lok. He was informed of their decisions which he duly communicated to the people in public assemblies. Although it was recognised in principle that the king had the right to modify or veto the decisions of these bodies, tradition has it that this right was hardly ever exercised. Thus organic growth of states proceeded as new compromises and expedients were devised to minimise conflict and promote harmony in society. But all these developments took place within the same political framework of the elders sharing in the process of decision making in matters of public importance. It is in this fundamental respect that the northern chiefdoms or kingdoms retained their traditional concept of political authority even when many more people came under a single umbrella of a kingdom which had expanded beyond the original ideal of a single clan.

Against this background we can now turn our attention to the consideration of the types of relationships that subsisted between these people in the period preceding the coming of European rule. This will be done bearing in mind the generalisation which was made at the beginning of this section and that is that the societies living nearest to each other were in more frequent contact than those living farther apart from each other. Like all general statements, this one is subject to some qualifications since there were some exceptions to this general tendency.

Nevertheless, these exceptions were too insignificant to affect the validity of the statement. In the communities of pre-colonial Uganda the demand for consumption goods, outside one's own community, was extremely limited largely because these communities were almost self-sufficient. Each of these communities produced most of the goods they needed for their own consumption and there was hardly any need for producing a surplus beyond the necessity of producing the kind of food that could be stored against bad times or to cover the intervals between one harvest and the next one. The range of consumption goods was itself limited since these consisted in nothing much more than food and domestic implements.

Despite these strictures, however, there were a few essential commodities which were beyond the means of certain communities to procure within their borders owing, largely, to natural or ecological factors. The most important of such commodities was salt. This explains why salt was the primary commodity around which trade was built in pre-colonial Uganda. To a very limited extent several communities of Uganda were able to supply their needs and those of their animals for salt from diverse improvised sources. For example, a type of grass found in swamps when burnt to ashes and strained is salty enough for purposes of food seasoning. In some areas, too, there existed marshes or springs whose water was imbued with different degrees of salinity so that it could be used for human and animal consumption. But these sources of salt were far too inadequate even for those areas in which they existed and they were wholly useless in those areas in which they did not exist. It was therefore to the salt mines—or area where natural salt existed—that every community was finally attracted in order to supply its needs. In the supply of this commodity nature had not been overgenerous with Uganda for the principal centres of salt extraction were Kibiro (on the eastern shore of Lake Albert), Katwo and Kasenyi (extinct since the beginning of this century). And until the first half of the 19th century all these centres were in the kingdom of Bunyoro—from about 1830 Katwe and Kasenyi became part of Toro kingdom which seceded from Bunyoro at about that date. The location of this most sought-after commodity had important consequences upon the interaction of the peoples in this region. In particular this is why Bunyoro became the principal link between the predominantly Nilotic speaking people of the north and the predominantly Bantu speaking people of the south. The fact that Bunyoro provided this link was not a result of deliberate policy; it was quite simply a result of the fact that the single commodity upon which all societies of Uganda placed an equal premium was to be found in Bunyoro and everything else followed from this unalterable fact.

There were other vicarious factors which facilitated the flow of trade in salt especially between Bunyoro and her northern neighbours and some of these were mainly historical in the sense that the connection between Bunyoro and her northern neighbours predated the exploitation of salt mines.

It has been observed that the ruling house of Bunyoro sprung from the same stock as that which was largely to populate northern Uganda and to furnish that region with the Luo language. This connection was maintained by frequent contacts since geographical proximity made this rather easy. Many of the Palwo who set up states in northern Uganda and as far afield as Busoga continued to attach some importance to their origin in Bunyoro. Thus such states as Payera, Patiko and Alero and the Alur chiefdoms Musongwa, Muswa and Jukoth just to mention a few examples, traced their origins to Bunyoro and kept this connection alive by occasional formal contacts. For such communities, therefore, trade with Bunyoro presented very few problems because, for some, it could be said that they were going back "home"—Pawir (or Chope) from where their ancestors had migrated in not too distant a past.

Besides the considerations of historical connections, trade between Bunyoro and other Uganda communities flourished because it was beneficial to all the parties engaged in it so that where historical or genetic connections existed, these served as agencies of promoting such trade but not as the cause of it. In the general northward direction trade involved several communities—principally the Alur, Lendu, Kebu, Madi and the Lugbara and the principal intermediaries between these communities and Bunyoro were the Parombo whose main area of settlement was modern Padyere county of West Nile district. The Parombo's close involvement in trade led them to establish another nucleus settlement in Okoro county to ensure that their role as middlemen in this trade was maintained intact.[5] The Parombo themselves were part of the Luo speakers who had migrated from northern Bunyoro and settled in their present home in Parombo during the first half of the 18th century and who by the 19th century, as a result of their long distance trade connections, had absorbed other ethnic groups, principally Bantu and Sudanic elements. Even today some clans among the Parombo admit their Bunyoro origin and the fact that over a period of time they have lost their language through the process of social and cultural interaction.

For the purpose of this trade there were two collecting centres on either shore of Lake Albert—Panyimur and Magungo on the eastern and western shores of Lake Albert respectively. This trade was based on specialised production which in turn was dictated by ecological factors rather than by deliberate choice. Thus the Alur and the Lugbara were farmers (both agricultural and livestock) while the Kebu were ironsmiths (largely because they had iron ore deposits) and also a clan of the Kakwa (the Nyangilia) had acquired specialised skills in making iron implements and they imported some of the iron ore from modern 'Zaire. Thus from the Kebu, Lugbara, Madi and Alur, the Parombo would obtain livestock, iron products and foodstuffs which they carried to Panyimur and thence across the narrow neck of the lake to Magungo. From here these were transported overland to Bunyoro and exchanged for salt and dried fish. The homeward journey took them to Magungo and across the Lake to Panyimur and thence to the various societies of northern Uganda with whom they exchanged these commodities for local ones and then they would get ready for the southward journey. By means of these shuttle journeys those goods were spread to the various communities—the Acholi, Langi and the Iteso and as far south as Buganda.

In the southwest in the present Toro district important trade connections developed around the salt mines of Katwe and Kasenyi and this trade fanned out in several directions. The salt obtained from these mines was transported southwards to Nkore, Kigezi, Rwanda and Karagwe (in Tanzania). The existence of the trade in salt—both that leading to the north and to the south—seems to have been of long standing and it seems reasonable to suggest that it was increasing in volume (and the absence of statistical data forbids one to make a more categorical statement than this) when it was interrupted by the coming of Arabs and Europeans in the 19th century. In the early period no regular markets, in the sense we understand this term today, developed. Each group of people engaged in this trade functioned as a market for purposes of bartering the different wares which were coming from various directions but all focusing on the salt mining locations. By the mid 19th century, however, European travellers were describing market scenes in Bunyoro in which the Banyoro Banyankore, Baganda, Langi and others were gathered to exchange their wares. By the 19th century, moreover, barkcloths, at the making of which the Baganda excelled, had found their way south into Ankole and as far north as the Alur highlands. Iron hoes from Bunyoro, the area that developed that skill before anyone else in Uganda, had already revolutionised agriculture in Teso and Busoga and they had already reached as far afield as Bukedi. There seems to have been one major difference between the trade based on Lake Katwe and Kasenyi salt mines and that built around Kibiro. In this southern trade no specialised trading community came into being to act as middlemen as was the case in the north where the Parombo had become effective middlemen and had taken steps to ensure the retention of their position by founding different settlements and making extensive intermarriages with the communities among whom they traded.

From the foregoing we can make two important observations. The first is that this trade involved a great many societies. The direct participants in the trade—that is the people who carried these commodities back and forth—had to traverse great distances; and more important, they had to travel through many communities different from their own. The important point to note is that these traders were not merely protected but were also warmly received among the communities with whom they traded. The main reason for this seems to be, as Shiroya has pointed out, that the leaders of the different communities saw to it that such traders as happened to come in their midst were protected since they had a vested interest in the continuance of the trade itself from which they and their people benefitted as much as the itinerant traders themselves. But this enlightened self-interest, if one may so term it, must have been based on an even more fundamental attitude of mind which was a result of an historical experience. This is that these communities were basically well-disposed towards each other. This statement does not mean that the communities which traded with each other had no differences with each other or that such differences did not occasionally get settled by force. Far from it. Such differences existed and such occasional clashes occurred. To even pretend otherwise would be to presume a degree of identity of human nature and an identity that has yet to be indicated by a concrete example since man inhabited this troubled planet. The point is that the existence of divergent interests between two or more communities at one time or another was not incompatible with the fact that there were other interests that were convergent. In other words, the two principal forms of relationship—co-operation and hostility—were not mutually exclusive in any meaningful sense. This is not even the casuistry that it might seem at first sight. And in order to illustrate this one may cite an example in societies neighbouring to Uganda. Talking about inter-community raids in pre-colonial Kenya, the late Jomo Kenyatta tells us that intermarriages and raids existed alongside each other between neighbouring societies and:

> "in territories where this (friendly) relationship was established, especially between the Kaptei Masai and the southern Gikuyu, the warriors of the two tribes joined together to invade another section of the Masai, like Mbeere or Tharaka.[6]

The point of this example is that neither the Gikuyu nor the Masai ceased to regard themselves as one people in spite or because of these alliances. In other words, the Loita and the Tharaka continued to be Masai and Kikuyu respectively in the wider social context.

The real point therefore is that wherever these occasional—and even where they were frequent—hostile encounters occurred, the objective and, more importantly, the scale of destruction was never of such intensity or duration that they could create enduring enmity. In Uganda there were no such phenomena as inter-ethnic total wars. When, for example, the Lugbara or the Kakwa fought the Alur, this meant no more than a few adjacent clansmen on either side of the boundary fighting in order to adjust the boundary between themselves. Even when we talk of the larger political entities such as the kingdoms of southern Uganda, this argument still holds good since there must always be a limit to which one society can freely interact with another which is an acknowledged enemy and that limit begins as it ends on the battlefield—not beyond if the involved parties subsist as independent entities. It is against this background that one feels justified to conclude that these communities were basically well-disposed towards each other and this is what made it possible for traders to feel safe enough to traverse so many cultural and political boundaries without the necessity of creating "trading armies" which would be strong enough to fight their way through any resistance or hostility as the Arabs had to do, not merely because they traded in humans but because they were also aliens in the real sense of that term. Our conclusion, from the foregoing, is that since the raid—and we shall soon attempt to show that few such hostile encounters deserved the term "war"—were neither extensive nor destructive (the weapons forestalled the latter possibility anyway) enough to lead to the creation of enemy societies. Our modern historians who have found it possible to describe some pre-colonial Uganda communities as "enemies" may have done so to fulfil the dictates of their emotions and not of their intellect.

The second observation we may take note of was the enduring friendship between Bunyoro and her northern neighbours. It must be stressed at the outset that although Bunyoro was far larger and more powerful than any of these communities individually, the relationship between Bunyoro and any one of them did not in any way imply subordination. It was co-operation between equals—equals who were politically independent of each other. To the extent that the dynasty of Bunyoro had any expansionist ambitions, these were never directed against her northern neighbours—they were directed southwards as we shall endeavour to show. Uzoigwe has explained this particular relationship by reference to a number of factors—the factor that, for instance, Bunyoro herself could not have attempted, with any hope of success, the subjugation of these peoples with their long history of democratic decentralisation and their being unused to accepting regal personal authority. He also explains the failure of these communities to take advantage of Bunyoro's weakness and multitude of problems to expand at her expense by reference to the fact that these communities had an exaggerated sense of Bunyoro's power even when her power in the whole region had actually declined. This was even true of those communities such as the Langi and the Iteso where no dynastic connection existed between them and Bunyoro.[7]

These explanations are sound and are in accordance with what we know of these societies. Nevertheless it can be added that there was more to it than that. The Acholi, for example, could not have refrained from attacking Bunyoro merely because they believed they could not win. The fundamental basis of this relationship was that the ties of friendship that had been established between Bunyoro and her northern neighbours over a long period of time had become strong enough to withstand and supersede other drives of sectional aggrandizement or aggression. This seems to be a reasonable explanation because the Acholi and the Langi, had been inclined to expand at the expense of their neighbour (Bunyoro), could not have been deterred by belief in the strength of their potential victim-strength, moreover, against which they had not measured their own.

This line of reasoning seems to be borne out by the coming of the Arabs in the middle of the 19th century. The Arabs were primarily interested in ivory and this commodity was much more abundant among the northern communities than in Bunyoro. Both Kamurasi and his more energetic son and successor, Kabarega, made every effort to keep this trade under their control. In the trading patterns which had existed before the arrival of the Arabs, the Banyoro had been the senior partners in trade because salt, the commodity around which trade was built, was to be found in their territory. In order to secure and maintain a near-monopoly of the ivory trade, both Kamurasi and Kabarega "turned to their traditional foreign markets: Bulega Angal, Alur, Acholi, Lango, etc."[8] These supplies were not secured by force but by diplomacy in particular by sending rich presents to the leaders of these societies and by occasionally giving military assistance to some of them. It is said, for instance, that sometimes Kabarega complied with requests of some of the Alur chiefs by sending them troops to raid the Lendu. Additionally the traditions of the Langi and of the Banyoro confirm that from the 19th century, the Langi aided Bunyoro rulers by supplying them with troops from time to time. It appears, for instance, that Langi fighting contingents played a significant role in the Kabarega/Kabugumire succession war which followed the death of Kamurasi around 1869.

It is also to be noted that when the Arabs came, they were allowed to take part in the trade but not to control it and Baker was driven out of the country by Kabarega because, among other things, he tried to control and divert the channels of this trade. Neither Baker, Gordon nor even the well-disposed Emin Pasha found willing collaborators among the Banyoro, Acholi or Langi. The bonds of common interests and the period over which these bonds had been forged and consolidated made the bonds of friendship too solid to be shaken or shattered by short-term and often evanescent benefits that could be reaped from collaboration with aliens. All this was of course changed by British colonisers because against the nature of their penetration and the apparent permanence of their presence, these societies had no adequate weapons. But even then reluctant collaboration and acquiescence was not obtained without a great deal of trouble as we shall see. Finally, one may note that when the might of imperialism finally overtook Kabarega during the closing years of the 19th century, that monarch fled to Acholi where he was sheltered and protected from his hunters and when Acholi became too hot, he went on to Lango where he was joined by Mwanga, another royal refugee from the forces of colonialism. In Lango the two fleeing monarchs were afforded shelter and sustenance until they were finally captured in 1899. That these societies sheltered important personalities who had already been branded "enemies" of the powers-that-be, and at a considerable risk of reprisals against themselves, cannot be explained away in terms of momentary aberration or the perversity of "natives". It must, at the very least, have been an expression of mutual esteem and friendship that had been built up over a long period of time.

When we turn to the southern societies, we find ourselves confronted by and large with a similar situation with one important exception— this being that the relationships of this region of Uganda were complicated by the fortunes and ambitions of the ruling families. This is the area, with an early exception of most of Kigezi district, where what might be termed authoritarian or centralised regimes developed. It is perhaps necessary to note that when we talk of northern and southern Uganda this is more a choice of conveniece and not of anything else and it is an arbitrary one at that. This is because on grounds of ethnicity and history, it would be exceedingly difficult to divide Uganda into meaningful units. Confronted with these problems, the present writer has taken Lake Kyoga to form a crude division of Uganda into two.

Apart from trading relationships which involved almost all these communities in varying degrees, the southern kingdoms were involved in frequent conflicts and the chief cause of these were dynastic ambitions of the ruling houses. It has already been noted that from the beginning, Bunyoro was the largest of these kingdoms. It was also the most ambitious and aggressive. Thus we find that early in the 16th century she mounted an attack against Buganda during the reign of Nakibinge and in the course of the fighting Nakibinge was slain in battle. The Banyoro, under their king Olimi I, withdrew from Buganda and invaded Nkore which was then ruled by Ntare I. As in Buganda, Bunyoro's invasion of Nkore was a success but, unlike in Buganda, Bunyoro armies occupied Nkore for some period. According to Kinyoro traditions the Banyoro withdrew because of an eclipse of the sun and this is now believed to have taken place in 1520[9]—a date that agrees with our estimate of the reign of Ntare I in Nkore. One feels bound to accept the Kinyoro tradition because, if present superstitions are any guide to the beliefs of the past, a solar eclipse, or "the sun falling from the heavens" as it is expressed, must have been an event of awesome magnitude for the victors as well as for the vanquished. Kinyoro traditions also explain that Bunyoro armies withdrew from Buganda after their impressive victory because the augurers advised against annexation of a sister kingdom, an assertion that is dismissed by Kiwanuka[10] who explains this withdrawal by saying that the war probably had exhausted the Banyoro as it had the Baganda and that is why the Banyoro withdrew without effecting political change in Buganda as the success of their arms might have suggested. This is a peculiar way of reasoning because an exhausted army could not have immediately invaded another kingdom (Nkore) and with great success. That the Banyoro withdrew from Buganda without effecting political changes may mean nothing more than that this was not their intention and that their intention, as indicated by their forays in Nkore, was to obtain cattle—a commodity that Buganda then and through the pre-colonial period did not possess in any numbers that merit mention. In fact the Banyoro carried off so many cattle from Nkore that their invasion was followed by a famine.

The importance of this invasion may thus lie in what it tells us about the circumstances obtaining in the three kingdoms involved. The first conclusion we can draw from this war is of chronological importance. The solar eclipse which took place immediately after the invasion of Buganda and during the invasion of Nkore has been dated by scientific means. We know that it took place in 1520 and we know who the rulers of these kingdoms were in that era. This date, being one of the firm dates, has thus been used as a peg on which to hang the chronological problems of this region—with varying degrees of success.

The second conclusion we can draw is that the invasion itself tells us the relative developments that had taken place in these kingdoms since their formation. It has already been stated that the rulers of these new states had to take a variety of measures to legitimise their rule in their new domains. It follows therefore that the Babito of Bunyoro had already consolidated their power in Bunyoro, at least by 1520, otherwise they could not have felt confident enough to wage two foreign wars in a row without fear of upsetting their own hegemony at home. It would also seem that this invasion may have made the Banyankore and the Baganda unite firmly behind their rulers because this was truly a foreign invasion. In material terms the invasion did a lot more economic damage to Nkore than to Buganda as we have already indicated.

Finally, the invasion tells us something about the relative strengths of the three kingdoms during this period. Of the three kingdoms, we deduce that Bunyoro was by far the strongest since she was able to beat Buganda and Nkore in succession without sustaining much damage. It is perhaps relevant to note that this was the last occasion on which Bunyoro invaded Buganda although a more determined attempt was to be made to subdue Nkore much later. It is from this particular point in time that one has to take up the organic growth which had taken place within these kingdoms to explain these developments and some of these have already been indicated. Mention has already been made of Buganda's centralising tendencies even before the occurrence of the war we have just outlined and it was noted that during the 17th and 18th centuries the rulers of Buganda had succeeded in creating an efficient hierarchy of chiefs all dependent on the Kabaka for the tenure of their offices. It was also observed that the rulers of Nkore fashioned, in the same period, a loose form of government and created a class society in which the possession of cattle counted for a great deal socially and politically. For the stability of their rule, it was from this class of cattle owners that the kings of Nkore selected their administrative agents or chiefs. In this set up an efficient administrative machine did not develop because the simple needs of a cattle–oriented government would have made little or no use of it.

It has also been suggested that Bunyoro developed a system of internal administration which, organically, had fissporous tendencies. This was not all. Initially Bunyoro also had extensive extra-territorial commitments. These were the small states which had been founded by the Babito or a related family of rulers—who continued to look upon Bunyoro as their spiritual home and metropolitan country. Some of these states were in Acholi and the Alur highlands as we have indicated. Some of these were to be found in the states of northern Busoga, the small Kingdom of Kooki and the conglomeration of the chiefdoms of Buddu. These small states did not just look upon Bunyoro merely as a spiritual home but also as a protector and this brings us to the consideration of one of the major problems that faced Bunyoro. This is that her extensive extra-territorial responsibilities as well as the administration of her own territory required a more centralised administrative and military organisation to keep everything and everyone under control. There was thus an inherent contradiction in Bunyoro's governmental system and her ambitions. This contradiction was that to keep an extensive territory, to seek to add to it by conquest (annexation) and to keep a string of client states under her protection was incompatible with a system of administration which left so much power in the hands of administrative agents. It could only be within the organs of a centralised administration at home that delegation of authority in the far flung dominions could be made without encouraging secession and other forms of disaffection.

It did not take long for the tightly knit kingdom of Buganda to take advantage of Bunyoro's cumbersome administrative system. Thus during the 17th century Butambala and Gomba fell to Buganda during the reigns of Kimbugwe and Kateregga. These were areas of some importance to the expanding state of Buganda as the way was open for her to the grazing lands of the west and Buganda lost no time in using the narrow fords of the Katonga river to mount raids against Nkore for cattle. Then during the reign of Mawanda in mid-18th century, Buganda gained more territory—most of Ssingo came under Buganda as did most of Kyaggwe which had been under a variety of clans who had owed some vague allegiance to Bunyoro in the past. The importance of the acquisition of Kyaggwe was that it gave Buganda access to the Nile and here dates her active interest in the states of Busoga. Mawanda was the first Kabaka remembered to have raided Busoga. Then towards the end of the 18th century Buddu also fell to Buganda, apparently with the assistance of Kooki, lately one of the client states of Bunyoro. This acquisition gave Buganda access and then control of the southern trade routes which, with the coming of the Zanzibar traders, were to assume so much importance during the 19th century. In addition to this and partly because of it the way was open between Buganda and the states of Buhaya so that we find that by mid-19th century Buganda was taking an active interest in the succession disputes of Karagwe and Kiziba kingdoms. In many ways Buddu was the most valuable addition to the kingdom of Buganda. Apart from her geographical location in relation to the coast-oriented trade, Buddu was also rich in food production and, by Buganda's standards, fairly rich in cattle of which Buganda was usually short as we have indicated. Moreover, Buddu brought to Buganda even more skilled bark-clothmakers and it has already been stated that this was

Buganda's chief speciality and chief item of trade with her neighbours. We have already mentioned that in the course of the 19th century the bark cloths graced royal personages in places as disparate as Nkore and Alur highlands and it was not long before this item percolated to the well-to-do commoners of those societies.

There is one aspect of Buganda's expansion at the expense of Bunyoro that needs more probing than it has received so far. It has almost become customary in the historiography of Uganda to describe these two kingdoms as "traditional enemies" and yet hardly anyone has bothered to determine whether this statement is true both in the pre-colonial and colonial periods. In the latter period a whole range of new factors materially altered the attitudes of these kingdoms towards each other and we shall deal with these factors at the appropriate moment in this survey. We now concern ourselves with the pre-colonial period. It has already been indicated that trade connections between the two kingdoms were of long standing and that these subsisted until the intrusion of colonialism which put an end to this economic interaction. This was not the doing of either Buganda or Bunyoro—it was part of the process of colonialism which devalued everything "native" so that the flow of pre-colonial trade went the way of "native" religions, administration, education and all in order to facilitate the establishment of a new order in all spheres of life.

We have also to consider the fact that in Buganda as in Bunyoro traditions there is no mention of any longstanding conflict or bitterness between the two rivals, one of whom had already lost so much territory to the other as Bunyoro had unquestionably lost territory to Buganda. Arising from this line of argument it seems appropriate to call into question the assumption that Buganda "conquered" all these provinces from Bunyoro by military invasion of the latter and the attendant corollary that the two states were therefore enemy states. This assumption seems to have arisen because of the notorious tendency of the traditions of this area to describe any kind of conflict or even mishap as "war". Every translator of these vernaculars has come up against this problem often enough to warrant giving it some attention. In his translation of Kagwa, for example, Kiwanuka points out Kagwa's indiscriminate use of the word "olutabalo" (rendered "war" in English) even when describing the tiniest of skirmishes. Nyakatura for Bunyoro and Katate and Kamugungunu for Nkore are just as guilty of this tendency. The argument is therefore that the provinces which Buganda took from Bunyoro were taken with a minimum of military conflict. Looking at Bunyoro's hold over her outlying provinces, it seems that this was minimal and was based on historical sentiment rather than on actual control that Bunyoro exercised over them. By the 18th century, outside the main core of Bunyoro itself, the kingdom seems to have been a conglomeration of substantial provinces in which each governor enjoyed a substantial degree of independence—or should one say a substantial degree of neglect—from the centre. In Kooki for instance:

> Bunyoro influence was still strong until the 1760s when she lost influence in this area to Buganda. Kooki owes her regalia to the generosity of Duhaga (King of Bunyoro) who gave many items of regalia to his departing brother.[11]

If the bonds connecting Kooki to Bunyoro were no stronger than this—and there appears to be nothing to suggest the contrary—then these could only subsist and grow if they were supported by the existence of a visibly strong kingdom of Bunyoro. There is no doubt, for instance, that by the 1760's Buganda had become the strongest of the two kingdoms and that the smaller entities—Busoga states, Bwera and Kooki—were aware of this fact. They had to be aware of it since their survival as kingdoms until the coming of British rule depended as much on their careful dealings with their more powerful neighbours as on their correct instincts as weather cocks to judge the shifting balance of power between the same neighbours. In a touching conclusion to his paper, for example, Lunyingo states:

> "In the process of survival Kooki contributed more to the development of her stronger neighbours (Buganda and Bunyoro) than to her own".

This is a pregnant summary of the tightrope walking that the smaller states of this region had to accomplish to avoid falling victims of the wrath of any of their powerful neighbours.

It should also be pointed out that what these smaller entities sought from their stronger neighbours was not so much "protection" as the freedom to be left alone to run their own affairs without molestation. Several examples can be cited to show that there was no meaningful protection that these "bigger brothers" could extend to the smaller ones. We noted earlier that the various clans were autonomous in Kyaggwe before the 17th century. They looked upon Bunyoro as their protector apparently for no better reason than that Bunyoro was the largest kingdom. We do not hear of Bunyoro giving them any particular form of aid in any context or against anyone and it may be safely assumed that such aid was perhaps never given or even asked for. When Buganda took them over, we do not hear that Bunyoro came to their aid to prevent the liquidation of their independent existence—even supposing these communities desired to preserve independent existence in an environment that was being increasingly dominated by larger political associations.

When by the end of the 18th century, Buganda could have assumed the mantle of this region's policeman by reason of her size and power, instead of Bunyoro whose shrinking outposts of influence had made the smaller entities wary of depending upon her, we do not see Buganda fighting wars to protect her new clients. To this there is a single exception which proves rather than vitiates the foregoing statement. This exception was a raid Buganda mounted against Nkore in the 1860's to avenge the death of Isansa, the ruler of Kooki, which had by that period become a protege of Buganda. Isansa had been killed in fighting when a Nkore expedition invaded Kooki to punish Isansa for having made a statement of fact but which, to Nkore rulers, was a punishable impertinence. He had sent an uncomplimentary message to king Mutambuka of Nkore and mentioned, among other things, his protruding teeth. This is a well documented story.[12] Kooki was invaded, Isansa killed and the Nkore expedition withdrew having administered the lesson they were presumably supposed to have administered. Then Mutesa I sent an expedition against Nkore which did not fare well—having even its leader slain in battle as both Buganda and Nkore sources agree[13]. But the failure of the expedition—or even its success had it been a success—is not the point. The point is that the expedition was sent long after the event when it could have changed nothing so that this type of protection was moral rather than physical. Had the position been otherwise these "protectors" should have devised means of protecting their proteges against such misfortunes instead of drumming up token means of redress long after the event and when the material damage done—the death of Isansa—could not be undone.

We may take one final but different example from the kingdom of Nkore. After many unsuccessful attempts Nkore finally succeeded in making the kingdoms of Buhweju, Buzimba and Kitagwenda and some of the principalities of the former kingdom of Mpororo into her vassal states during the 19th century. We do not find at any given period that Nkore had to fight to defend the integrity of these states. What all these examples seem to amount to is that the role of being a "protector" in this period and in these circumstances was more honorary than actual and that, in political terms, it was a matter of prestige rather than a definition of extended political or other material obligations. One is therefore justified to coclude that, with reference to Buganda and Bunyoro and in the circumstances of the change in the balance of power between the two states, Buganda had acceded to these "obligations" of protecting states smaller than herself but that this accession did not impose upon her any more onerous exactions than it had upon her predecessor in a similar situation. As before, these were honorary obligations.

We can conclude further that the provinces that Buganda was able to annex were those in which Bunyoro's political and military presence was minimal or non-existent and if one accepts Bunyoro's internal structure of government, one has also to accept the fact that this was the most ill-suited for the control not only of her own rather extensive territory but also for the control of her extensive interests outside Bunyoro itself.

That Buganda was able to absorb these provinces without undue stress can be explained in terms of the organic developments within Buganda itself. Within these outlying provinces of Bunyoro—and this seems to be the correct terminology since Buganda never found it necessary or possible to invade Bunyoro kingdom proper—the presence of a powerful ruler could not have been unwelcome given the insecurity that was being felt all round the small political entities. This, on its own, would not have been enough. The greater explanation has to be found in Buganda's administrative and social devices which made it impossible for a foreigner to feel an outsider in the mobile Kiganda court society. As Kiwanuka says,[14] Kiganda society had the flexibility that could allow even a Musoga distinguished dancer to become important in the political hierarchy. The fact that some of the states of Busoga had effectively become tributary to Buganda did not debar men from such states from advancement in Buganda society or politics. It would therefore seem that Buganda's success in geographical expansion and in assimilating those elements whose emotional attachment was to Bunyoro rather than to Buganda lay in her flexible social system of giving personal merit its due. Thus a recent Musoga or Mukooki felt he lost nothing by transferring his allegiance to Buganda since this in no way hindered his own advancement and yet it had the added advantage of being attached to a state that was obviously powerful enough to "protect" his society of origin should such an eventuality arise. The fact that such an eventuality did not arise is immaterial in this context. Thus Buganda was a society open to talent and in this one's origins did not pose a stumbling block to material progress. It may also be said that the full fruition of these mechanisms of social adjustment was not realised because their natural development was stopped by colonialism.

Nor would it be correct to explain Buganda's expansion as that of a predatory kingdom as Wrigley has done.[15] Buganda was an exceedingly industrious society and the proposition that Buganda was predatory because their staple food was the banana which the women could look after thereby freeing their men for fighting is, at best, very unhelpful. In almost all the societies of pre-colonial Uganda, the maintenance of crops was done by women and it would be curious to argue that the Baganda were an exception because they depended on bananas rather than grain or some other foodstuffs. Buganda like any other society in pre-colonial Uganda, was never a nation-in-arms. Her raiding expeditions were limited affairs both in objective and in numbers of men involved on any given occasion. Within these complex and criss-crossing relationships, some interests became more important to maintain than others. Thus in time Buganda's opening to the Nile became of sufficient importance to her to take an active interest in the internal politics of Busoga states whose internal rivalry was endemic. In the 1860's Buganda aided Rumanyika to drive out his rival, Rwegira, in a succession war that lasted some years not only because Mutesa I wanted to secure Rumanyika's friendship but also in order to ensure that prolonged civil war conditions in Karagwe did not endanger the southern trade routes that had become of such economic importance to Buganda by that date. In other words, in both Busoga and Karagwe Buganda had established interests to protect and the chief method by which such protection was ensured was to have a well-disposed ruler in power in these areas by intervening in a succession war against one contender. It was rare to impose a candidate who was not in the running by direct intervention and some of Buganda's attempts at this method came to grief in Busoga as the experience of Luuka in mid-19th century showed.

Immediately to the south of Bunyoro and west of Buganda was the small kingdom of Nkore and we can now deal briefly with her relations with her bigger neighbours. Taking relations with Bunyoro first, mention has already been made of the invasion that Bunyoro mounted against Nkore early in the 16th century. We have seen that this was a successful invasion and that the Banyoro were probably disturbed in their occupation of the Kingdom by the solar eclipse which took place in 1520. Then early in the 18th century an even greater invasion of Nkore was mounted by Bunyoro, led in person by her king, Cwa I, better known to history as Cwamali. On this occasion in Nkore there ruled one of the most enterprising kings of the dynasty Ntare IV (C.1699-C.1727). The purpose of this invasion, according to Kinyoro sources, was to replenish the supply of cattle because an epidemic is said to have decimated Bunyoro cattle soon after the accession of Cwamali. The invasion was overwhelmingly successful; so successful in fact that even the royal drum of Nkore was captured and held for a period by the invaders. This is not the appropriate context in which to explain the importance of the capture of the royal drum—the most embracing symbol of Nkore's statehood. It is sufficient to state that its capture proved as nothing else could have proved so conclusively that the Banyankore had been defeated. Nkore was occupied for some three years according to both Kinyankore and Kinyoro sources.[16] The occupation seems to have been leisurely accomplished since the Banyoro took time off to make extensive water wells to ensure their supplies of water. These water wells are still identifiable today. Then, so the story goes, the king of Bunyoro decided to invade Rwanda, farther south, for more cattle and by undertaking this new venture, the ruler of Bunyoro seems to have overstretched his resources for he perished in that campaign and the surviving leaderless Bunyoro troops made their weary way back to Nkore only to be set upon and chased out of the kingdom by the Banyankore.

This campaign, like the earlier one, merits the term "invasion" because they were on a very large scale and the occupation of the invaded country was accomplished even though this was not on a permanent basis. They are the only two campaigns that merit that label throughout the pre-colonial period for Bunyoro did not invade Nkore again and did not even raid her. From the beginning of the 19th century Nkore was able to mount limited raids against Bunyoro's border villages for cattle and, even once, to interfere in a succession dispute there. The occasion for the latter was the succession war between Kabarega and Kabugumire following the death of Kamurasi around 1869. At the request of Kabugumire, the ruler of Nkore, Mutambuka, sent a contingent of warriors to aid him and the contingent was almost entirely wiped out by Kabarega's forces and, fearing another debacle or worse, the ruler of Nkore refused to send more help to Kabugumire. The fact that Nkore made raids against Bunyoro and that she even unsuccessfully attempted to intervene in a succession dispute there does not mean that the balance of power between the two kingdoms had changed in favour of Nkore. These raids were of very limited objectives and they never even extended to the centre of Bunyoro itself. That such raids were carried out without provoking retaliation may mean no more than that the raids inflicted little or no material damage upon Bunyoro and that during the 19th century Bunyoro was engaged in containing greater situations to spare the forces to abate this nuisance. The lasting contacts between Bunyoro and Nkore continued to be through trade since Bunyoro remained the principal source of salt for the Banyankore until the advent of colonial rule.

Between Buganda and Nkore there existed a curious relationship which differs markedly from the patterns that we have been surveying. This is so because although the two kingdoms were adjacent to each other, their contacts did not become frequent or intimate as this geographical proximity might suggest. Again although Nkore was rich in cattle and Buganda in agricultural produce, no economic exchange patterns developed between the two to any degree that merits mention. In terms of power and size Buganda was the larger and the more powerful and yet she did not seek to invade or annex Nkore territory or even impose tributary status upon her as she had done elsewhere. Buganda's only interest in her western neighbour consisted in occasional raids for cattle and women but even these were never mounted on any substantial scale and, during the 19th century, they became increasingly unsuccessful. We have already referred to one such unsuccessful raid which was led by chief Senkoloto Muganda in the late 1860's.

One other instance of military contact between Buganda and Nkore that merits mention was the military assistance given to Mukwenda, who was one of Nkore princes fighting for the throne around 1875. But this aid, unlike the aid that Buganda occasionally gave to some princes of Busoga, was a casual affair in that Buganda had no particular interest to defend or promote in Nkore. In fact Mukwenda who was assisted did not even win the contest. It seems reasonable to conclude that Mutesa had given this aid in the hope of securing a friendly ruler on his western border primarily because his last years on the throne were full of internal troubles. That the Banyankore did not take this intrusion seriously is shown by the fact that Ntare V, the prince who won the succession war and against whom military aid had been given, was giving asylum to the Baganda refugees of the religious wars only a few years later.[17] It seems reasonable to conclude therefore that little or no political importance could be read into this military adventure nor indeed into the occasional raids that Buganda made against Nkore. In neither case was the intention or the outcome the establishment or maintenance of political hegemony. It might perhaps be pointed out, in concluding this paragraph, that Buganda was to expand by taking most of Kabula county which had belonged to Nkore. But this was during the colonial period and it was solely as a result of British policy for it was admitted by colonial officials that "Kabula was once truly Ankole territory" but that it had been necessary to incorporate it in Buganda as one of the measures aimed at defeating Mwanga whom the British had deposed and whose supporters were operating in that area.[18]

Before we conclude this survey of relationships, it is necessary to outline the existence of two other kingdoms which came into being later. These were the kingdoms of Mpororo and Toro and we shall deal with Toro first although Mpororo was founded earlier. It is convenient to deal with Toro first because this was a breakaway province of the earlier kingdom of Bunyoro and it broke away under a prince of Bunyoro so that it was not a new kingdom under a new dynasty in the same sense as Mpororo was.

We have already seen that the administrative decentralization of Bunyoro had in-built tendencies for secession. Toro, under prince Kaboyo, broke away from Bunyoro as an independent kingdom around 1830. His father, either because of his advanced age—he is said to have grown so old that his sons became impatient for succession—or because of military and administrative problems, did not attempt to put down his rebellious son. It was Kabarega in the 1870s who reconquered Toro only to be frustrated by the vanguard of British rule who restored Toro's independence. Even while Toro was independent and before Kabarega's invasions, she regarded Bunyoro as her friend and spiritual mentor and this for understandable reasons since her rulers were directly descended from those of Bunyoro and the population had recognised the legitimacy of Bunyoro's rule for centuries in the past. The two countries were therefore culturally and historically one so that even the incursions of Kabarega, though a manifestation of strength and ambition, could not have been without sympathisers in Toro itself. This consideration, apart from the weakness of Toro vis-a-vis Bunyoro, may not have been an insignificant contribution to Kabarega's easy success on the occasions he attempted to regain Toro.

Of the two new kingdoms Mpororo is by far of greater historical interest. This is because it came on the scene earlier than Toro, disintegrated earlier owing to internal problems and left a people that are not only still recognisable despite their dispersion over a long period of time, but who have also maintained an attachment to their past separate and independent existence to a degree that has puzzled casual observers to the present day.

According to the traditions of this area, the kingdom made its appearance around the middle of the 17th century and its existence did not last much more than a century, if that. It is said that the founder of the kingdom came from Rwanda and that he was related to the ruling house of Rwanda although the precise nature of this relationship is still obscure. It does not seem possible, in the absence of more concrete supportive evidence, to attach any particular importance or draw any definitive conclusion from this piece of tradition about the relationship between the rulers of Rwanda and Mpororo. Only two kings of the dynasty are remembered i.e. Kahaya, the son of Murari, usually known quite simply as Kamurari, and his son and successor who was also known as Kahaya Rutindangyezi. It is said that the first Kahaya came to Mpororo and found the Amazonian queen, Kitami, whose subjects were all women. He eventually married her and procured from her the royal drum, Murorwa, and thus founded a kingdom that came to be known as Mpororo.[19] It was during the reign of the second Kahaya that Mpororo is said to have greatly expanded so that by the time he died, around the middle of the 18th century, it included most of the counties of Western Ankole, most of Kigezi district and a portion of northern Rwanda. This approximate territorial extent as well as the date of the disintegration of the kingdom is corraborated by Nkore traditions and also by the distribution of all those people known as Bahororo—the people indigenous to the former kingdom of Mpororo—on the advent of colonial rule until well into the 1920s.

During the life-time of Kahaya Rutindangyezi, that is the second Kahaya, he had several sons whom he appointed as his administrative agents over the provinces into which his kingdom was divided. When he died, his kingdom broke up into independent principalities corresponding to the provinces over which his sons had ruled and they therefore became independent rulers of these principalities. Mpororo traditions explain this break up by saying that the second Kahaya had been so angry with his disobedient sons that he buried the royal drum so that none of them might succeed him. Although it is true that the royal drum was in fact lost in circumstances that can only be described as mysterious, this does not seem to be an adequate explanation for such a momentous event as the disintegration of a kingdom. After all we know that one of the same Kahaya's sons, named Mafundo, made his own drum and founded the kingdom of Igara which subsisted as an independent kingdom until the colonial administration incorporated it into Ankole in 1901. The point is that if Mafundo could fashion a drum and it could be accepted as a royal drum of the particular kingdom as it was, there was nothing to prevent any of Kahaya's sons to make one and keep the integrity of the kingdom under one ruler. It would seem therefore that the causes of the disintegration of that kingdom were much deeper than Mpororo traditions would have us believe.

In the first instance Mpororo seems to have had a loose system of government such as that which obtained in Nkore—the neighbouring kingdom that was to benefit so handsomely from this disintegration. But for Mpororo this could not have been anything but disadvantageous since in size she was much greater than Nkore so that any substantial part of it was an attraction to any prince bent on becoming an independent ruler. This factor explains, in part, the survival of Nkore during the late 18th and early 19th century in spite of several succession wars. Princes always fought for the whole rather than for portions of the small kingdom. In other words Mpororo was beset by much the same political and administrative problems as those which beset Bunyoro.

Additionally, Kahaya compounded his difficulties by appointing his own sons as administrative agents because to the subjects those sons were as of royal blood as the king himself and hence equally legitimate rulers. Any prince raising the standard of rebellion commanded natural loyalty in whichever part of the kingdom he happened to be. This problem was not unique to Mpororo for it beset other kingdoms which found themselves in similar circumstances. Some states of Busoga, for example, disintegrated into yet smaller units each under a discontented prince of the same royal family. This happened to Busiki and Kigulu during the 19th century and the other rulers of Busoga took the cue and began appointing commoners as their administrative agents to stem the tide. Thus it would appear that these were some of the internal problems that led to the break up of Mpororo and that the disappearance of the royal drum could not have been more than a minor contributing factor.

Since the disintegration of Mpororo, around the middle of the 18th century, the principalities which had constituted it maintained different degrees of independence *vis-a-vis* their larger neighbours until the advent of colonial rule at the end of the last century. Then these were merged into Ankole and Kigezi districts of Uganda so that the name Mpororo went out of use and did not figure on any map of Uganda. But her people, dispersed as they were, have tenaciously remained Bahororo in everything but geographical terminology whose absence does not seem to have made any impression upon them. During the colonial period, right up to independence, petition upon petition was to be lodged with the colonial officials for the creation of a Mpororo district based on the reconstitution of their former kingdom. That their attempts failed is of far less importance than the fact that those attempts were made for this proved that they had not lost their identity. This, incidentally, should make the reader appreciate the diversities within Uganda society which is one of the cardinal points of this venture.

By way of concluding this survey, one can make a few observations of general application to the societies we have been concerned with. One such observation is that territorial expansion, whenever it occurred in Uganda, was a function of internal control rather than being a result of deliberate foreign policy. As we have seen, Buganda was the state that expanded greatly and it does not seem to be a mere coincidence that this expansion went hand in hand with the enhancement of the powers of the king at the expense of other centres of power in the kingdom. The argument is, therefore, that wherever rulers or leaders undertook foreign ventures, these were prompted by the desire to better their personal standing at home rather than undertaking those adventures for their own sake or as a matter of calculated foreign policy.

The second observation refers to the historiography of Uganda which has for so long been obsessed with *Bunyoro's decline* being one of the major, if not the major, developments of this region's history during the 19th century[20]. This theme has more of the quality of rhetoric rather than of historical judgement. If the importance of the alleged development is supposed to lie in the relative sizes of Buganda and Bunyoro, then this is a factual error since Buganda had virtually ceased to expand by the 19th century and whatever territory was added to her by the British, this was done during the colonial period when neither Buganda nor Bunyoro existed as an independent state anyway.

Moreover, if by the decline of Bunyoro one means that the kingdom had so degenerated that it was on the verge of total collapse, this would be a demonstrable untruth. From the 1860s Bunyoro had successfully kept intruders at bay, and without anyone's assistance, and this was well appreciated by colonial intruders. Explaining why it became possible in 1897 to mount a punitive expedition against the Kenya communities of the Mau escarpment, Matson says that the year (1897) looked propitious because "....... Bunyoro, which had tied down the bulk of the Protectorate's forces for many years, was quiet. It was largely because of the government's pre-occupation with Kabarega in the past that pacification of the Eastern province had been deferred ......"[21] This could not possibly be an achievement of a society for so long in a state of decay. To explain this achievement solely by reference to the character of Kabarega would be a gross oversimplification. It is true that the personality of Kabarega contributed to this. But to have achieved so much, Kabarega must have built on foundations that existed before him— and these could not have been decayed foundations. It is not reasonable to suggest that a single man—Kabarega—could "revitalize" a system of government and, much more important, a society that had been in such a state of demoralisation in the space of a single reign that did not even run its full course.

"One has to belong to the intelligentsia to believe things like that; no ordinary man could be such a fool".

So said George Orwell in a different context. Perhaps contexts are far less universal that circumstances.

Thirdly, it is difficult to say or to attempt to predict what organic evolution could have followed upon these contacts, institutional developments etc. had they not been interrupted and then halted altogether at a time when they had not assumed anything like their permanent form. Would, for instance, the small state systems which prevailed in northern Uganda have disintegrated into accephalous societies or coalesced into bigger political units? In either case would the history of Uganda have changed course? Would the segmentary societies such as the Bakiga and Iteso, for instance, who had, by the advent of colonialism, achieved such absolute cultural identity, have transformed that identity into wider political association? Such questions and others of a similar nature can be posed but hardly answered so that these must remain the great ifs of our history because however much we can speculate upon them, we cannot adduce meaningful answers to them. Colonialism came to Uganda when most of the societies that consituted it were still in the process of fashioning the mechanisms of their social and political organisation and when the various forms of relationship that had subsisted between them had not assumed permanent patterns. Then almost everything we have considered became immediately irrelevant as colonial rule was extended over the protectorate that was called Uganda.

1. M. S. M. Kiwanuka: *A History of Buganda,* (Longman, 1971), Chapter 2.
2. M. S. M. Kiwanuka: *Ibid:* p. 111–22.
3. S. R. Karugire: *A History of the Kingdom of Nkore in Western Uganda (Clarendon, 1971), p. 33–80.*
4. Based on J. B. Webster: "State formation and the Development of Political Institutions in Eastern Acholi", *M. S. P.* /3/70/71 p. 2–7.
5. This account is largely derived from: O. J. Shiroya: "Northwestern Uganda in the 19th Century: Inter-ethnic Trade" *M.S.P.* 21/70/71.
6. J. Kenyatta: *Facing Mount Kenya,* (Mercury Books, 1961 edition), p. 210.
7. G. N. Uzoigwe: in *Tarikh* Vol. 3/2/1970.
8. O. J. Shiroya: *M.S.P.* 21/70/71, p. 7.
9. R. Gray: "A Preliminary List of References to Solar Eclipses in Africa South of the Sahara", *Journal of African History,* 9/1/1968, p. 147–57.
10. M. S. M. Kiwanuka: *op. cit.* p. 60–63.
11. S. Lwanga-Lunyiigo: in *M.S.P.* 6/72/73.
12. Sir Apolo Kagwa: *Ba Seekabaka be Buganda* (London, 1927), p. 133 and for a summary see S. R. Karugire. *op. cit.* p. 122.
13. Sir Apolo Kagwa: *op. cit.* p. 133 Katate and Kamugungunu: *Abagabe b'Ankole,* p. 113.
14. M. S. M. Kiwanuka: *op. cit.* Chapter 6.
15. L. A. Fallers: *The King's Men,* (O.U.P. 1964), p. 18.
16. Katate and A. G. Kamugungunu: *Op. cit.* p. 65–71. J. W. Nyakatura: *Abakama ba Bunyoro-Kitara,* (Canada, 1947), p. 95–8.

17. Sir Apolo Kagwa: *op. cit.* p. 148–50—Kagwa was one of them. Katate and Kamugungunu: *op. cit.* p. 127.
18. See H. M. Commissioner, Uganda, to Sub-Commissioner Ankole District, Despatch No. 15 of 10/9/1899 (Mbarara Archives).
19. For details see: H. F. Morris: "Kingdom of Mpororo" *Uganda Journal*, Vol. 19 (1955). S. R. Karugire: *op. cit.* p. 190–5.
20. See M. S. M. Kiwanuka: "Bunyoro and the British: reappraisal of the decline and fall of an African Kingdom", *Journal of African History*, Vol. 9/4/1968.
21. A. T. Matson: *Nandi Resistance to British Rule, 1890–1906* E.A.P.H., 1962), p. 239.

CHAPTER TWO

THE BEGINNING OF RELIGIO-POLITICAL POLARISATION (1860-1900)

And so to the coming of colonial rule to Uganda. In this confused period of Uganda history, we shall mainly be concerned with the events in Buganda because this is the kingdom in which the unsettling influence of alien instrusion was concentrated. Such attention as was paid to the other areas of Uganda was secondary for the main centre of events—Buganda. It is proper to begin this section by observing that by the time the interest of the European powers was directed towards this region of Africa, the Europeans had developed, almost to perfection, three potent weapons against which the African societies and their way of life could not possibly muster any defence. These were the gun, the bible and the 'anthropologist'. These were so uniquely complementary that it is not easy to determine which of them was the most effective and perhaps this determination is superfluous since each was important for a different purpose. Of the first two weapons we shall speak presently and of the third we may note that it was by the grace of the anthropologist that we got the term *tribe* to apply to Africans and to mean a debased form of nationhood and other perjurous connotations that no longer need recounting. A casual glance at the Concise Oxford (English) Dictionary tells the reader that "tribe is a Group of barbarous clans under recognised chiefs; (in Rom. Hist) each of the political divisions (originally three, probably representing clans, ultimately 35) of the Romans . . . ." Earlier the same source informs the reader that a "community" means "Joint ownership . . . identity of character, fellowship . . . organised political, municipal or social body; body of men living in the same locality; body of men having religion, profession etc. in common . . . ." In the light of the fact that Uganda was colonised by Britons, whose native language is English—at the official level anyway—it does not take a great deal of imagination to see why the term "tribe" rather than "community" or any other term was preferred and for reasons that had nothing to do with English grammar.

For the short term needs of colonial occupation, the Europeans were preceded by or they arrived simultaneously with the most conveniently timed epidemics—smallpox, rinderpest, tetanus, jiggers, famine and a host of other smaller scourges. In Uganda, as in Kenya and mainland Tanzania, these epidemics ravaged the African societies and their livestock just as the vanguard of colonial rule pitched their tents everywhere. Even where the Europeans preceded the epidemics, these still followed them as if to prove the permanence of the new order. For instance, the Nyakwai of northern Uganda had been spared these calamities and in 1898 a small detachment of Macdonald's expedition, which was exploring that area, wandered among them. The Nyakwai destroyed the party, including its European leader, Captain Kirkpatrick. The following year (1899) the Nyakwai had a terrible visitation of smallpox which they firmly believed to be the Europeans' way of punishing them for having killed one of their number.[1] The point is that many African societies believed that their misfortunes had been brought by the Europeans since the arrival of the latter coincided with those misfortunes. These epidemics had a very considerable effect and, by sapping the physical energies of the Africans, made the acceptance of alien rulers much easier than it would otherwise have been. Thus these epidemics were the most important psychological allies that the new masters could have devised and the fact that they did not actually devise them is irrelevant since their potential adversaries believed they did. It is not possible to estimate just how much, in terms of troops, money and arms, these natural disasters saved the colonial rulers but that they did cannot be doubted. This statement is as true of the Kikuyu of Kenya whose land was taken away while they were sheltering from these epidemics as it is of the Nyakwai of Uganda to whom a smallpox epidemic seemed to be a pointed rebuke about the error of their ways—i.e. having killed a European some months before the outbreak of the scourge.

There is a superficial sense in which Uganda was not scrambled for by the European powers. This is that there were no pitched battles between the British, the French, the Belgians or the Germans—the principal European powers which were interested in this region. But these heroics had long been played out in India and North America, especially between Britain and France and while the latter had lost the actual battles the former had come to doubt the "morality" of it all. By the 19th century the very idea of pitched battles over colonial possessions had become obsolete and by the 1880's there was a general consensus among the colonial powers that it would be unnecessary to shed European blood in dividing up the African continent—this could be achieved by simply agreeing on spheres of influence within which each power could do what it pleased with the "native savages" therein. This is the only marginal importance that one could attach to the Berlin Conference of 1884–5. It confirmed the vague rules by which the European powers had been carving out spheres of influence in Africa. The conference certainly did not usher in the scramble for Africa since this had started before the conference was convened and it did not determine the territorial partition of the continent since this would have imposed specific obligations and boundaries some of the European powers—notably Britain—were not keen to accept then. For Britain, the greatest imperial power of the period, it was sufficient to obtain vague spheres of influence in order to restrict other European powers—especially Germany whose agents did not seem inclined to follow the rules of the game: and indeed the Germans did not even play cricket, a matter of no small concern to the men who ruled the British Foreign Office and empire. This would give time to Britain, more especially to the Liberal Party, to argue whether it was worthwhile to have African possessions at all or, in the case of East Africa, as Gladstone is reputed to have said, to gain control of a country "behind the mountain with an unrememberable name" referring to Tanzania (mainland) and Kilimanjaro, respectively.

The fact that a Liberal Government was returned to power in 1892 at a time when the question of retaining Uganda (by which term it was primarily meant the kingdom of Buganda) was something of a public debate tended to confirm the view that the British reluctantly accepted the "burden" of administering Uganda in order to accommodate the pressure of missionaries and their allies in Britain. There is no doubt that much of the propaganda for retaining Uganda was centred on the "precarious" situation of the missionaries "labouring" in Uganda and, of all things, the suppression of slave trade[2]—just as the fact that the disorders that were raging in Buganda in the same period had been caused by the missionaries was ignored. Moreover, so the argument runs, Mutesa I of Buganda had actually "invited" the missionaries to his country and it would be un-British to let him down—this refers to the now famous letter said to have been written by Stanley at the request of Mutesa and which letter eventually appeared in London's *Daily Telegraph* appealing for missionaries to come to Buganda. What is not clear, at least to the present writer, is how much of that letter was Stanley's and how much of it was Mutesa's idea. But perhaps this is a moot point and what is not is the subsequent statement that Mutesa had invited the British to establish a protectorate over his country. This, for some strange reason, has been assumed as a matter of course in the historiography of Uganda. Thus in a work published as recently as 1973 we are told that, "It is true to say Mutesa I "invited" the

British to establish a Protectorate over his kingdom which at the time was called Uganda by the British."[3] The source of such a statement is obscure but that it gained wide currency is beyond doubt, especially in the late 1950s when this "invitation" was put to a variety of bewildering uses. Yet some of the available literature of the period does not bear out such a claim. We may, for example, refer to Mutesa's letter to Colonel Gordon of 24th March 1876 in which he reiterated his desire to be a "friend of the white men", and in which he made a number of requests which included a priest to teach the way of God to his people, clothing for himself and for his people and "excellent guns and good cannons"[4] and so on. When one bears in mind that this was the period when the Egyptian government was still sending military expeditions to annex Bunyoro and Buganda; a threat to which Mutesa was very much alive, one would be justified to conclude that Mutesa wanted supplies with which to defend his kingdom rather than aliens to protect his country.

Mwanga, Mutesa's ill-fated successor, was even more specific. On 26th April 1890, amid the disorders reigning in his kingdom, he wrote to Euan Smith, the British consul in Zanzibar. This was after the Christian parties had defeated Muslims. Mwanga informed Euan Smith that Britain, France or Germany could send any of their representatives to Buganda and that if they wanted to help him, they should name the price of such help because, "I do not want to give them (or you) my land. I want all Europeans of all nations to come to Uganda, to build and to trade as they like."[5] The import of this letter is too clear to be mistaken for an invitation to protect Buganda since it emphasises Mwanga's desire to befriend all Europeans while retaining the independence of his kingdom.

The point is that it was not the safety of the missionaries or an invitation from Mutesa (even supposing that such an invitation existed) which led the British to come to Uganda. To even suppose this is to ignore the wider strategies of imperialism which made such factors—missionaries or African potentates—side issues, if at all. There is ample evidence to show that there were more fundamental factors which made it imperative for the British government to decide to occupy Uganda and that these factors would still have been uppermost in the minds of the British leaders whether or not missionaries and Mutesa existed. We may, for instance, refer to Britain's obsession with the security of India; an obsession that was as real as it defied all known facts of physical geography. This is well documented and perhaps the following summary of it is as good as any. Colin Cross tells us that the British entanglement in Africa resulted, in part, from the great central entanglement in India. He continues to say:

"Africa lay on the way to India and whether the route were around
the Cape or through the Suez Canal it was regarded as essential to
prevent hostile European powers establishing bases there. This
was as much a rationalisation as an operative cause; but pushful
British pioneers on the spot could always claim London support
by using the argument of communications with India. The most
obvious chain of conquest on these lines had been that in East
Africa. To protect the Suez Canal it was regarded as essential to
control Egypt. To control Egypt it was essential to control the
hinterland, Sudan. To control Sudan and the source of the Nile,
on which Egypt depended, it was necessary to control Uganda.
To control Uganda it was necessary to have a railway running from
the East Coast. To control the railway it was necessary to control
Kenya, the territory which the railway crossed."[6]

This chain reasoning is compelling, not so much because of its
accuracy as because of its simplicity. It did not matter from which
part of the globe one started, the Indian empire was threatened all the
same. The measures to ensure the security of India, moreover, could
be as bizarre as the belief in its vulnerability itself. The point is that
that belief—a cardinal article of faith for the imperial defence strategists of the period—could hardly have been modified by such insignificant considerations as a handful of cantankerous missionaries, less
still by ill-formulated wishes of a "native" potentate somewhere in
the middle of the "dark" continent where one could not even send a
gunboat when the situation warranted it.

We may, secondly, refer to the views of the actual agents of imperial
rule regarding the desirability of acquiring Uganda as a British possession. We can take the example of the views of Lord Lugard who, as
much as anyone else, epitomised the pioneers of imperialism in Uganda.
He informed his countrymen that:

The "Scramble for Africa" by the nations of Europe—an incident
without parallel in the history of the world—was due to the growing
commercial rivalry, which brought home to the civilised nations
the vital necessity of securing the only remaining fields for industrial
enterprise and expansion. It is well, then, to realise that it is for
our *advantage* [emphasis in original]— and not alone at the dictates
of duty—that we have undertaken responsibilities in East Africa.
It is in order to foster the growth of the trade of this country, and
to find an outlet for our manufactures and our surplus energy,
that our farseeing statesmen and our commercial men advocate
colonial expansion.[7]

Just so that nobody should miss the message, Lugard went on to
elaborate on this theme as follows:

"There are some who say we have no *right* [emphasis in original] in Africa at all, that "it belongs to the natives". I hold that our right is the necessity that is upon us to provide for our ever-growing population—either by opening new fields of emigration, or by providing work and employment which the development of overseas extension entails—and to stimulate trade by finding new markets, since *we know what misery trade depression brings at home*"[8] (*my emphasis*).

He concluded this spirited enunciation of the doctrine that might is right by the misplaced caution that although East Africa held the promise of commercial potential, it was not an El Dorado.[9]

In a leading article, the *London Times* of 28th September 1892, threw its considerable weight behind those agitating for the occupation of Uganda, but in a language far less intemperate than Lugard's as one might expect from such an august British institution as the *Times*. The paper stated:

"Such a withdrawal [from Uganda] would be nothing short of a national calamity. It would mean not only the loss of a great amount of capital already expended, but the destruction of our influence and prestige throughout Central Africa, the practical defeat of our anti-slavery policy, the persecution of the numerous missionaries labouring in Uganda, and the reconquest by Mohammedan fanatics of the only African state that has shown disposition to accept Christianity. Whether we desire it or not, the British East African Company must be identified for all practical purposes with national policy."[10]

With minor exceptions of hyperbole (such as the reference to numerous missionaries) and irrelevant issues (such as slave trade) this is Lugard written in a more temperate language and shorn of the emphasis on material rewards in order, one presumes, to make these arguments more palatable to the rulling class of Britain who, then as now, constitute the principal local readership for that paper.

The argument therefore is that the coming of the British rule to Uganda owed nothing to local initiative within Uganda. The tempo or momentum of imperialism was such that Uganda would have been colonised irrespective of the existence of Christian missionaries and a well-disposed king in Buganda. The factors upon which the decision to occupy Uganda was based were of more importance than Uganda itself and to use Mutesa's unproven invitation and labouring missionaries is to obscure the real issues by promoting excuses to occupy the position of causes. It was in terms of British influence and material advantages that Sir Gerald Portal recommended that the British government take over the "responsibilities" of the Company because

Uganda "dominated the north and the west of Lake Victoria, held access to Lakes Albert and Edward and controlled the headwaters of the Nile" so that its abandonment would "imperil" British interests and confine her "influence to the Coast."[11] On the basis of this report a protectorate was declared over Uganda. It was therefore the wider imperial interests which led Britain to occupy Uganda and to the extent that Christian missionaries and a well-disposed kingdom could be used to mollify a Parliament that was increasingly becoming restive about colonial expenditures, one could say that these were useful excuses, but they were no more than that. It has been felt necessary to dwell briefly on British motives for occupying Uganda in order to clear the air of the hoary theories of the "civilising mission" and other "higher purposes"[12] which the British felt for Africa and other less well-endowed lands. We have simply been inundated with these specious bogeys for much too long. If these had been the motives of colonialism, Britain would not have been so anxious to exclude countries like France and Germany from sharing this "burden" for these countries were just as civilised as Britain, the unpopularity of cricket in France and Germany notwithstanding.

In retrospect it is correct to say that British imperialism was extended to Uganda in three phases spreading over the last four decades of the 19th century. These phases are best distinguished not so much by distinct periods as by interest groups of Britons who came to Uganda. The first of these were what came to be known as "explorers". In the case of Uganda this group includes Speke, Grant, Baker and Stanley, among others. The second group of people were the Christian missionaries and the third were the actual agents of imperial rule. We are justified in classifying these groups as but part of the same process of colonialism quite simply because they were. It is possible to argue, for instance, that the "explorers" were merely interested in gathering scientific knowledge in the lands in which they travelled and that therefore they were not part of the process of colonialism. But this would be a superficial argument and one is quickly disabused of such ideas when one considers the fact that the areas visited by such "explorers" were soon claimed by their respective nations. Nineteenth century materialism quite simply had very little room for scientific knowledge which could not further the cause of trade and industry and hence of profits—especially in far away "barbarous" lands. There were, of course, a few individual exceptions to this statement: that is to say, there were individuals or societies to whom such information was of intellectual value, but these were the exceptions, not the rule. The "explorers" nevertheless went ahead to "discover" not merely the lands, lakes and mountains of Africa but the African

people as well and to name the African lakes and mountains, etc.
oblivious to the fact that these features had been known to the
African people for centuries and it was the Africans who had led
Europeans to them. Since then the term "discovery" has adorned our
history text-books despite its historical invalidity and its insulting
connotations—in particular the connotation that the Africans were
somewhat less than "people" otherwise they could not be discovered
any more than their lakes could be.

We may now turn our attention to the actual process and personnel
involved in spreading colonial rule to Uganda.[13] It is convenient to
begin with northern Uganda because it was through the north—Egypt
and the Sudan—that the Europeans had hoped to extend their influence
farther south. Subsequently, political upheavals in Egypt and the Sudan
and then in Bunyoro saddled this route with intractable problems so
that eventually the east coast offered the easier access to the interior
of East Africa. The first alien intruders to get into contact with northern
Uganda were private adventurers seeking personal fortunes principally
through trade in slaves and ivory. A Maltese by the name of de Bono
was the first among the foreign adventurers to set foot in Acholiland.
Using Gondokoro as a staging post, these bands of adventurers
penetrated as far south as Bunyoro. The main body of these well-
armed slavers were from Khartoum under European leadership.
We have already observed that most of the political units of northern
Uganda were small and it was relatively easy for these marauding
bands to aid one community against the next and then to enslave the
vanquished—and often their allies in the bargain as well. The continous
warfare generated by these bands caused untold damage in this region—
deserted or burnt out villages had become a common sight by the
time a big game hunter, Samuel Baker, arrived in this region early
in the 1860s. Enroute southwards Baker and his wife met Captains
Grant and Speke who told them of the existence of a big lake farther
south as yet unknown to Europeans and it was this information which
led the Bakers to Bunyoro, arriving at Kamurasi's court in February
1864. On their way to Bunyoro the Bakers had encountered slaving
expeditions and sometimes they were compelled to join them in order
to continue their journey at all since the forces at their disposal were
too meagre to disperse or deter the slave traders much as they wished
to do so. Eventually the Bakers were led to the lake they had come to
seek and they proceeded to name it Lake Albert. But Baker's stay in
Bunyoro was far from pleasant because he was tactless and arrogant
and his relations with the reigning Omukama (King) Kamurasi were
strained. Happily for both parties nothing untoward happened and

the Bakers were able to leave the country in the same year (1864) and
proceed to Gondokoro and thence to Britain. But to Samuel Baker
Kamurasi was a coward who was also greedy and treacherous—a
judgement that was to pass to Baker's countrymen in his reports and
was to be believed since Kamurasi did not write reports about Baker
which, in all probability, would have been just as unflattering of Baker.
Soon, however, Baker was to return to Bunyoro—a return that was
far more eventful than his earlier sojourn in that kingdom.

By way of relevant digression, it is to be borne in mind that since
1821 Egypt had exercised overlordship of sorts over the Sudan. In
1863 Ismail became the ruler of Egypt. Ismail was a man cast in a
greater imperial mould than his immediate predecessors and he was
therefore desirous of expanding his dominions—especially to transform
his vague claims in the Sudan and northern Uganda into actual annexations. To that end, therefore, he engaged the services of Samuel Baker
to whom he assigned the title of Governor General of Equatoria
province (a territory of uncertain boundaries but which was assumed
to include at least Southern Sudan and northern Uganda). Thus in
1871 Baker (by then Sir Samuel) was once more at Gondokoro but
on this occasion flying the Egyptian flag and commanding Egyptian
troops. Baker understood his new territory not merely to include
northern Uganda but also Bunyoro and Buganda as well and that
these latter kingdoms he was to take over by formal annexation.
In 1872 Baker was once again in Bunyoro. He found that the mild
Kamurasi had died a few years before and that he had been succeeded
by his martial son Kabarega. The relations between the new Governor
and the new monarch of Bunyoro rapidly deteriorated.

"On 14th May 1872 he (Baker) publicly annexed Kabalega's
country to the Egyptian empire. The young monarch was now
convinced that his fears were justified. He attacked Baker's
garrison at Masindi . . . . . . Forced to withdraw ignominiously to
northern Uganda, Baker published, in 1874, his *Ismailia* in which,
in an attempt to justify his failure, he deliberately poisoned
his countrymen's minds against Kabalega and his kingdom."[14]

It was from this point in time that the Europeans' conception of
Bunyoro's hostility to themselves was accepted for a fact and British
officials' attitude to Bunyoro was conditioned against this background.
Kabarega, like his father before him, could not write his own version
of these events and perhaps this would have availed him nothing for
his version would have been that of a "native" against Baker's (a white
man's version). It is not an exaggeration to say that Baker's most
remarkable achievement in Uganda was the creation of lasting mis-

understanding between Bunyoro and British officials. The importance of this will become apparent as our story progresses.

As Governor of Equatoria province, Baker was succeeded by Col. Gordon whose knowledge of Kabarega and his kingdom was solely obtained from Baker's accounts—the worst possible source by any standards. For the purpose of checking slave trade in southern Sudan and northern Uganda, a number of forts were constructed by Gordon and garrisoned with Egyptian and Sudanese troops, but some of these forts were constructed in northern Bunyoro without Kabarega's permission or knowledge. But Kabarega refrained from attacking these forts and this may account for the absence of open rapture between Kabarega and Gordon during the latter's term of governorship. Gordon's successor from 1878, Emin Pasha, was able to establish his presence in Acholi and West Nile which districts were, for a period, regarded as a part of Egypt's Equatoria province. Emin was to be the last European official of consequence to be on good terms with Kabarega and this may not be unrelated to the fact that he wanted to follow the evidence of his experience rather than swallow Baker's propaganda wholesale. But even Emin observed that Kabarega was suspicious of all Europeans; an observation that was as accurate as Kabarega's attitude was only to be expected since his experience of Europeans could hardly have fostered any other attitude.

Emin's goodwill towards the Africans was marred by his inability to control the raiding propensities of his Egyptian and Sudanese troops, most of whom were slave dealers in their own right. The presence of these troops in northern Uganda was as much of a threat to the population as the slavers had been before the advent of Egyptian "administration"—because the forts in which they were quartered became the centres from which the surrounding country was laid waste. Emin's governship was brought to an abrupt end by the Sudanese nationalist rising—known to history as the Mahdist rebellion—which broke out in 1883. This was a rising aimed against, among other things, Egyptian imperialism in the Sudan. For our purposes it is sufficient to note that this rising cut off Emin Pasha's contact with the north and he was forced to withdraw in 1889 from which date the Acholi, the Madi and other peoples of northern Uganda became their own masters once again. Two consequences followed from this rebellion and Emin's abandonment of his governorship. The first was that northern Uganda was left alone—or rather was left to cope with the slave and ivory traders as best it could. Secondly, it confirmed to the European potential colonisers of Uganda that the best way to get into Uganda was from the east coast and not from the north. A corollary to these events was that the relatively warm relations

between Bunyoro and the Europeans which had subsisted during
Emin's governorship effectively came to an end.

The events that we have considered deterred rather than encouraged
the European penetration of Uganda from the north. But there existed
a more congenial route from the east coast to Buganda and it was
through this route that the effective occupation of Uganda was to be
effected. It was not that this route was unknown until the 1880's.
It had been long established by caravan traders based in Zanzibar.
The first foreign traders to set foot in Buganda did so in the 1840's
using this route although foreign goods coming from the coast had
reached Buganda towards the end of the 18th century. These were
Arab and Swahili traders. Beginning from the east coast and by a
series of concentric movements from Bagamoyo westwards these
traders had effected the penetration of the mainland of East Africa.
From the coast trading posts were set up and these in turn served as
staging posts for further penetration inland. By inciting inter-
community feuds these traders were able to get slaves and ivory
which commodities were then despatched to the coast. But by the time
they reached Buganda their raiding propensities were reduced because
their line of communication with the coast had been stretched. They
could not risk unnecessary confrontations in case they found their
line of retreat blocked. But more important than this, in Buganda they
found a tightly organised kingdom in which foreigners, for the sake
of their own safety among other things, were not free to wander all
over the kingdom. Their transactions had therefore to be carried out
at the court of the king and under his control. Moreover, in Buganda,
unlike among most of the communities along the route from the coast,
the time–honoured device of setting one ethnic group against the
next one quite simply could not work. The Baganda were a single
ethnic group under one king. Within the kingdom of Buganda these
traders had to carry out their transactions by negotiations with the
king and largely on his own terms because it was on his goodwill that
their security depended. This brings us to the first major difference
between the north and the south of Uganda with regard to colonial
penetration. That is, foreign penetration of the area south and east
of the Nile involved far less suffering of the African population than
was the case northwards. The explanation for this disparity of experience seems to be that the first foreigners to reach the south first came
to the well-organised kingdom of Buganda and that their initial
impact could not disrupt the cohesion of that kingdom. Failing in
this and in the light of the fact that, in case of confrontation and defeat,
these traders knew that their line of retreat to the coast was hopelessly

overstreched, they had to deal with the king of Buganda on his own terms. In the north, as we have seen, the scale of political organisation was such that these adventurers found it relatively easy to set one community against the next one and thus to intensify disorder. These Arab and Swahili traders came to the mainland of East Africa seeking ivory and slaves in exchange for their firearms, cotton cloths and a few other trinkets of doubtful decorative value.

More than their wares of trade the Arabs also brought their religion, Islam. But because their main concern was trade rather than the conversion of the Africans to their faith, this latter remained a secondary issue so that no special effort was made to convert Baganda to Islam— at least not until the coming of the Christian missionaries. In fact Suna II, the Kabaka of Buganda at the time, expressed some intermittent interest in Islam but he was not converted and towards the end of his reign he became positively hostile to all foreign traders and banned them from his kingdom.

Much more pertinent for the history of Uganda was the coming of Europeans to Buganda—Captains Grant and Speke — early in 1862. Speke had been to East Africa earlier (1856-59) in search of the source of the Nile.   But he had travelled from the east coast to Lakes Tanganyika and Victoria and had gone back without positively vindicating his theories about the source of the Nile and without therefore locating it. It was this follow-up expedition to complete his earlier journey that brought him to Buganda in 1862. The two Britons were favourably impressed by Mutesa as were many foreigners who came into contact with him. Speke conceived the idea of missionary endeavours in this region of Africa using Buganda as a base, but the C.M.S. in England were not enthusiastic about the scheme and with Speke's untimely death in England in 1864, the idea of missionaries coming to Buganda was put on ice for a while. From the departure of Speke and Grant from Buganda the flow of traders and their wares from the coast increased with Mutesa's encouragement. For a period, too, it looked as if Buganda might become an Islamic state of sorts because Mutesa permitted the adoption of the Islamic calendar and Kagwa tells us that between 1867 and 1876 Mutesa even observed the Ramadhan. Gifts were exchanged between Mutesa's Buganda and Zanzibar. But Mutesa was never fully converted to Islam and the arrival of Christian missionaries soon made this possibility academic.

Reference has already been made to the arrival of Stanley and to the letter which was sent to England appealing for missionaries to come to Buganda. When the letter was published in London's *Daily Telegraph* in November, 1875, there was a warm response by way of private financial donations reaching the C.M.S. to make such a venture possible. Nevertheless the C.M.S. did not decide for Buganda whole-heartedly since the objections which had been raised when Speke broached the subject a few years earlier were still extant. A missionary post in Buganda would be completely isolated and vulnerable to attack should the Baganda and their rulers change their minds about the presence of missionaries in their country. In such a contingency there would be no secure line of retreat and hardly any means of rescue (this being the age of gunboats, instruments of imperialism which were inapplicable against a landlocked kingdom such as Buganda)· At the same time there was no question of sending missionaries to or through Bunyoro in the 1870s since that country was locked in conflict with Egyptian expansionist agents. In any case Bunyoro was already adjudged to be hostile to Europeans as we have seen so that the question of sending missionaries there did not arise. The point therefore is that the C.M.S. did not take the decision to venture into Buganda without a certain amount of misgivings. It is possible—perhaps probable—that the C.M.S. would have got cold feet about the whole venture had they even suspected what seems to have been Mutesa's real motives in sending for missionaries so readily when Stanley suggested it. It seems that Mutesa's real interest in Christian missionaries—better still in European missionaries—was to have foreigners in his kingdom to act as a counterweight to the Egyptian threat to Buganda. The Egyptian activities to the north of his kingdom were not lost on Mutesa. This motive seems to have been the uppermost consideration in Mutesa's mind in this period rather than the zeal for western religions about which he could not have known enough to be enthusiastic anyway. Additionally, Mutesa was too much of an astitute politician to be swayed by untested foreign doctrines so that whatever impressions of Christianity he might have gathered from Stanley could not have been weighed outside the political realities of the day.

In fact Mutesa was soon to learn that Egypt had not given up designs upon his kingdom for in 1876 Gordon sent an armed expedition under an Egyptian officer, Neuhr Aga, to hoist the Egyptian flag on the shores of Lake Victoria, in Mutesa's territory. Mutesa's tact averted what might well have turned into an open confrontation between the representatives of the Egyptian government and Buganda and Neuhr Aga and his troops were rescued from virtual imprisonment through the good offices of Emin Pasha. More than this, however, the British government had come to the conclusion that the Egyptian expansion southwards was undesirable and should accordingly be discouraged. To this end therefore Gordon's last attempt to annex Buganda and Bunyoro to the Egyptian empire was positively discouraged by the

British government through the agency of the British Consul at Zanzibar who was then the virtual ruler of those islands and the principal agent to oversee British interests on the mainland of East Africa. One might also observe in passing that the British government's decision to discourage Egyptian expansion southwards did not stem from any desire to maintain, less still to enhance, the independence of either Bunyoro or Buganda but rather to save the region from the spread of Islam. British imperialism and Islam had been seen to be incompatible and this was the parting of their ways as far as Uganda was concerned, but it was to take another sixteen years before this could be overtly pursued as the official British policy. The upshot of all this was that by 1877 the possibility of Egyptian expansion into Bunyoro and Buganda had passed out of the realm of practical politics and for reasons that had little or nothing to do with Bunyoro or Buganda as such.

On 30th June 1877 the vanguard of the C.M.S. missionaries in the persons of Lt. Shergold Smith and Rev. C. T. Wilson arrived in Buganda to be followed, at the beginning of 1879, by the Roman Catholic White Fathers. With the arrival of the Christian missionaries began the real colonisation not only of Buganda but of Uganda as the whole British protectorate was soon to be known.[15] It might appear strange that one can make a general statement such as the foregoing one without qualification. The point of it is that in Uganda, unlike in any of her mainland neighbours, the missionaries were the most effective agents of colonialism—initially more effective than even the agents of the British government themselves. This is not to suggest that in Kenya or mainland Tanzania missionaries were not an important arm of colonialism, for they were. But the point is that in Uganda, to a much greater extent than in her two neighbours, the missionaries were the most important arm of colonialism. In mainland Tanzania, for example, missionaries and their activities hardly became a national issue at all. In Kenya it took the Africans, especially in the Central province, only a few years to realise that there was no difference between a White settler and the missionary, *Gutiri mubea na muthungu*, as the Kikuyu laconically expressed it. In Uganda the most effective agency of transition from the traditional way of life to colonialism was the missionary and the issues of religion have dominated public life in Uganda to the present day. In order to get a proper perspective it is necessary to turn our attention to the activities of the Christian missionaries in Buganda as these explain events in the subsequent Uganda Protectorate—the name Uganda itself owing its origin to the kingdom of Buganda, apparently for no better reason than that the Swahili interpreters of the European colonialists found it difficult to pronounce the word Buganda.

The arrival of the Christian missionaries—the C.M.S. Anglicans, called Protestants in Uganda and in this survey, and the White Fathers —was a momentous event. As it has been indicated, Buganda was the staging post for the new order—religion, colonial rule, cash crops etc.—all these began in Buganda and were then extended to the rest of the protectorate with different degrees of success. The relations between the Baganda—especially the Kabaka—and their new guests were initially curious. The Baganda could not readily understand, less still accept, the missionaries' contention that they were interested in teaching their religion and in nothing else besides. For their part the missionaries were nonplussed as to what else they were expected to do and why. But we have seen the background against which Mutesa had asked for missionaries to come to his country. Moreover, Buganda's experience of religious teaching, if such it could be termed, prior to the coming of the C.M.S. personnel, was limited to the rudiments of Christianity which Stanley had imparted to them and to the equally peripatetic teaching of Islam by their Arab guests. Yet neither Stanley nor the Arabs had claimed that they were solely interested in the teaching of religion alone. Both the Arabs and Stanley had taught their respective religions but this had not deterred them from trading in firearms and, occasionally, from joining the Kabaka's armies to raid his neighbours. Stanley, for example, who came from the same country as the C.M.S. missionaries and who had interested Mutesa in his religion, had assisted the Baganda to raid the islands of Buvuma in Lake Victoria. The Baganda were therefore justified in expecting their new European guests to teach their religion but also to give them the benefits of their superior technology—especially firearms. Mutesa in particular must have felt let down since, as we have postulated, one of the reasons he wanted missionaries in a country was to bolster his strength in relation to Egyptian expansionism. That these Europeans insited on teaching religion only and not in making or trading in firearms must have greatly devalued their utility in Mutesa's eyes.

Then, as we have indicated, before this dilemma of intentions and utility was resolved, Father Lourdel and Brother Amans landed at Entebbe on 23rd February 1879 and these were reinforced, in June of the same year, by Fathers Barbot, Girault and Livinhac. These were the vanguard of the Roman Catholic order of the White Fathers. What had been a state of bemused curiosity in Buganda turned into complete confusion because the arrival of yet another batch of "teachers of religion" was not originally a source of enlightenment in Buganda— it was a source of confusion. The new arrivals also claimed to be teachers of Christian religion but of a more valid Christianity than that of the C.M.S. who had preceded them in Buganda. One can easily imagine why this was confusing to the aspiring Baganda Christians-to-be. Father Lourdel and Mackay, the respective leaders of the Catholic and Protestant missions, were men of excessive zeal in the true Christian crusading sense of old and their endless doctrinal disputes before Mutesa and his subjects must at best have appeared pointless to their Baganda audience. This situation was not made any easier by the fact that these Christian leaders were exceedingly intolerant of views not conforming to their own and that the art of compromise was foreign to their nature. If their doctrinal debates appeared pointless, their collective inability to provide firearms or any kind of military advantage rendered their presence in Buganda even more undesirable. To compound this confusion, the Muslim Arabs who had hitherto not been interested in conversion as an end in itself took every opportunity to discredit the Christian missionaries before Mutesa and such opportunities were legion. As a result of these goings-on, Mutesa's attitude towards the Christian missions cooled visibly. The traditional religions and their ministers who had lost ground at court to the new religions revived. In fact Mutesa became so unfriendly that the Catholic missionaries thought it prudent to remove themselves from Buganda in November, 1882 and to establish a temporary station at Kagei, just south of Lake Victoria and there they were to remain until Mwanga, Mutesa's successor, summoned them again to Rubaga where they arrived in July 1885. Then the political climate in Buganda underwent a rapid change.

In the course of 1883 news reached Buganda that a European (Joseph Thomson) had reached the northern end of Lake Victoria by the direct route from the Coast through Masailand; this being the route no Europeans had taken before. But, more important than this, that was also the route the Baganda believed and feared would bring the conquerors of their country—a fear since heightened by the Egyptian incursions of a few years before. Then in October 1884 Mutesa died and was succeeded by his youthful and headstrong son, Mwanga. Mutesa's death, as much as anything else, altered the course of public affairs in Buganda and, as it turned out, in Uganda. In order to get this in its proper perspective, it is necessary to go a little backwards in history so as to assess the importance of Mutesa's death at that particular moment of his kingdom's history.

By the time the Europeans came to Buganda Mutesa was a mature and prestigious ruler as all who came into contact with him readily testify. His control over his kingdom was complete. As a matter of policy strangers were not allowed to wander over the kingdom for whatever purpose. Any transactions they wished to carry out in Buganda were closely supervised by the Kabaka or by his chiefs. This policy seems to have originated as much from the need to ensure the safety of their persons as from the desirability of keeping track of their activities while they sojourned in Buganda. This policy had affected the coastal traders, British explorers and it was also applied to missionaries. Before Mutesa's death some conversion of chiefs and pages had taken place at court where the missionaries had begun their "labours". This was very important for the subsequent history of Buganda because it meant that the missions had converted Buganda's chiefs and future chiefs before converting the peasants. The young pages at court who were converted were in the process of being groomed for public office in the future. In the light of the fact that Buganda state system was hierarchical and authoritarian, the conversion of Buganda's leadership secured a powerful and sympathetic base in the state structure for the Christian missions. Mwanga, who succeeded Mutesa, did not have anything like the experience or the prestige that his father had acquired over the period of his long reign. And yet Mwanga was taking over a kingdom in which the seeds of disorder and disunity had been sown by the Christian missionaries even if this may not have been done deliberately. These divisions were moreover exercerbated by the manner in which the new religions themselves came to Uganda. The C.M.S. were not only Protestants but Britons by nationality and the Catholic White Fathers were French. Thus along with these new doctrines there were imported into Uganda the national antipathies of Britain and France which antipathies were themselves ancient and still subsist in more subtle forms even today. This fact contributed substantially to the rapid transformation of religious faiths into political parties or factions as we shall see presently. The upshot of all this was that Mwanga found himself beset with numerous problems which he was not properly equipped to deal with by reason of his inexperience and temperament.

In the year 1885 more news reached Buganda that another European (Dr. Karl Peters) was making "treaties" in the interior of mainland East Africa, opposite Zanzibar. It was also in that same year that the news of the approach of James Hannington reached Mwanga. Hannington was the newly appointed first Anglican Bishop of Eastern Equatorial Africa and he had come to the interior of East Africa by the same route as that taken by Joseph Thomson. Mwanga was perturbed by these events—especially by the activities of Europeans, since it appeared that they were closing in on his kingdom for as yet unspecified but sinister purpose. It also seems probable that the Arabs at his court persuaded him (if any persuasion was necessary) that all these activities were a co-ordinated effort on the part of the Europeans to do harm to his kingdom. Mwanga reacted—and, with the benefit of hindsight, some might say he overreacted. When Hannington reached Busoga, he was arrested, detained for about a week and then put to death on Mwanga's orders. The hapless Hannington had been mistaken for one of the empire builders and he thus met his death. We have already explained the relationship between Buganda and some of the states of Busoga and it was against that background that Mwanga's orders could have effect in Busoga. Simultaneously the Christian converts in Buganda were persecuted lest they became the agents of these sinister forces at large. In 1886 those who would not renounce their faith were burnt alive at Namugongo, a few miles outside Kampala. (These were the now celebrated Uganda Martyrs in whose memory a shrine was erected at the sight on which they were massacred and which shrine was concecrated by Pope Paul VI in 1969—the first Pontiff in modern times to visit the African continent.)

As so often in the history of Christianity before and since the Donation of Constantine, this persecution had the effect of increasing rather than decreasing the number of converts—much to Mwanga's understandable annoyance. Much more important than merely annoying Mwanga, the attitude of the missionaries changed as a result of this persecution and massacre. Hitherto the missionaries had been content to work within Buganda's establishment without seeking to change it. After the massacre, the missionaries were determined to have a political base within that establishment to ensure the future success of their endeavours. In other words they sought to install their own converts in positions of authority. Such men would not only be sympathetic to the missionaries but would also be a great deal more amenable to their ideas and, if necessary, defend them against royal excesses. The stage was thus set for the revolution that was to change the institutions of Buganda which had been carefully fashioned over the past four or so centuries. That this revolution was possible was itself due to two principal factors. Firstly, Mwanga, who presided over Buganda during this eventful period, was demonstrably unequal to the task of controlling the foreigners who were subverting his kingdom under his very nose. He did not have the experience or the prestige that had enabled his father to keep foreigners in their place within his kingdom. Secondly, it was comparatively easy for the Christian missions to secure the political base they desired because by and large the evangelisation of Buganda had affected the court—or the leadership of Buganda as we have indicated. Within this elite the influence of the missionaries was tremendous as the course of events was soon to show.

Mwanga fearfully watched the influence these foreigners wielded over his subjects—influence, moreover, that was growing day by day as his own was correspondingly dwindling. The Baganda converts' zeal for the new religions made them impatient with the "old ways of doing things" and one of such old ways was the unquestionable power of the Kabaka which these "new men" were ever questioning Daily incidents of insurbodination and insolence among his pages and the equally frequent moral lectures by the missionaries increasingly became unbearable to Mwanga. In 1888 he decided to rid his kingdom of all foreigners and the "readers", as the Baganda converts were known. The plan was to lure them onto canoes and then maroon them on some island in Lake Victoria and leave them there to starve to death. By this stroke Mwanga hoped to regain control of his kingdom and also to get rid of irksome subjects and visitors at a go.

In fact everything turned out differently. The plot had no chance of success right from the beginning because Mwanga no longer had the means to carry it out. To begin with, it was leaked out prematurely by the very people who were supposed to implement it. The chiefs, young and old alike, no longer obeyed the Kabaka's command without question. The young chiefs especially had come to regard themselves as the arbiters of Buganda and they did not see why they should obey a Kabaka who was not even a reader like themselves. The older chiefs—those who were not readers—had for sometime lost influence at court and Mwanga's excesses against them had effectively alienated them. These excesses, which included public humiliation of some of the most respected of the old chiefs, are catalogued by Wright and they need not detain us here.[16] The readers, moreover, had by 1888 fashioned private armies—the Christian factions and the Muslim one had each their own guns. And they were not reluctant to use them even against their own Kabaka. Since the massacres of a few years before each of these parties was determined to defend itself against royal excesses to which there seemed to be no end. When it came to the execution of the plot, Mwanga found that it could not be carried out because each of the parties of the readers was fully prepared for a showdown. The moment of truth for Mwanga had arrived. On 10th September, 1888 the three parties combined and deposed Mwanga with, no doubt, the approval of the Christian missions. These parties had come to the conclusion that Mwanga's continued occupation of the throne was a physical danger to themselves since there seemed to be no let-up in his schemes for their liquidation.

Before we follow the course of these momentous events it is appropriate that we pause in order to estimate the magnitude of the changes that had taken place in the Kiganda state system and of which changes the removal of Mwanga from his throne was only an external visible symbol. Within a decade of their arrival, the missionaries had created a new class in Buganda—the "readers"—which rapidly became the most powerful interest group in the kingdom. That an interest group could oust a king of Buganda was something that no one could have dared contemplate let alone attempt only a few years before 1888. Yet that is exactly what happened then. The fundamental precepts upon which the governance of Buganda was based had been changed beyond recognition in 1888. It is something of an exaggeration to say, as Wright says approvingly, that "Mwanga's fundamental weakness on his accession in 1884 was that he was an unbeliever in the age of faith,"[17] because both the Muslim and the Christian parties had by 1888 become consciously political parties as much as they were religious faiths. Additionally, the wars of this period were as much aimed at preserving the new faiths in Buganda as they were aimed at the political control of the kingdom. In the final analysis it was the political ambitions of the converts that were the fundamental causes of the conflict for it can scarcely be maintained that the wars between Christians and Muslims and then between the Christian parties themselves were aimed at the preservation of any faith. Moreover, it can hardly be overemphasised that the number of converts, as a proportion of the whole population of Buganda, was infinitesimal and today, nearly a hundred years later, the adherents of these religions are still a minority. It would therefore be incorrect to call the 1880s "the age of faith"— it was the period when a minority of readers seized the control of Buganda kingdom. That this was possible at all was due to the authoritarian nature of the Kiganda political system to which reference has been made. Moreover, it was the readers who had a monopoly of firearms so that even if the peasantry had been inclined to rise against them—a remote possibility in the light of what we know of Buganda's political system of the period—the readers would have in all probability won. Mwanga therefore did not have a dog's chance against the forces ranged against him. Wright, almost ecstatically, quotes Mwanga as having told Peters in 1890, that:

> "I am Mutesa's son, and what Mutesa was in Buganda that I will also be, and against those who will not have it so I shall make war."[18]

This ambition we are supposed to accept as an explanation for Mwanga's downfall. Mwanga was quite right to seek to be the master in his own kingdom just as his forefathers had been, all his excesses and faults of character notwithstanding. Some of his predecessors had been guilty of worse acts of cruelty and injustice and nothing drastic had befallen them. In other words even if all the charges levelled against Mwanga by his numerous Christian and Muslim detractors were true, he was still right to claim supreme authority in the kingdom of his forefathers. One can justly accuse Mwanga of failing to see that the essential base of his authority had been effectively subverted by the new religio-political groupings. Just as Buganda had been saved the ravages of slave raiders and other adventurers because of her political and social cohesion in the past, so also when the new religious undermined that cohesion the king, who was the symbolic as well as the active embodiment of it, lost his pre-eminence in the state structure. This is the sense in which the wars of the 1880's and 1890's and their outcome can be, and should be, called a revolution.

To compound the confusion in Buganda, the Muslims (especially the Arabs), who had preceded the Christian missions in Buganda and who all along had been content with trade rather than the control of the kingdom, had definitely become interested in Buganda politics by the 1880's. They, like Mwanga, but for different reasons, were anxious that European influence should as far as possible be curbed. And the instruments of European influence in Buganda were the Christian missionaries and their African converts. This is what makes the alliance of September 1888 so unnatural and it is the main explanation for its rapid disintegration. In October 1888, hardly a month after the readers had turned Mwanga off his throne, the Muslims turned against their Christian allies and chased them out of the capital. When Kiwewa, who had been installed in succession to Mwanga, temporised about being circumcised, he was deposed and replaced with his brother, Kalema, who was promptly circumcised. Thus for a brief period Buganda became an Islamic state of sorts. We are told by several writers on this over-researched period of Buganda's history that the immediate cause of the Muslims' discontent was the feeling that they had not been given a fair share of the offices of state by their Christian allies after the deposition of Mwanga. But this could only have been an excuse rather than a cause since the fundamental rivalry and hostility between the Muslim and Christian parties had not been removed by the threat posed by Mwanga to all the parties of readers—it had merely been shelved in the face of a graver danger and when this danger was removed, i.e. when Mwanga was deposed, that rivalry and hostility came to the fore in Muslim and Christian politics.

After the eviction of the Christian parties by the Muslims, the Catholics had fled to the south of Lake Victoria and the protestants to Nkore—or Ankole as it was soon to be renamed. Both Christian parties realised their fundamental weakness in that they did not have a prince of the blood to put on the throne should they eventually succeed in ousting their recent allies and even more recent enemies—the Muslims. Twice, but separately, both the Catholics and the Protestants had attempted to oust the Muslims but they had been beaten off by Kalema's forces. The Catholics, most of whom had found their way into Buddu, had been joined by Mwanga. Messages were exchanged between the Catholics in Buddu and the Protestants in Ankole the result of which was the agreement between the two parties to mount a joint invasion of Buganda and to restore Mwanga—this latter had been agreed upon because the two sides had failed to secure a prince around whom to rally and fight their way back to Buganda and into power. Thus it happened that in October 1889 the Christian parties converged on Mengo, defeated the Muslims and Mwanga once again sat on his increasingly precarious throne. This victory, however, was anything but complete because the Muslim forces had beaten an orderly retreat northwards, gained the friendship of Bunyoro's Kabarega and obtained more troops so that in November 1889 the Muslims were once again in control of the capital and the Christians parties in flight. It was not until February 1890 that the combined Christian parties decisively defeated the Muslims and scattered them. Mwanga once more uneasily sat on his throne.

What was the outcome of these wars? By finally winning the wars, Mwanga had lost his major point. This was that originally he had chafed at the influence which was exercised by the missionaries and their Baganda converts in his kingdom and he had sought to regain control of his kingdom. The course of the civil wars decisively proved that the Christian chiefs had become the masters of Buganda and that the Kabaka would only rule at their pleasure. He had become their instrument and no longer their master. A more undesirable outcome, Mwanga could not have contemplated. As a matter of fact it would be more correct to say that the chiefs had won the wars and then in the absence of a more suitable candidate, had reinstated Mwanga in order to assuage the peasant populace which was getting increasingly restive. Secondly, and much more important for what was soon to be Uganda Protectorate, these wars established the principle that religious affiliation would henceforth be the basis of political association and action. It is perhaps necessary to explain that in Buganda as in the rest of Uganda the unconverted populace (called "pagans" in the Christian and Islamic literature) remained the overwhelming majority. But these had forfeited access to political power as the old values were discarded for new ones, the access to which was, for a very long time, exclusively controlled by the missionaries. This practice was enhanced by the fact that when formal education began to spread in Uganda, it was also

controlled by the missionaries who were the sole providers of that
rapidly much sought–after commodity for the Protectorate government did not seriously concern itself with the education of "natives"
until well into the thirties. In turn this explains why the Muslims
increasingly fell behind their Christian counterparts in the management
of public affairs in Uganda—they did not have the missionaries to
give them education.

The victory of the Christian parties over the Muslims did not mean
the end of the upheavals in Buganda; more disorders were still in
store. The explanation for this lay in the fact that the unity between
the Catholics and the Protestants had been an expedient forced upon
those parties by the necessity of overcoming their Muslim rivals.
The rivalry and hostility between them had by no means come to an
end. Just as all the readers had combined to depose Mwanga who
had posed a threat to all of them, so also did the Christian parties
combine in order to dispose of a common threat to their position—the
Muslims. Once this threat had been removed, the Christian parties
turned against each other. It is from this period that one can date the
preponderance of opportunism over principle in the management of
public affairs in Uganda—a preponderance that is still with us today.
For Mwanga these wars were a great misfortune in a fundamental
way. It has already been observed that the Christian victory over the
Muslims had established those parties as the most poweful political
groups in the country and had turned Mwanga into a mere tool of
the Christian chiefs. This was not all. In Mwanga's restoration, the
Catholics had played a prominent role and, when the fortunes of war
were still going against the Christian parties, Mwanga had been kept
by the Catholic party and with this party he was increasingly identified.
What this meant was that Mwanga was seen by the Protestant party
as belonging to the Catholic party and not as a Kabaka of all Buganda
as the other Kabakas had been before him so that Mwanga's authority
was undermined among the most powerful section of his subjects.

The local troubles in Buganda were soon overtaken by external
events of much wider significance—events that were to move Uganda
from the era of informal contacts with adventurers and missionaries
into the era of colonial rule. This was brought about by what has come
to be known as the "scramble for Africa" by European nations, an
event to which reference has been made and which event gathered
momentum at about the same time as the Christian and Muslim
parties were fighting for the control of Buganda. The Berlin Conference
of 1884-5 had confirmed what was already a fact and this was that
Germany had entered the field of colonisation as earnestly as Britain

and France had done for some years. German contacts with East Africa had been firmly established by the middle of the 19th century (the German trading firm of Hertz, for example, had been established in Zanzibar in 1844). During the 19th century German explorers were among the Europeans who undertook the exploration and the mapping of East Africa and like their counterparts of other European nations, these German explorers tried to persuade their Government to take active steps and acquire the territories through which they had wandered. This agitation was given greater weight by the German Chamber of Commerce who saw that German industry would need tropical products and that these could be best secured through the acquisition of tropical dependencies. But the German Government was for sometime unconvinced of the wisdom of acquiring colonies in Africa. Bismarck, for instance, is reported to have said that:

"No success could be hoped for by transplanting the Prussian government assessor and his bureacratic system to Africa."

Moreover, this remarkable statesman believed that a string of colonies without a fleet to defend them would be vulnerable and would lead to unnecessary international complications of which he had more than a handful during this period. Among the German public, moreover, Africa was an unknown quantity and for this reason some of the promoters of German colonisation advocated the colonisation of South America instead of Africa, ignoring the existence of the Monroe Doctrine which, by this period, the United States was strong enough to enforce.

This attitude of official disinterest was soon to change primarily because of European rivalry all over the globe and because of the initiative of private individuals—in the case of East Africa mainly because of the initiative of Dr. Karl Peters. In 1884 Karl Peters founded a society for German colonisation of which he became the President and he secured his government's approval to make Zanzibar his society's staging post for operations into the interior of East Africa. Karl Peters and his associates reasoned that their activities in East Africa would not be impeded because Zanzibar on her own was weak and her protector, Britain, was deeply involved in other international troubles to bother about a few German adventurers wandering in the interior of East Africa. This reasoning proved to be correct because Britain was engaged in quelling a nationalist rebellion in the Sudan and she was also locked in other imperial disputes with Russia in the Far East. Thus from November 1884 Karl Peters and his associates proceeded inland and made "treaties" of protection with whoever they thought was an African chief.[19] These "treaties" were recognised by the German government which granted Peters an imperial charter in February 1885 and the right to administer the area the Company's leaders claimed to have acquired by treaty. Thus almost overnight Germany acquired the largest tract of territory on the mainland of East Africa—the territory that came to be known as Tanganyika (mainland Tanzania of today).

The activities of the German agents in the interior of East Africa woke Britain to the possibility that their interests might be excluded from East Africa altogether. Hence by the Anglo-German agreement of 1886 the British and the German governments divided the territory between the Tana and Ruvuma rivers into their respective "Spheres of influence"—a terminology that suited the British mood at the time since it did not commit Britain to any particular course of action while, at the same time, her interests, whatever these might prove to be in the future, were safeguarded. The division of the region into spheres of influence was as far as Britain was willing to go. Yet this division left the position of Uganda uncertain because the imaginary line between the two spheres only extended to the eastern shore of Lake Victoria. The British government temporised and private initiative stepped in.

In 1886 Sir William Mackinnon, the Chairman of British India Steamship Company, set up a different company by the name British East Africa Company with the object of ascertaining the resources of the British sphere of influence and he offered to administer the region on behalf of the British Government through the agency of his company. To the British government this was the easiest way out of a problem they had not quite made up their minds how to dispose of. The Company was granted an imperial Charter and renamed Imperial British East African Company (hereafter I.B.E.A. Co.) and given the responsibility to govern the region between Mombasa and Lake Victoria. And so, early in 1889 F. J. Jackson, the first Company agent, was despatched to explore the area under the Company's jurisdiction.

By the time of Jackson's appointment, news of the disturbances in Buganda had reached the coast and before he set off for the interior, Jackson was instructed by his superiors not to enter Buganda because the Company's slender resources could not permit the undertaking of expensive risks. But in June 1889 he received an appeal for help from Mwanga in a letter written from Sesse islands soon after which he also got news of Mwanga's victory over Kalema (i.e. the victory of October, 1889). Jackson was unsure of what course of action to take since he had clearly been instructed not to go to Buganda and the news of Mwanga's victory seemed to make his assistance unnecessary. He therefore sent emissaries to Buganda to inquire whether his assistance was still required and he stipulated that should this be the case, he would, in return, require compensation and a treaty from Mwanga. The nature of such a treaty was not specified and Mwanga's reply was vague because he did not immediately need Jackson's assistance. In these circumstances, Jackson moved off towards Mt. Elgon, apparently to hunt for big game.

We have already noted that after the first Christian victory over the Muslims, the latter had withdrawn northwards, regrouped and had been reinforced by Kabarega so that they had returned and chased the Christians and their Mwanga from the capital in November, 1889. Now, in desperation, Mwanga once again wrote to Jackson for assistance and on this occasion he accepted Jackson's earlier terms. But then Jackson was absent on his travels and he did not get the letter until March 1890 by which time the Christians had finally ousted their Muslim rivals. In February 1890, however, Dr. Karl Peters had entered Jackson's camp in the latter's absence and had read his mail among which mail there was Mwanga's second letter of appeal to Jackson. After reading Jackson's mail, Peters hastened to Buganda and, in order to promote German interests, he promptly offered a treaty to Mwanga on behalf of his own chartered Company. Mwanga accepted the treaty not only because it was a fair one to him, but also because the Catholic faction was strongly in favour of it. The Catholics preferred a German Company to a British one because they reasoned, quite rightly as it turned out, that a British Company would only favour their Protestant rivals to their own detriment. It took a lot of cajoling for the Protestant chiefs to sign the treaty because their missionaries had advised against it as they were in favour of a British Company for obvious reasons. In fact Karl Peters' *coup* dissolved into this air just as soon as it seemed to have been executed. After getting his treaty signed, he heard that Jackson was heading for Buganda and he withdrew to the south of Lake Victoria as speedily as he had come. As soon as he arrived, Jackson, too, offered a treaty of protection on behalf of his Company but Mwanga, on the advice of the Catholic missionaries, refused to sign it on the grounds, it is alleged, that its terms were much more stringent than those which had been offered by Karl Peters. As he had no further instructions from his directors, Jackson decided to withdraw from Buganda, leaving behind Edward Gedge with a small force (presumably to keep British presence visible because the German agents were lurking about in the region.)

As it turned out, the efforts of both Peters and Jackson were rendered irrelevant by events in Europe for on 1st July 1890 an agreement was signed between Britain and Germany—the agreement known as the Heligoland Treaty. Although Uganda figured in this treaty, she was not one of the causes leading to it. The treaty was meant to reduce tensions between the signatory powers over those areas all over the world and also within Europe where their rival claims and ambitions clashed. It provided, among other things, that the territory known as Uganda was to become a British sphere of influence and that in return the island of Heligoland, in the North Sea, was to be ceded to Germany by Britain. There were several other provisions of the treaty which do not concern us here; it is sufficient to note that this was the period when chunks of territory on the African continent and elsewhere were traded about with abandon without reference to the wishes of the people who occupied them. Uganda, like many an African country, was merely a pawn in the game of European diplomacy. What the Heligoland treaty did for Uganda was to end the uncertainty as to which European country would take it over.

Now that the area of the Company's "responsibility" had been defined and extended, it was decided to send Captain Lugard to Buganda as the first fully accredited representative of the Company. Other events increased the tempo of the coming of colonialism to Buganda and then to Uganda. Lugard was already in the employment of the Company and when he received his orders to proceed to Buganda with the utmost speed, he was already in Kikuyuland making "treaties" and setting up Company stations in the country that was ultimately to become Kenya. The real reason for his summary despatch to Buganda, however, was not that the area under the company's juris-diction had just been extended, but rather that during the wars in Buganda after which Jackson had failed to obtain a treaty from Mwanga, news had reached London about a large expedition under the leadership of Emin Pasha which was said to be heading for the interior and which was suspected of heading for Buganda. Additionally, it was also believed that Charles Stokes, a one-time missionary who had turned into an ivory trader,[20] was carrying a large consign-ment of arms and was heading for Buganda. It was felt that if Mwanga got all those arms, he would be difficult to come to terms with. Hence Lugard's summary despatch to Buganda was aimed at forestalling Emin's expedition should it be heading for that kingdom and to prevent Stokes selling arms to Mwanga. For this twin objective speed was essential: hence the haste with which Lugard was ordered to march to Buganda.

Lugard's major mission was to secure the control of Buganda for the Company by means of an agreement to that effect. Among his other instructions there was one directing him to consolidate the position of the Protestant party while, at the same time, reconciling the Catholic party. Apparently this latter instruction did not appear contradictory to Lugard's superiors and it was to prove impossible to carry out in practice. Lugard duly arrived in Kampala on 18th December, 1890, and set about negotiating for a treaty with Mwanga. This was not as easy as he had anticipated because his arrival had been seen as a triumph of the Protestants by all the parties. The Catholic party was hostile and so was Mwanga whose sympathies lay with them. Lugard managed to get Mwanga and the Catholic party to sign the agreement by bluff and threats for he had a small but trained and disciplined force and, of course, a maxim gun. Some of the Protestant chiefs were suspicious of Lugard's motives and were reluctant to sign the treaty but Lugard's threat to leave the country if they did not sign was enough to secure their co-operation since they were the minority and they did not want Lugard to abandon them to the mercies of their more numerous and recent allies between whom and themselves antagonism was rapidly mounting.

Soon after the signing of the agreement, Lugard helped in beating off one of the Muslim incursions into Buganda from Bunyoro so that it looked as if the protection just offered under the agreement might serve a useful purpose after all. But, as has already been observed, with Muslims ceasing to be a material threat, hostility between the Christian parties mounted. This was exercerbated by the curious provision in the agreement that in the event of any chief (of whatever rank) changing his religion, he would also lose his official post together with the usufruct rights to land attached to that post. The provision had been insisted upon by the Protestant party in order, apparently, to keep the balance of political power because the Catholics were not only more numerous, but they also had the sympathies of the Kabaka. The Protestants therefore feared that their members might desert their faith and join the one which seemed to have the support of the Kabaka. In fact this fear proved to be unfounded for no such changes of faith occurred on any scale that merits mention. But such was the degree of hostility and polarisation of attitudes that anything seemed possible. What is more, each of the Christian parties had large armed groups of men which were prepared to fight it out should the tension prove impossible to resolve by any other means. Lugard therefore found himself increasingly playing the role of mediator (a biased one it might be added) between two armed and hostile camps.

Before the tension between the Christian parties worked itself out, Lugard decided to undertake a journey to the western parts of Uganda. It would appear that the tension which was building up between the Christian parties had convinced Lugard that sooner or later hostilities would break out and he would be involved. He therefore sought the means of increasing the forces at his command if his intervention in such a conflict was to be decisive since the force he had brought from

Kenya was quite small. He wanted to enlist the Sudanese troops which were under the command of Selim Bey. These were the troops left behind by Emin Pasha, in the neighbourhood of Lake Albert, when he was finally compelled to abandon Equatorial Province as a result of the nationalist rising in the Sudan. Besides the need to provide against this eventuality, the Company also was anxious to augment its meagre resources[21] by finding local items of trade—especially ivory. Lugard therefore also undertook this journey to explore the possibilities of ivory trade in this region. Finally, it seems also that perhaps a more compelling reason for making the journey was to hoist the company's flag in this area.

Thus Lugard headed for the west and to look after the affairs of the company or rather of Buganda, he left his second-in-command, a Captain Williams. This latter agent of the company had arrived in Buganda towards the end of January 1891 with a contingent of 75 Sudanese and 100 Swahili troops and—even more important than these human reinforcements—another maxim gun. Whatever qualities Capt. Williams may have had as a soldier, he was an unfortunate choice as an arbiter and doubly so in so heavily charged an atmosphere as that which obtained in Buganda at the period. It did not occur to him that in order to contain the tension between the parties he had to be absolutely impartial; instead he was openly partial to the Protestant faction; a policy that could only enrage the Catholics who were already saturated with ill-will towards the Company generally and the Protestants particularly. Moreover, the Protestants, owing to their numerical weakness, were spoiling for a fight to preserve the *status quo* for they felt reasonably certain that the Company would come to their aid should fighting break out. Williams was demonstrably unequal to the task of cooling these excessive passions so that the political tension in Buganda mounted with every day that passed.

Meanwhile, Lugard was engaged in extending the territorial claims of the Company to the west of Buganda presumably, owing to the state of communications in Ùganda then, oblivious to the mounting crisis for the Company in Buganda. Thus on his way to Lake Albert he signed a "treaty" with the representatives of Ntare V of Nkore on 1st July 1891. Lugard believed that Nkore was of strategic value because some of the arms reaching Kabarega were brought through Nkore by traders originating from the coast via Karagwe and this is why one of the clauses of the so-called treaty provided that Ntare would not allow the traffic of arms through his kingdom—a provision that Ntare had no means of enforcing even supposing that he had any inclination to do so. The important provision of the treaty, so far as the strategy of imperialism was concerned, was that offering the

Company's "protection" to Ntare would also prohibit Ntare from entering into treaty relations with any foreign power without the company's consent. This was important because such a "treaty" could be used to substantiate the claim of the Company's suzereignty over Nkore should another European power claim the same area at some future date. Lugard then headed farther westward to Toro with Kabarega's troops retreating before him as he advanced. In Toro, he reinstated Kasagama whom he had brought along with him from Buganda where the latter had been a refugee since he was deposed by Kabarega a short while before the arrival of Lugard into the country. Kasagama also signed a "treaty" accepting the "protection" of the company, the contents of which were similar to that signed in Nkore.

Capt. Lugard eventually found the Sudanese troops he was looking for at the southern end of Lake Albert. After some protracted negotiations, their commander, Selim Bey, agreed that his troops enlist in the service of the Company on condition that subsequently the Company would obtain permission from the Kedive of Egypt in whose service these troops technically were since they had been part of the force given to the governor of Equatoria Province. Some of these troops were posted in forts which were constructed along the Toro/Bunyoro border by Lugard. Their primary function was to contain the incursions of Kabarega into Toro and thus to ensure the security of Kasagama's throne. The rest of the troops agreed to accompany Lugard to Buganda. Thus in December 1891 Lugard arrived in Kampala with some 300 Sudanese troops (including Selim Bey himself) to find the political atmosphere very tense. To make matters worse, from Lugard's point of view, he found orders from his employers ordering him to withdraw from Buganda immediately. The Company had run into financial difficulties and could no longer afford to maintain a representative in Buganda or to defray the expenses of Lugard's military compaigns. He was thus ordered to withdraw to Dagoretti in Kenya.

But to Lugard such a withdraw was a calamity both for the Company and for his personal ambitions. For a start his withdrawal would leave the Protestant party, by then his tacit allies, in a very vulnerable position especially vis-a-vis the Catholic party. Additionally, if he withdrew, his recent treaties in Ankole and Toro would be rendered valueless thus opening up the possibility of either Muslims or Kabarega gaining the upper hand in the area, both of which possibilities were equally distasteful to Lugard. Besides, Kabarega and the Muslims, there was always the possibility that another European power could step in and successfully claim the region and Lugard, an imperialist to boot, was not the type of man to let a chance—his first chance—of extending the British empire slip by him merely because his directors willed it so from so far away. He decided to take matters into his own hands and stay on, regardless of the orders of his directors, so as to resolve the political tensions in Buganda in one way or another. That he was able to defy the company's orders successfully was due to a number of factors. In the first place, De Winton, who was the company administrator at the coast, continued to send arms and other supplies to Lugard despite the fact that his directors in London had instructed him not to do so. Hence Lugard was not starved of supplies for had this been the case, he would in all probability have been forced to withdraw because his military effectiveness would have been greatly reduced. Secondly, the state of communications between the coast and the interior was so poor that often directives arrived in the interior long after they had ceased to have relevance to the particular circumstances so that agents like Lugard who were operating far inland usually had much more freedom of action than those stationed at the coast. In connection with the state of communications, one might observe that just when Lugard made up his mind to stay on in Buganda, other orders, countermanding those of withdrawal, were on their way to him. The C.M.S. had managed to raise enough funds to enable the company to stay on in Uganda for a further year (i.e. up to the end of 1892), but these new orders had not reached Kampala.

The tense situation in the Capital of Buganda boiled over on 24th January 1892. The events leading to the outbreak of violence were straightforward enough. A Catholic shot and killed a Protestant in circumstances that many judged to justify a plea of self-defence. Mwanga tried him and duly acquitted him. Lugard demanded that the man be handed over to him for retrial and execution and Mwanga, rightly believing this to be an infringement of his authority, refused. Lugard then decided to settle the issue by force. He issued guns to the Protestants and took the Protestant missionaries into his fort. Wright's contention that Mwanga, without the urging of "Catholic extremists", could not have taken such a decision of defiance which was also a wrong one,[22] is really beside the point and this seems to be due to the fact that he sees no single virtue in Mwanga and no single fault in Lugard. The point is that whether Mwanga's decision to acquit the Catholic was right or wrong—and even this depends on who is telling the story—Lugard had no legitimate right to question it. When he demanded the retrial of the man, he did not even claim any customary or other right to do so; he did so because he had Sudanese soldiers and two maxim guns which Mwanga did not have. Whatever faults Mwanga may have had, he was unquestionably the legitimate Kabaka of Buganda as Lugard unquestionably was not and to confuse physical force for legitimacy seems to me to be inexcusable in a writer who claims that his understanding of Baganda's predicaments in this period "must surely excite sympathy, admiration and, above all, respect."[23]

With Lugard issuing guns to the Protestants, the Catholics also made final preparations for the showdown. In this heavily charged atmosphere, it seems to be a moot point to seek to establish who fired the first shot—each side accused the other of firing first. The point is that the situation was ripe for a showdown and, for Lugard, time was a vital factor since he had been ordered to leave Buganda and he did not want to leave before making the position of the Protestant party reasonably secure—this being one of the factors which had prompted him to disobey his employers and stay on in Buganda. In fact if any one individual was responsible for the outbreak of this war, it was Lugard.

When fighting broke out, Lugard's troops fought on the side of the Protestants as expected and a few shots from his maxim gun easily and quickly determined the outcome of the fighting in favour of the Protestants. The lines of the Catholics which were converging on Protestant positions were mowed down, their ranks broken and Rubaga itself was stormed so that the Catholics were once again in flight to Bulingugwe island. It would appear that at this stage of the fighting, when the outcome was no longer in doubt, Lugard wished to bring hostilities to an end and, apparently, sent emissaries to Mwanga and the Catholic Party asking them to return to the capital and to arrange the terms of peace. But this offer was rejected, whereupon Lugard dispatched Capt. Williams with a contingent of Sudanese troops and a maxim gun and Bulingugwe islands were stormed. Mwanga and most of his followers at first fled to Bukoba (mainland Tanzania) and then made their way back into Buddu. The return of Mwanga and his Catholic subjects to Buddu occasioned great chaos in that province for it caused a confused exodus of the Protestants who were fleeing in the opposite direction, trying to get out of Buddu and away from the Catholics. For a brief period it looked as if a general civil war would break out in the provinces, but fortunately this did not happen and only minor skirmishes took place.

By winning the war for his Protestant allies, Lugard created an entirely new problem. The capital became a dismal place without the Kabaka who, traditionally, was the linchpin of court life and the axis of Buganda's social life. Lugard and his Protestant allies might villify Mwanga, but they could not fill his place in the eyes of the Buganda populace. Additionally, so long as Mwanga remained a fugitive, it was impossible to make any enduring settlement that the Baganda could accept. Lugard increasingly became anxious as inci-

dents of violence increased both in frequency and scale in the provinces
—an ominous pointer to the peasants' restlessness at the continued
absence of the Kabaka from the capital. And, above all, Lugard knew
that time was not on his side. This is why he was anxious to resolve this
tangled situation as quickly as possible. It would appear that Lugard
or the leaders of the Protestant party or both sent secret emissaries to
Mwanga and assured him that he would be welcome to his capital
if he elected to return and, accordingly, Mwanga reappeared in
Kampala on 30th March 1892—and almost immediately the fighting in
the provinces ceased. A new "treaty" with Mwanga was signed by
which the company's authority was recognised formally for the first
time—this was in fact the first formal declaration of Buganda's loss
of independence; a fact Mwanga recognised and resented but could
not alter. By this treaty also offices of state were shared out between
the religio-political parties—the Catholics were given the county of
Buddu and Sesse islands were divided between the Catholics and the
Protestants owing to their strategic importance and the Protestants
got the rest of the counties except the three small counties of Busujju,
Gomba and Butambala which were given to the Muslims thereby
effectively sandwitching them between their more numerous Christian
rivals as they were soon to complain with justification.[24] Subsequent
to this settlement a story went round that Lugard had wished to make
a more generous settlement in respect of the territory given to the
Catholics but that he had been prevented by his Protestant allies
from doing so. This story, whose origin seems to be Lugard himself,
does not seem to have any substance since both Lugard and the Protestant party knew that it was Lugard's intervention at a crucial moment
which had determined the outcome of the war so that had he been
disposed to give more territory to the Catholics, he would have been
able to do so without much difficulty. He was in a position strong
enough to dictate the terms of settlement.

The consequences of this war for the history of Buganda and of
Uganda were of far more fundamental importance than the mere
re-arrangement of chiefships in Buganda. Firstly, Lugard's presence
and intervention in the conflict at the right moment ensured that
Buganda and eventually Uganda would be a British colony, or protectorate as they preferred to term it, because if the Catholics had won,
it seems doubtful that the Company could have maintained a foothold
in Uganda and the subsequent spirited compaigns in Britain by the
C.M.S. and their supporters for the retention of Uganda might not
have materialised. This seems all the more probable when one considers
that the British government was reluctant to get involved in uncertain
colonial ventures in a world that was increasingly beset by a series of

international crises. Another consequence of Lugard's victory is that it ensured that the control of the major organs of government both in Buganda and in Uganda would remain in the hands of the Protestants and this practice was to endure for the next eighty years. To this latter consequence we shall return time and again in the course of this survey not as an exercise in boredom but because it was so pervasive in the management of public affairs in Uganda.

Lugard had beaten the Catholic party and consolidated the political position of the Protestant party, but this was not the end of the story for this victory created international complications that neither Lugard nor his maxim guns could help solve. The French government, on behalf of their missionaries, formally protested to the British government and demanded compensation for the losses sustained by the French missionaries in Buganda during the war. These were tabulated as being: 1 Cathedral (for Rubaga Cathedral had been destroyed before it was completed), 60 chapels, 12 schools and 50,000 Catholic converts alleged to have been sold into slavery by the Protestants. These claims, which could not be very well brushed aside, raised a host of new issues in British government circles. In particular it became necessary to determine the extent to which a British government could be held responsible for actions of a chartered company. Lord Halsbury, the Lord Chancellor of the day, gave it as his opinion that the mere granting of a charter of incorporation would not in itself entail responsibility by the British government for the actions of the Company so incorporated. But then he added that since the British government, in terms of the charter, assumed control of the activities of the company (the provision which required that the company's dealings with foreign powers would be subject to the direction of the Secretary of State whose opinion on all matters would be deferred to), could be construed to entail responsibility by government for the company's actions. Eventually the British government worked out a typically British solution to this problem. They did not admit responsibility but they nonetheless paid out a compensation to the Catholic missionaries of £10,000 in 1898. But this incident as well as the increasing German competition in East Africa, just as on the Niger before, made the British government doubt the efficacy of exercising influence in overseas territories through the agency of traders, consuls and naval squadrons (the latter in the case of Uganda was useless anyway). It was thus necessary to work out a new policy and then to implement it.

After signing the second treaty, Lugard left for England in June where he arrived in October. In Britain, a Liberal administration had just been returned to power by the time Lugard got there and the question of abandoning or retaining Uganda had become something of a public issue. And the Liberal government, unlike its Tory predecessor, had mixed feelings over the whole question of Uganda. But the question as to whether Britain retained or abandoned Uganda was not left to the Liberal government alone to decide because the C.M.S., fearing for the safety of their missionaries and their converts and for their very future in the whole region, had mounted a thrill campaign for the retention of Uganda. This campaign had got off ground by the time Lugard arrived in England to add his own extensive propaganda in support of the C.M.S. and its other supporters. He addressed public gatherings and Chambers of Commerce up and down the country and he, along with others, wrote letters to infleuntial papers, all in the cause of retaining Uganda. Lurid pictures were drawn of the terrible suffering that would befall Christians and "savages" alike if the British were to withdraw from Uganda and what a blot such a step would be on the march of "civilisation". The trick worked for the public took up the issue with gusto.[25] The Liberal government was in something of a quandry since the cabinet itself was divided on the issue and yet public pressure was such that the issue of Uganda could not just be swept under the carpet. This division centred on the personalities of Gladstone and Rosebery. Gladstone, the ageing colossus of the Liberal party who was soon to retire as Prime Minister, was opposed to further acquisition of colonies and Rosebery, the Foreign Secretary, and strongman of the cabinet who was slated to succeed Gladstone to the Premiership, belonged to the wing of the Liberal party known as Liberal imperialists, and it should be borne in mind that this was the period before the word imperialism had become an international insult). He was therefore in favour of maintaining a foothold in Uganda.

When, therefore, the question of Uganda came before the cabinet at a time when public campaign through the press, public meetings and through deputations to the government, was in full swing, Roseberry and his supporters were able to press and get the government to settle for a compromise in order to buy time. Instead of making a decision to retain or quit Uganda, it was decided to prolong the decision by granting a subsidy to enable the company to stay on in Uganda until 31st March 1893 instead of 31st December 1892. Furthermore, in November 1892 the government adopted the time honoured British device of defusing hot issues on which British Parliament or cabinet were divided. They appointed a Commissioner to advise on the future of Uganda. The Commissioner appointed for this task was Sir Gerald Portal.

Portal duly arrived in Buganda in March 1893 and found the

Christian parties enduring an uneasy peace. As soon as he arrived, moreover, he was flooded with petitions from all parties alleging all kinds of violations of existing agreements. The Christian missionaries also presented a petition about the ravages that were being inflicted on the Batoro by the Sudanese troops garrisoning the Toro borders and this was true and serious enough for Portal to dispatch an expedition to withdraw those troops from Toro. At least on one point the Christian missions were in complete agreement and this was that Britain should not withdraw from Uganda. This position reflected a considerable metamorphosis in the thinking of the White Fathers since, as we have seen, they were originally opposed to the British occupation of Uganda largely because this would give a competitive advantage to their C.M.S. rivals. Yet by the time Portal arrived in the country both European missions had come to the conclusion that their efforts would be best rewarded under the umbrella of imperial rule. The recent unheavals in Buganda had opened their eyes to the probability that in the event of a civil war, they would be unable to restore order or control events without external European aid. Thus even for the White Fathers British rule, undesirable as it was, was far better than the absence of any European rule at all. Portal duly hoisted the Union Jack at Kampala on 1st April 1893, thereby initiating the first step in bringing the shortlived but eventful company rule in Buganda (and in Uganda and Kenya as it turned out) to an end.

Subsequently, a new "treaty" was signed with Mwanga on 29th May 1893 by which Mwanga accepted British "protection" and surrendered to the same the right to levy and spend taxes. In the new arrangement for the governance of Buganda, Portal inserted the curious and cumbersome provision that henceforth there would be two Prime Ministers (Katikiros), two Gabungas and two Bajasi (respectively the Commander of the canoes and of the army); one being a Protestant and another a Catholic in each case. This bizarre arrangement remained in force until the 1900 Buganda Agreement altered it.

But then the Commissioner fell ill and he also heard of the death of his brother, Capt. Raymond Portal, whom he had sent among the expedition to withdraw Sudanese troops from Toro forts. He therefore left Buganda for the coast en route to Britain and he left Macdonald to act as Commissioner in his place. Eventually Portal made his report and, as expected, he recommended the retention of Uganda. His major recommendations were that the Company's Charter should be evoked so that the British government assume full responsibility for Uganda excluding Bunyoro and Toro, at least initially. He also recommended that a railway be built from the coast to Kikuyuland to speed up communication between the coast and the interior. He additionally adduced arguments to back up his recommendations. He pointed out, for instance, that although Uganda would for some time not be a good commercial proposition and would not even defray the expenses of its occupation (i.e. Uganda would be unable to pay for the privilege of being occupied), withdrawal might nevertheless open up the country to the influence of Islam, to the detriment of Christian "civilising influence", one assumes. Alternatively, he argued, if Britain withdrew, some other power would step in and fill the vacuum thus created. He dismissed the suggestion from some government officials of handing over the country to Zanzibar on the grounds that this would be handing over Christian missions to Muslims. Additionally, and perhaps more importantly, he argued that to leave the natural key of the Nile (an old bogey this one) "unprotected" and unnoticed could not fail to attract the attention of other powers merely because a British Company had failed to hold it. This last argument, as we saw earlier, loomed large in the minds of the imperial strategists of the period. In fact one could argue that this consideration rather than the claptrap of "civilisation" was the overriding one otherwise Portal would not have been so anxious to exclude other European powers from the burden of "civilising natives." Besides, the term "protection" was itself a convenient alibi to cloak other motives since it was far from clear as to what or whom Uganda was to be protected against for Uganda had as much to fear from British intrusion as from the intrusion of any other alien power. The decision to retain Uganda was announced in both Houses of Parliament on 12th April 1894—Gladstone, the main opponent of imperial annexations in Africa, having finally retired in March of that year. British "protection" was formally declared over Uganda in the London Gazette of 27th August 1894. With this declaration the period of Uganda's informal contact with alien powers came to an end. Colonial rule had arrived— or perhaps more correctly was knocking on the door for there were still more troubles in store for the British.

Soon after the departure of Sir Gerald Portal, Macdonald found himself in trouble in Buganda and this time the trouble came from the Muslims and not the Christian parties. The hostility and rivalry between the Christian parties had somewhat subsided with the signing of the Portal's treaty so that this had ceased to be a source of anxiety for the Baganda and for the nascent British administration by the time Portal left Buganda. In the course of 1893 the Muslims began agitating for more territory, especially for the county of Busiro, to be added to the three small ones allocated to them under Portal's agreement. They put forward, with a certain amount of justification, the complaint that their territory was uncomfortably hemmed in between the territories of their more numerous rivals—the Catholics and the Protestants. These complaints on their own would not have unduly perturbed the British officials in Kampala but for the fact that the Muslim grievances had considerable support of the Sudanese troops under the command of Selim Bey. What is more, it seems that Macdonald had created this delicate situation of confidence for himself. It would appear that both Captains Lugard and Williams had treated Selim Bey as an equal rather than a servant—more likely than not out of necessity. But Macdonald seems to have treated him as a servant thereby incurring Selim Bey's resentment and hostility. Moreover, Selim's hostility meant also the hostility of the enlisted as well as unenlisted Sudanese whose leader he was. Thus when Muslim Baganda threatened rebellion and the Sudanese troops openly supported them, Macdonald's alarm verged on panic. And he had every reason to panic because a combination of Muslim Baganda and trained Sudanese troops could easily overwhelm him and effect a political change in Buganda.

In order to reduce the number of Sudanese in Kampala, Macdonald requested Selim Bey to send all the unenlisted Sudanese to Entebbe and the latter firmly turned down the request. In desperation, Macdonald even wrote to Sir Gerald Portal, who was on his way to the Coast, asking him to return and handle the crisis, but Portal would not return —he only sent a small force under Lt. Villiers to reinforce Macdonald. Mocdonald then paid up all the troops and ordered Selim Bey and his troops to Entebbe to prevent the possibility of these troops making joint planning with the Baganda Muslims in and around Kampala. This order was obeyed but the troops went looting and causing havoc all the way and when they arrived at Entebbe, they refused to take orders from the European officer incharge of the station there.[26] Selim Bey, moreover, warned Macdonald to restrain Mwanga from making war upon Baganda Muslims as he and his troops would regard such an action as a hostile act against themselves. Macdonald decided to take pre-emptive measures and on June 18th 1893 the Sudanese troops stationed in Kampala were disarmed under the cover of the rifles of a Swahili force and two maxim guns manned by European officers. This was achieved without untoward incident. And on the same day the Muslims who had been taking up positions around Kampala took up arms but they were quickly defeated by a large force of Baganda Christians, mostly Protestants since most of the Catholics had retreated to Buddu for safety as tension mounted in the capital. The very next day Macdonald assembled a large force, the core of which was composed of Swahili troops, and marched on Entebbe but the Sudanese troops there did not offer any resistance; they simply laid down their arms and they did not even protest the arrest of their leader, Selim Bey, who was promptly tried for mutinous conduct, convicted and sentenced to deportation to the Coast. But Selim Bey was already an old and dying man—in fact he died at Nakuru before reaching his destination. Both Lugard and Portal thought that Macdonald's attitude to the Sudanese troops was unnecessarily alarmist although of course this did nothing to alter the fate of Selim Bey about which Lugard was to lament:

"There must have been a strong want of tact to convert a loyalty so sincere into hostility when Selim was a dying man . . . ."[27]

Thus ended the career of a man who had put his soldiers as well as his own fighting skills at the disposal of Lugard in the Company's bleakest moment. But then the advance of colonialism did not weigh such matters: the moment Selim Bey voiced concern for his followers and his co-religionists, he was disposed of. Collaborators, just like resisters, became expendable the moment there was the slightest doubt about their total submission and loyalty to the interests of the colonial masters.

As a result of these drastic measures, Kampala was once again saved for the British. Furthermore, as a result of these upheavals, the territorial settlement established by Portal was modified. The counties of Gomba and Busujju were taken away from the Muslims and given to the Protestant and Catholic factions respectively so that the Muslims who had rallied to the British cause were left with only the obscure county of Butambala.

But this settlement did not hearald the end of the Acting Commissioner's woes, for hardly had the dust of these turbulent events settled down over Kampala than fresh troubles erupted in Toro and Bunyoro. Many of the Muslims who had fled Kampala had gone to Bunyoro, which country by then had become the collecting centre of all elements opposed to the advance of British control. The British officer stationed in Toro, Owen, was in danger of being overrun and he was accordingly ordered to withdraw to Ssingo (Buganda) with the Omukama Kamurasi. But he could not withdraw because his line of retreat was blocked by Muslim levies. What made the situation in Toro even more threatening was that the Muslim refugees in Bunyoro were seeking to make contacts with the Sudanese troops in the west of Uganda which had also heard of the news of the defeat of their co-religionists in Kampala. The unofficial leader of these troops was Bilal who, apparently with a group of his followers, was planning to murder Owen and set up an Islamic kingdom in Toro itself. But Owen kept his head and opened negotiations with Bilal whose hostility he disarmed by the trick of formally appointing him the Commander of all enlisted Sudanese troops. Bilal agreed to support the British cause and from this point onwards Bilal did not cause any more trouble for the British whose faithful ally he remained throughout.

But all these events, unsettling though they were, were secondary for the main problem was Bunyoro and its ruler Kabarega. At this time (1893) the British interest in Bunyoro was to ascertain whether any French or Belgian agents had reached the Nile Valley through the west. It is also to be borne in mind that since the days of Sir Samuel Baker the Banyoro, and especially their king Kabarega, were not all well disposed towards the British or towards any Europeans owing to the unhappy experiences of the past encounters as we indicated earlier. The British for their part returned this sentiment in the same, if not more, measure since their attitude to Bunyoro and her king was based on Baker's accounts and a worse source could hardly be found as it has also been indicated. As part of Portal's settlement, the troops which were guarding Tororo's borders with Bunyoro were to be withdrawn. This step had become necessary because their looting propensities had laid the country all round their forts waste and as a result of the pressure brought to bear on Sir Gerald Portal, especially by the Christian missionaries, the Commissioner had decided to withdraw them to Buganda where their activities could be more closely supervised. But as soon as this withdrawal was only partially accomplished, Kabarega took advantage of the situation and invaded Toro. The Omukama Kasagama, who had been reinstated by Lugard hardly two years earlier, once again found himself a refugee in the Rwenzori mountains. Kabarega's raids became so daring that Owen was compelled to evacuate some of the frontier forts. Macdonald then came to the conclusion, as Portal had done before him, that a full-scale invasion of Bunyoro and the subjugation of Kabarega was the only course open to him if *pax Brittanica* was to be secured in the region. But unlike Portal who had concluded that no useful purpose would be served by such a military venture, Macdonald decided that such a military invasion was necessary and in September 1893 he instructed Owen to start preparations for the invasion of Bunyoro—the same Owen who had been compelled by Kabarega's harassment to abandon some of his defensive positions in southern Bunyoro.

Before the plans for the invasion were finalised, Col. Colvile arrived in November as the new Commissioner and took over from Macdonald who became his Chief of Staff. Colvile's instructions included, among other things, the checking of a suspected Belgian advance in the region and the protection of British interests generally in the Nile Basin so that a military campaign in the west of Uganda fitted in well with his instructions. Moreover, by the time Colvile arrived in Uganda, Kabarega's raids were extending as far afield as Busoga. In December, therefore, Colvile himself led a massive punitive expedition against Bunyoro aimed at defeating Kabarega and dictating the terms of settlement for he was convinced that Bunyoro could neither be pacified nor cajoled into accepting British presence by any other means except force. It was not just the intransigence of Bunyoro alone that had led the British officials to this conclusion: Bunyoro had also consistently given asylum to Muslim dissidents and to almost everyone else who was opposed to British rule. The expedition consisted of 8 European officers, 2 maxim guns, one steel boat which was transported in sections, about 450 Sudanese troops and a vast number of Baganda rifle and spearmen variously estimated to be between 20 and 43 thousand strong.[28]

The invading force expected Kabarega to attempt to stop them at the River Kafu crossing, but this did not happen. Kabarega, after burning his capital behind him, withdrew northwards in an orderly fashion, harassing Colvile's advance guard as he retreated. Eventually he, his numerous followers and a vast number of cattle disappeared into Budongo forest without offering Colvile the chance of fighting a pitched battle. Kabarega's tactics compelled Colvile to change his own. He decided to divide Bunyoro by a line of forts from Kibiro on Lake Albert eastwards through Hoima and beyond, thereby cutting off the southern portion of Kabarega's kingdom and confining his influence to the northern portion of it. Capt. Thruston was left in command of Bunyoro with the primary responsibility of keeping an eye on the river Kafu crossing. Budongo forest itself was besieged in the hope that Kabarega would run out of supplies and come out of the forest. By these measures the ground was laid for the *lost counties* controversy that was to bedevil Uganda's politics in the fifties and 'sixties and about which controversy we shall say more in due course. Colvile himself returned to Buganda in February 1894. In the heavily invested Bunyoro, Kabarega carried out a guerilla campaign against British positions but in the course of 1894 his attacks became increasingly unsuccessful and his losses in men became heavier and heavier.

In August 1894 Colvile formally announced the Protectorate to have come into force over Buganda before an assembly of the Kabaka and his chiefs at Mengo and at the conclusion of that ceremony Mwanga and Colvile signed yet another "treaty" the terms of which were similar to Portal's earlier treaty. On that very day Kabarega mounted his biggest assault, which was also to be the last serious one, against the British fort at Hoima. Wave after wave of Banyoro hurled themselves at the fort but they were repulsed with crippling losses. This attack convinced Thruston that if he confined his strategy to defending positions already held, this would enable Kabarega to regroup his forces for more attacks, thus rendering the conflict interminable. He therefore launched an attack on the fugitive Kabarega and in November 1894 the Omukama of Bunyoro was compelled, for the first time, to flee his kingdom and to take refuge first in Acholi and then in Lango where for the next five years he was to carry out an intermittent struggle against the forces sent against him by the British. The final campaign that dislodged Kabarega from his stronghold has been described, in glowing terms, by Bartlett as having been:

> "one of the keenest actions ever fought by the Sudanese, and success was largely due to the excellent leadership displayed by the native officers."[29]

But the victory had been costly and this convinced Colvile that in order to further hamstring Kabarega it was necessary to establish a British post in Ankole (as Nkore was henceforth known) so as to prevent the supplies of arms through German East Africa (mainland Tanzania) and Ankole reaching Kabarega. To this end therefore Capt. Cunningham was dispatched to Ankole for the purpose of securing a "treaty" with the Omugabe, Ntare V. Ntare resolutely refused to meet any European and therefore Cunningham on 29th August 1894, signed the "treaty" on behalf of the British government while Mbaguta signed, or rather thumbmarked, on behalf of Ntare V. There was nothing new in the so-called treaty because it was the standard proforma "agreement" like the ones we have encountered before and by which "agreements" the African rulers thumbmarked away their sovereignty in exchange for British "protection" which, at the time, was of doubtful value. This was the first formal agreement between the agents of the British government and Ankole. In spite of this agreement, however, Ntare firmly refused the offer, by the British agents, to establish a military post in his country and, initially at least, the aims of the British agents were thwarted since the major consideration for entering Ankole at all was to stop arms getting to Kabarega through the area and a military posts in Ankole would have contributed towards the achievement of that objective a great deal more than the rulers of Ankole ever could and did.

The formal declaration of a protectorate over Uganda—and this principally meant the kingom of Buganda—also meant the ratification of Portal's treaty. In June 1895 Berkeley arrived in Uganda as the first British Commissioner of Uganda protectorate. But the Commissioner's domain was an exceedingly troubled one. For one thing Bunyoro was still up in arms and there seemed to be no prospect of resolving the conflict and restoring normalcy in Bunyoro. For this situation Kabarega was not entirely to blame for he seems to have made overtures for peace—overtures that were unsuccessful partly because some of his important chiefs had no desire for peace and more often than not such chiefs continued to raid British positions inspite of Kabarega's instructions to the contrary. It would also seem that the Baganda collaborators successfully misrepresented every move made by the Banyoro to the British. Not that the Baganda needed to try too hard—the British agents were already convinced of the hostility and intractability of the Banyoro and they did not need the Baganda to embellish that conviction: Sir Samuel Baker had done a thorough job! For Bunyoro the conflict was a misfortune from every angle. Because her territory had become the battleground, her economy was shattered and, especially, her long distance trade, to which we referred earlier, was completely disrupted. Additionally, some of her territory was excised for with the second restoration of Kasagama another "agreement" was signed with him in March 1894 as a result of which the Toro confederacy was set up. This was a much larger territory than the original kingdom of Toro for to it was added the Bunyoro areas of Mwenge, Kyaka and Nyakibamba and also the formerly small independent kingdom of Kitagwenda. On Berkeley's arrival in Uganda, therefore, he found an unpacified, decimated, impoverished but hostile kingdom of Bunyoro.

And Bunyoro was by no means the only headache to afflict the new Commissioner, for Buganda was heading for yet another crisis. After the defeat of Bunyoro and the dispersal of the Muslims an uneasy calm had settled over Buganda—calm in the sense that there was no actual war. But Mwanga was getting restive because of the political restraints forced on him by Portal's settlement. Even more irksome for Mwanga was the overbearing attitude of his Christian chiefs and the tiresome moral lectures of their equally tiresome missionaries. In this he was not alone for the conservative Baganda chiefs—i.e. those who had not been converted to the new religions—were equally resentful of the enormous political influence wielded by the European missionaries and their Baganda converts. These "readers" had, within a period of twenty years, become the most powerful single group in the kingdom. In July 1897, therefore, Mwanga slipped out of his capital and made his way to Buddu where he raised an army with which he hoped to expel the Europeans and their collaborators from his kingdom once and for all. But once again Mwanga had misread the signs for his attempt to oust these usurpers was doomed to failure before it even started. He simply could not muster enough forces to beat the Europeans and their African supporters—especially their professional Sudanese troops. Major Ternan, at the head of Sudanese regulars and Baganda auxiliaries, met Mwanga's force and decisively routed it. Outmanned and outgunned, Mwanga fled to Bukoba where he was held captive by the German agents in that territory. By August 1897 operations against what was termed "Mwanga's rebellion" were over and so also was Mwanga's eventful and turbulent reign for he was finally deposed and in his place was installed his one year-old infant son, Chwa. Buganda settled down to the rule of the British agents and their Christian chiefs; three of the latter having been chosen to act as Regents during Chwa's minority.

Just as during the wars of the 1880s and 1890s in Buganda, Ankole once again became a refuge for those elements which were fleeing from the war against Mwanga. For this reason the British officials felt that in order to secure their hold over Buganda more firmly, it was essential to prevent Ankole from providing an asylum for those opposed to the British. Ankole, moreover, had become another front from which the Baganda who were loyal to Mwanga were raiding Buganda—notably one Gabulyeri Kintu who up to 1899 had succeeded in virtually closing the Ankole/Buganda boarder to all but well-armed caravans by his daring exploits. Largely as a result of these exploits, the county of Kabula was handed over to Buganda for administrative purposes in order to round up Mwanga's supporters, but when these operations were over, Kabula was not returned to Ankole. All these factors rendered it necessary to establish control over Ankole itself.

The decision to establish a post in Ankole was taken at an opportune moment for Ankole itself was in a state of the greatest possible confusion and demoralisation. The closing years of the 19th Century had been singularly unfortunate for the Banyankore and their king, Ntare V. In rapid succession crippling epidemics had struck Ntare's kingdom: tetanus, the jigger epidemic (this became the more devastating because no one had any idea of how to combat the pestilence since it was unknown in the country then) and rinderpest. These epidemics, moreover, struck a population that was painfully recovering from a smallpox epidemic which had taken a heavy toll of life, including Ntare's only son, Kabumbire. Additionaly, these scourges struck Ankole's economy at its most sensitive link for by wiping out almost all the cattle, the rinderpest had rendered the pastoralists, who were the ruling class and the soldiers, completely destitute. The jigger epidemic had crippled the agricultural population so that in many parts of the country food production decreased and in some areas it was halted altogether. It is not necessary to elaborate the softening effect these epidemics had on Ankole's population and how they were instrumental in preparing the Banyankore to accept British rule almost without resistance since we have already indicated this in respect of other societies. As if all these misfortunes were not enough, the Banyarwanda invaded Ankole in great numbers early in 1895. In the prevailing circumstances, it was not surprising that the Banyarwanda made rapid advance in the country without meeting any serious resistance and it seems probable that, had the king of Rwanda not fallen ill in the course of the campaign which event compelled his troops to withdraw from Ankole—the Banyankore would not have managed to rid themselves of the invaders.[30]

The crowning misfortune of them all was the death of Ntare V in the middle of 1895. To a society that had been beset by continuous misfortunes for the past fifteen or so years, the death of Ntare came as an unbelievable shock. The fact that nearly all the princes in direct line for the throne had been killed in the succession war of a generation before (out of which succession war Ntare had emerged the victor) and the additional fact that Ntare had died without a male heir (for his only son had died before him), nearly broke the kingdom into pieces upon his death. This perilous situation was aggravated by Ankole's quaint rules of succession because in the circumstances there were two princes, one of whom could have become the Omugabe. These were Igumira, who was Ntare's half brother, and Kahitsi, who was Ntare's first cousin (brother in Runyankore). But Igumira had one eye and Kahitsi was left-handed and both of these conditions were effective disqualifications for the throne since custom decreed that no one could strike the Bagyendamwa (Ankole's royal drum) i.e. become Omugabe, unless he was absolutely free of any physical deformity. In the circumstances a compromise was reached to give the throne to Kahaya, the youthful son of Igumira, and even this was achieved after a brief succession war.

It was in this vaccum of authority and public disquiet that the first British Collector (these were renamed District Commissioners later) pitched his tents at Muti (soon to be renamed Mbarara) in 1898 to regularise British occupation of Ankole, the sanction for which had been obtained from the British Foreign Secretary as early as 1896. Against the background of what we have considered there was little likelihood of resistance to the British presence and none was initially forthcoming.

However, before the arrival at Mbarara of MacAllister (the first British Collector in Ankole) a more serious crisis which was to threaten the very presence of the British in the whole region of East Africa was slowly unfolding. This was what came to be known to history as the

Sudanese Mutiny. Major Macdonald had been detailed to command an expedition to survey the northern portion of British East Africa (the country that came to be known as Kenya). For this task he was to be furnished with an escort of Sudanese and Zanzibari troops. Col. Ternan, who was incharge of these troops, had informed the Foreign office in London that the pay for the Sudanese troops had been in arrears for a very long time and he requested that this oversight be remedied but, apparently, this was not done. After the conclusion of the war against Mwanga, Ternan agreed to reinforce Macdonald's expedition with 3 companies of Sudanese troops and, accordingly, Companies 4, 7 and 9 were detailed for the task—these being regarded as some of the best troops under Ternan's command. But much more than this, these were also the troops that had done the most prolonged fighting of the recent years. They had taken part in the campaign against Kabarega at the conclusion of which they had been marched straight back eastwards to fight the Nandi and the Turgen people of the Rift Valley of Kenya. Before this latter campaign was fully concluded, they had been marched right back to Buganda to fight against Mwanga.[31] And yet these troops had been led to believe that after the campaign against Kabarega, they would be given a long period of rest during which they would be reunited with their families instead of which they found themselves fighting two more actions (in the Rift Valley and in Buganda). At the conclusion of these latter two campaigns, they learnt that they were not getting anywhere near their long-promised leave but that they had been selected to accompany Macdonald's expedition to an unknown destination for an indefinite period and, to make matters worse, that on this new expedition they would not be allowed to take their wives with them. There were, moreover, other standing grievances apart from ceaseless campaigns and these concerned low pay, which was usually very late, and also inadequate supplies of food and clothing. Additionally, just before the outbreak of the mutiny, Ternan had meted harsh punishments to these very troops—punishments which included the reduction in rank of several of their number. These troops felt, with justification it would seem, that these were humiliating punishments for a force that had fought for so long to enable the British to maintain control over East Africa. But then, as so often happened in the annals of colonialism, European officers believed in being tough with the natives in order to keep them in their proper place. This, no doubt, was one such instance.

In August 1897 Ternan went home on leave after ordering the three companies to join Macdonald's expedition at Eldama Ravine, which they did. Soon after their arrival, they presented their grievances to Macdonald but, it would seem, nothing concrete was done about them beyond Macdonald's promise that he would allow them to take their wives with them. In September of the same year, the main body of the Sudanese troops deserted at night and headed for Uganda, sending messages to their Muslim co-religionists in Buganda and pillaging and looting as they advanced. They headed for Luba's fort in Busoga, a little south west of Jinja, on the banks of the Nile. Major Thruston, who had been warned of their intended destination, hastened to Luba's fort and got there before the oncoming rebellious troops. But Thruston and his other European companion, Norman Wilson, were overwhelmed by the Sudanese rebels and were held prisoner in the fort they had come to defend. They were soon joined by a third European, Scott, who was the engineer of a steam launch which was also captured by the rebels. The hapless Scott had stumbled into trouble by fluke for on seeing a British flag flying over the fort, he assumed that British officials were in occupation of it and hence he entered the fort only to find that the only Britons there were prisoners. Then reinforcements began pouring in—Indian troops were brought up from Mombasa and other troops from other locations in Kenya and a massive force of Baganda auxiliaries were all brought into Busoga. All these forces laid siege on the fort. The three European captives were put to death and during the night of 7th/8th January 1898, the mutineers broke out of the fort and by means of canoes and the captured steam launch, headed for Bunyoro. As a pre-emptive measure the Sudanese garrison at Kampala was disarmed lest they join their rebellious comrades and the Sudanese troops in Bunyoro, whose loyalty was in doubt, were matched to Kampala and similarly disarmed for the same reasons.

To compound the complication of a situation already hopelessly confounded, Mwanga escaped from captivity in German East Africa, declared himself a Muslim and joined Kabarega in northern Uganda at a time when the main body of mutineers was concentrated around Lake Kyoga. Thus the campaign to dislodge the mutineers and Kabarega and Mwanga became intensified. On 4th August 1898, the last stronghold of the mutineers was destroyed in a bombing by a much larger force than the mutineers could muster. On 4th April of the following year both Kabarega and Mwanga were captured in a surprise attack and were promptly exiled, first to Kismayu and then to the Seychelles.

We may now pause and make a few observations at this point. The Sudanese Mutiny was by far the most serious crisis that faced the British in the process of occupying Uganda. It was much more serious than the threat posed by Kabarega's intransigence and Mwanga's intermittent and ineffectual rebellions because the Sudanese troops were not only well armed and professional soldiers, but they had also been the chief instrument by which the British agents had been able to defeat all elements in East Africa which were opposed to their rule. That the British agents were able to quell the Sudanese mutiny was due to the former's ability to obtain more collaborators to fight for their cause since this campaign was largely won by Indian, Zanzibari and African troops. In all these campaigns the British military personnel was negligible. The essence, therefore, of the success of Britain's conquest and occupation of Uganda lay largely in the ability of her agents to make other people fight her wars. Finally, the Sudanese mutiny itself illustrates a fundamental point in the advance of colonialism and this is that the role of a collaborator was almost an impossible one to fulfill. So long as these troops were willing to fight continuously, sometimes under trying and often appalling conditions, they were useful and valuable to the colonial machine—witness the glowing tribute paid to them by European officers for their part in the campaign against Kabarega to which tribute reference has just been made. But as soon as they started complaining about overfighting and other shortcomings in their terms of service, then they became a threat to that machine and as such they had to be denigrated, humiliated (lest other "natives" miss the lesson) and disbanded. Collaboration was in fact a misnomer since it was all a one-sided affair—*the Europeans were doing all the ordering and the Africans all the obeying all the time*. Otherwise the system could not work at all.

The persistent disorders in Uganda provoked public criticism in Britain about the mishandling of the affairs in Uganda by British agents and in the British Parliament many questions critical of the government were asked. Moreover, the protectorate was becoming too expensive to maintain for in 1899 the imperial grant-in-aid was close to £400,000 and that for a protectorate in which no single promising commodity of trade had as yet been found. As a result of these criticisms and probing questions, a special Commissioner was appointed and, in the words of the Marquis of Salisbury, "The main object of your (Special Commissioner's) appointment is to place the Administration of the present protectorate on a permanent satisfactory footing." The Special Commissioner entrusted with this task was Sir Harry Johnston who had had a distinguished career in the administration of colonies. He had served as Vice-Consul in the Oil Rivers and Cameroon (in West Africa) and as Commissioner in British Central Africa (Malawi) and in this latter posting he had instituted a hut tax and a civil administration earlier than elsewhere in East and Central Africa.[32] With Johnston's appointment, a new chapter was opened in Uganda's history for the period of half-hearted occupation of

Uganda came to an end. Colonial rule had arrived at last and in earnest.

1. J. Barber: *The Imperial Frontier,* (E.A.P.H. 1968), p. 83–4.
2. See for example: D. A. Low: "British Public Opinion and the Uganda Question: October-December 1892", *Uganda Journal,* Vol. 18 (1954).
3. G. S. K. Ibingira: *The Forging of an African Nation,* (Viking, 1973) p. 116.

4. D. A. Low: *The Mind of Buganda: Documents of the Modern History of an African Kingdom,* (University of California, 1971), p. 5.
5. D. A. Low: *Ibid:* p. 26.
6. Colin Cross: *The Fall of the British Empire,* (London, 1968), p. 80.
7. F. D. Lugard: *The Rise of our East African Empire,* Vol. I (London, 1893), p. 381.
8. F. D. Lugard; *Ibid.* p. 382.
9. F. D. Lugard *Ibid.* p. 398.
10. Quoted in D. A. Low—Footnote 2 above.
11. Moyes Bartlett: *The King's African Rifles: A Study in Military History of East and Central Africa,* (Aldershot, 1956), p. 56.
12. See for instance: Margery Perham, "Letter to the Editor", Times (London, July 29th, 1969).
13. There is ample literature on this period of Uganda history and perhaps the most comprehensive is G. S. K. Ibingira: *The Forging of an African Nation.* Here we shall attempt to summarise events and, where applicable, give fresh

    interpretation to those events.
14. G. N. Uzoigwe: "The Agreement States and the Making of Uganda," (an unpublished manuscript kindly made available to me by the author), p 22..
15. Missionaries, travellers and others have written extensively on this period of Uganda history and what is offered here is a summary of some of this literature. See for example: F. B. Welbourn: *Religion and Politics in Uganda—1952-62* (E.A.P.H., 1965), J. Taylor: *The Growth of the Church in Buganda,* C.M.S. Press, 1958), and D. A. Low: *Buganda in Modern History,* (London, 1971).
16. M. Wright: *Buganda in the Heroic Age,* (O.U.P. Nairobi, 1971), p. 14–19.
17. M. Wright: *Ibid.* p. 21–4.
18. M. Wright: *Ibid.* p. 11.
19. The account of German colonisation is based on: J. Iliffe: *Tanganyika Under German Rule, 1905-1912,* (Cambridge, 1969).
20. Charles Stokes had come to Uganda as a lay missionary of the C.M.S., but when he married an African wife, he was promptly dismissed by the C.M.S. and he took to ivory trading. It is a telling comment on the ethics of a society— the C.M.S.—which had come to teach the universal brotherhood of man in Christ that it did not extend that doctrine to the marriage of black and white. See Anne Luck: *Charles Stokes in Africa,* (E.A.P.H., 1972), Chapter 4.
21. See for example; R. Oliver, "Some factors in the British Occupation of East Africa," *Uganda Journal,* Vol. 15/1/March 1951, p. 56.

22. M. Wright: *op. cit.* p. 126–7.
23. M. Wright: *Ibid,* p. xiii.
24. Again these events and the period itself are covered by extensive literature. Perhaps D. E. Apter's *The Political Kingdom in Uganda: A Study in Bureaucratic Nationalism* Chapter 3 is as good a summary as any.

25. For a detailed account of this compaign see: D. A. Low: "British Public Opinion and the Uganda Question: October-December 1892." *Uganda Journal*, Vol. 18 (1954).

26. There exists considerable literature on this troubled period of Uganda history and perhaps the most detailed though by no means the easiest to read is Moyse-Bartlett: *The King's African Rifles: A Study of Military History of East and Central Africa, 1890–1945*, (Aldershot, 1956).

27. Quoated in Moyse-Bartlett: *op. cit.* p. 56.

28. Moyse-Bartlett: *Ibid.* p. 57–9.

29. Moyse-Bartlett: *Ibid.* p. 59.

30. For a detailed discussion of these events see: S. R. Karugire: *A History of the Kingdom of Nkore*, Chapter 5.

31. Detailed acoounts of these happenings may be found, among other sources, in A. B. Thruston: *African Incidents*, (London, 1900).

32. R. A. Oliver: *Sir Harry Johnstone and the Scramble for Africa*, (London, 1957), is a good account of the career of Johnston.

CHAPTER THREE

COALESCENCE AND
DIFERENTIATION (1900-1921)

In this part of our survey we shall primarily concern ourselves with the general examination of the methods which the British employed in bringing Uganda under their rule. For purposes of clarity we shall take, in turn, each of the four regions into which Uganda was ultimately divided for administrative purposes. Such a procedure, however, is not justifiable on chronological grounds since, apart from Buganda, there was no systematic sequence by which each region or province was added to the protectorate. Indeed the process of acquiring Uganda did not proceed according to a logically worked out programme or plan. The main explanation for the haphazard nature of the process by which British rule was extended over the whole of Uganda seems to be that the procedure of carefully laid out plans and programmes was un-British—one associated these procedures with the Germans or the Belgians. When, therefore, we deal with the extension of British rule in Eastern Uganda before we talk about Western Uganda, it does not mean that *all* districts in Eastern province were brought under British rule before *all* the districts of the Western province. This was far from being the case as we shall endeavour to show in the subsequent pages. The justification for this procedure is, therefore, that taking the whole protectorate together would almost certainly lead to confusion because each of the Ugandan districts was incorporated into the protectorate when and if it was judged desirable or necessary and the factors upon which such decisions were based were not only legion but some were also misleading. We shall therefore begin with the survey of Buganda which was the staging post for colonial expansion. We shall then deal with the Eastern province next, largely because this was an area of considerable interest to the British— the interest centering on Busoga and her geographical proximity to the Nile. The Western and Northern provinces will be dealt with in that order because that is in fact the order in which they were brought under British "protection".

So far as Buganda was concerned, when Johnston arrived at Kampala on 20th September 1899, he was not viewed as an agent who was going to establish a new order over the kingdom. To the British as well as to the Baganda, British rule was already a fact and to the Baganda, especially, the new Commissioner could not have been much more than a successor to those other agents of imperial rule who had been among them before. But to the British government, the Special Commissioner's chief task was to establish an orderly administration in the kingdom and, more particularly, to bring to an end the civil disorders that had plagued the kingdom and consequently made the expenses of British presence soar. "The main object of your appointment is to place the administration of the present protectorate on a permanent satisfactory footing," so the Marquis of Salisbury had enjoined the Special Commissioner. In order to achieve this, it was necessary to end the incessant civil wars in Buganda and, as a necessary accompanying corollary to this, to carry out the reforms that would enable the kingdom—for the protectorate at this time meant not much more than Buganda—to pay for its administration thereby relieving the British tax-payer of this additional burden. This latter consideration was important not merely on economic grounds but also on political ones since, as it has been indicated, the British Parliament was getting critical of huge expenditures for which there did not seem to be reasonable prospects of returns even according to the "men on the spot."

To his new appointment Johnston brought unbridled enthusiasm that was so characteristic of the men who helped build the British empire and his sense of mission was the more enhanced by the knowledge that this appointment would in all probability be his last venture in African dependencies, having served in British West and Central African possessions with some distinction. Even before he reached Buganda, Johnston had formulated the reforms he intended to carry out in Buganda and he anticipated no serious problems in getting them accepted so that he would be able to leave the protectorate in a couple of weeks or so. At any rate that is what he thought. With the benefit of hindsight it is comparatively easy to criticise Johnston for his misplaced optimism in assuming that his task would be so easy. This criticism would run as follows: the Baganda had been exposed to western influence for nearly twenty five years and had been in contact with British administrative agents for nearly ten years so that one could not but expect them to have a say in the affairs of governing their kingdom. On what basis, then, could Johnston expect that his pet ideas would simply be accepted without demur? This is the substance of the criticisms made against Johnston by Law and Pratt among other writers.[1]

It is true that Christian missionaries had been in Buganda for nearly a quarter of a century prior to the arrival of Johnston and it is also true that, as we have seen, their evangelisation had taken root—evangelisation and western civilisation were one and the same thing. All this Johnston could have reasonably foreseen and accordingly been prepared for. To this extent Johnston can be rightly criticised. But this would only be half the story and, in the opinion of the present writer, a lesser important half at that! For what Johnston did not foresee and could not have foreseen was that both the European missionaries and their Baganda converts were members not just of their respective faiths but also of two opposing political "parties". These were parties, moreover, whose history of the previous decade did not abound with examples of readiness to accept compromise. This latter consideration was itself a consequence of an even more fundamental complication. For although the Protestants and the Catholics were political "parties", they were partly western political parties but also, and more importantly, African political parties. The contention of this statement is that the basis of political association in Buganda had changed only on the surface—the clan was still the most important and fundamental basis of political association and religion was merely the "officially" recognised basis. It is improbable that even the missionaries, who for the most part championed Buganda's point of view, fully appreciated this factor. Johnston could therefore be excused for assuming that whereas he would consult the missionaries on some aspects of his reforms, he would not encounter much opposition from the Baganda themselves. His previous career in Africa had taught him as much. But the European missionaries and their Baganda converts were parties deeply interested in the proposed reforms. And whereas the European missionaries could talk the language of Johnston and his Europeans subordinates, they could only half-comprehend, at best, the fears of their Baganda converts whom they did not want to feel "let down" by a British administration with which the missionaries naturally identified themselves. The protracted negotiations were in the main due to the fact that Johnston and the Baganda chiefs (assisted by the European missionaries) often misunderstood the import of each other's position: witness Johnston's exasperation when he received a letter from Baganda negotiators complaining that he was treating them like the Masai or the "Wakavirondo"; a letter that is unlikely to have gone to the Special Commissioner without the knowledge and parhaps the approval of the missionaries. Johnston wrote to one of his subordinates (Jackson) that if the Baganda chiefs had not been blind, they would have realised that "they are only ten years and two pieces of barkcloth ahead of the Wakavirondo." And the Special Commissioner is not remembered to have placed any meaningful premium on barkcloths, in whatever quantity.

Despite all these setbacks, however, the "agreement" was finally signed on 10th March 1900 amid as much pomp and circumstance as could be mustered, no doubt, much to the bewilderment of the Kabaka Chwa of Buganda who had then attained the age of four years. We have already observed the circumstances in which his father, Mwanga, had been deposed and three Regents installed to rule Chwa's minority. Although much has been written about this particular Buganda Agreement,[2] it is necessary for our purposes here to give the broad categories of its provisions in order to keep a proper balance in this narrative and also in order to assess its place in the changes that were brought by colonial rule in Buganda and in Uganda. For this purpose therefore it has been found convenient to divide these provisions into four broad categories and, it must be admitted at the outset, that this categorisation is somewhat arbitrary. This is because the agreement was a political rather than a legal document which tried at one and the same time to reconcile all imperial and local interests to the extent that these interests were identifiable and could be reconciled. Briefly then these categories are (a) those provisions which defined Buganda's subordination; (b) provisions dealing with the new administrative arrangements of the kingdom; (c) financial provisions and (d) provisions of a general nature falling outside the categories we have already enumerated.

In category (a) we are primarily referring to clauses 5, 6, 8, 13 and 20 of the agreement. These provisions made the recognition of the Kabaka and his government conditional upon their loyalty to the Protectorate administration and the procedure of selecting future Kabakas of Buganda was laid down. The jurisdiction of Buganda courts in civil and criminal matters was limited in such a way that Buganda courts were made subordinate to the Protectorate courts and the Kabaka lost his traditional power of arming and maintaining an army. The British also reserved to themselves the right to abrogate the agreement unilaterally if the Kabaka and his government failed to remit the stipulated amounts of the hut and gun taxes to the protectorate administration.

In the second category—administrative provisions—clauses 1, 2, 3, 5, 9, 10 11 and 14 defined the boundaries of Buganda for the first time since in pre-colonial Uganda the concept of definite boundaries was usually unknown save in those rare cases where natural boundaries such as lakes or mountains existed between different territories Buganda was divided into twenty administrative counties and the kingdom was made a province of the protectorate with the same status as the other provinces which, as yet, were to be demarcated. By these same provisions Buganda renounced, in favour of the British government, any territorial claims against her neighbours—this primarily referred to the states of Busoga from whom, as we have seen, Buganda had occasionally extracted tribute. Duties and remuneration of Buganda ministers and chiefs were defined and the Lukiiko (Parliament) was formally instituted and its functions defined and subjected to the overall control of the Protectorate government.

The financial provisions—clauses 4, 7, 12, 15, 16 and 17—dealt with the imposition of hut and gun taxes and the control by the Protectorate government of the revenues derived from these sources. By the same provisions grants of salaries were made for some of the Buganda officials and some members of the royal family. Even more important than the foregoing, clause 15 dealt with land allotment. This was foremost in Johnston's scheme of things since he had intended that as much land as possible should be reserved for the Protectorate administration so that in the event of mineral and other wealth being discovered, the exploitation of such wealth by the Protectorate government should not be hampered in any way. The rights to minerals were also defined but the question of forest utilisation was deferred pending an accurate knowledge of their extent and economic viability.

Finally, under the category of general clauses—15, 18, 19, 21 and 22—we have again to consider land allocation from the Baganda's point of view, for as we observed earlier, land in Buganda was both an economic asset as well as an instrument of political control. This was the main reason why clause 15 was the most scrutinised provision of the agreement by the Baganda negotiators and it may also be said that it was in this provision of the settlement that the twin-bark-clothed Baganda outsmarted the bowler-hatted Johnston because by allowing the Lukiiko to demarcate the freehold land allocated to them (known as *mailo land* in Buganda), the Protectorate government ultimately found itself owning the most unproductive areas of Buganda. Under these clauses also cash payments, upon signature of the agreement, were made from the British Exchequer to the Kabaka, the three Regents and prince Mbogo, who was the leader of the Muslims, presumably as a further inducement to the recipients to persuade the lesser chiefs and other Baganda to be well-disposed towards the agreement. The last two provisions dealt with definitions and the interpretation of the agreement—interpretation in the sense that it was laid down that the English version of the agreement, not the Luganda one, would be binding on both parties—and, of course, none of the Baganda signatories understood English.

Briefly, then, this was the substance of the Buganda agreement about which so much has been written and which agreement was believed to define the relationship between the British protecting power and the

Buganda establishment and public. Before we assess the consequences of this agreement, it is appropriate that we also get a rough picture of what was going on in other parts of the protectorate so that we can evaluate the Buganda Agreement along with the other agreements that the British signed with some of the other areas of Uganda.

We have already noted that Busoga's proximity to the Nile and her geographical position in relation to the route to the coast had made the British take a keen interest in the area. While the centre of interest was Buganda, efforts were made to establish British rule in Busoga at about the same time as British control was being formally established in Buganda. The major difference was that in Busoga, as elsewhere in the protectorate, the establishment of British rule was not preceded by elaborate negotiations as had been the case in Buganda. For the purpose of keeping the line of communication with the coast open, a succession of British officers had been posted to Busoga since 1891. We have already observed that some of the small states of Busoga had intermittently paid tribute to Buganda and one of the major concerns of the British officers was to replace Buganda's overlordship over Busoga with their own. By the "Uganda-Usoga" agreement of 1895—a wholly British document in inception and construction despite the title—Buganda surrendered her claims over Busoga to the British in return for which Buganda was to receive regular and regulated tribute from Busoga. But even this tribute was stopped by the 1900 agreement as we have seen. Soon after the 1895 agreement Busoga was incorporated into the protectorate before a legal enactment to that effect was even made in London. Thus to the Protectorate was added a very large and potentially rich district without much fuss.

So far as the extension of British rule into the rest of what was to become the Eastern province of Uganda is concerned, the man most responsible for this feat was not even a Briton: he was a Ugandan by the name of Semei Lwakirenzi Kakungulu.[3] Before Kabarega and Mwanga were finally captured in 1899, the British officials were increasingly getting concerned about the area around and north of Lake Kyoga—the area in which the fugitive rulers had been hiding for so long. Additionally, very little was known about the peoples in this region. The nascent Protectorate administration sent Kakungulu to get in touch with the people inhabiting this region and to try and bring those "tribes", who were believed to be unruly, under some kind of settled government and also to persuade them to be well-disposed towards European presence. Kakungulu's choice was as much due to his own merits as to the politics of Buganda's leadership at this period. He was already a famous, if somewhat controversial, general by the time he was dispatched northwards. He had, among several exploits, commanded the vast Baganda levies which had accompanied Col. Colvile in the invasion of Bunyoro towards the end of 1893. But he had fallen out with the awesome Apolo Kagwa, who was unquestionably the leader of the Protestant party in Buganda. And it was partly due to the rivalry between the two men that Kakungulu had been selected to command the Baganda levies, much to Mwanga's helpless annoyance since he would have preferred to get his overmighty subject, Kagwa, out of Buganda at least for a period. But then Kagwa had the support of the protestant party, which Kakungulu did not have, and the Protestant party did not want Kagwa to take part in this campaign and to be exposed to the attendant risks of war. Additionally, the two men were cast in a mould that made accommodation difficult so that Kakungulu was looking for an opening to utilise his abilities and fulfill his ambitions. His new assignment was therefore a welcome reprieve from the limitations placed upon him in a Buganda regency in which Kagwa was the most powerful personality.

Whatever his precise instructions may have been—and these are difficult to ascertain—Kakungulu understood them to mean that he was authorised to undertake a military occupation of "Bukedi"—a term that then included Bukedi itself, Bugisu, Teso and Lango. Accordingly, in January 1896 he established a line of temporary stockades along the shores of Lake Kyoga right into Teso. The latter country became the centre of his operations. One of the objectives he was supposed to achieve was to dissuade the people of this region from giving shelter and supplies to the fugitive kings and also to rid the area of the small pockets of Sudanese mutineers who were still operating There. For this purpose Kakungulu had been given a small quantity of government guns but no other subsidy—not even government troops. This then meant that for the duties he was expected to carry out, he had to rely on his own considerable Baganda followers and his own resourcefulness.

By the time Kakungulu made his way into Teso, that country was suffering constant raids from the Langi and he therefore made common cause with the Iteso and during the first half of 1896, with the assistance of Teso warriors, he attacked the Langi. But the expedition came to grief for he ran short of ammunition and suffered heavy casualties in men lost. He was forced to beat a disorderly retreat so that the Langi managed to stay out of Kakungulu's area of influence. When he had another go at the Langi in 1899, he was equally firmly repulsed. Thus by the time the Buganda Agreement of 1900 was signed, Kakungulu's area of influence was confined to the Kumam people of the Kyoga peninsula and the surrounding Iteso people. In this limited area, Kakungulu established the rudiments of an orderly administration, based on the Kiganda model and in this he was aided by the large number of Baganda assistants who had followed him into the area lured by the prospects of getting better and larger estates than they could have hoped to get in Buganda.

Early in 1900 Kakungulu made a special trip to Entebbe to see the Special Commissioner about his own position in "Bukedi". During the course of their meeting, Johnston gave Kakungulu fresh instructions to the effect that he should extend his influence eastwards through Teso and it was this mission that was to bring Kakungulu into Bukedi proper and then into Bugisu. He set up his headquarters at a place he named Mpumudde (the present Nabumali) and it was here that, early in 1901, the C.M.S. missionary, Rev. Crabtree and his wife, found him. The Crabtrees were so impressed with Kakungulu's work that they decided to stay on at Nabumali as missionaries. It was also at Nabumali that Johnston found Kakungulu in April 1901. The former was on his way to the coast and thence to England at the conclusion of his commission. After Johnston's departure, Kakungulu gave up his headquarters at Nabumali to the Crabtrees to be converted into a C.M.S. station and he set up his new headquarters at Budaka. He set about consolidating his authority. He divided the area into counties and over these he appointed his Baganda followers who were given the same chiefly titles as those of Buganda chiefs. He even made land grants to his followers along the lines of the 1900 land distribution in Buganda. Over much of the present Bukedi and Teso districts Kakungulu's agents had roads constructed and a sound foundation for an effective and unified administration was laid. Next, Kakungulu's attention was claimed by the well-cultivated western slopes of Mt. Elgon (or Masaba as the Bagisu call it), but the Bagisu were far less willing to entertain the new order than their neighbours and their mountain home enabled them to keep Kakungulu and his agents at bay for a period while raids and counter raids between Kakungulu's agents and the Bagisu increased in frequency.

Then, as so often in the fortunes of many an African collaborator, Kakungulu's own fortunes began a downward path. This turn of events was inherent in the logic of colonialism itself. Kakungulu had succeeded in establishing rudiments of an orderly administration in most of eastern Uganda almost entirely on his own resources. Neither he himself nor his agents were paid for the work they did despite the fact that frequently European officials and missionaries had nothing but praise for his achievements. In order to maintain himself and his followers Kakungulu had therefore to live on the country—cattle, goats and other produce of the land extracted from the peasants over whom he was establishing his rule or, rather, over whom he was establishing British rule. This, in turn, created resentment among the people of "Bukedi" and reports of this resentment filtered through to the British officials at Entebbe. To make matters worse, Kakungulu had failed to collect taxes, especially hut tax, from his own followers and yet the imposition and collection of tax was one of the cardinal aims of extending the protectorate into the area. Moreover, the payment of tax was the first real sign that the people concerned had accepted the new order. The result of all this was that at the beginning of 1902 Kakungulu's station at Budaka was taken over by a European official from whom henceforth Kakungulu was to take orders in the governance of an area he had done so much to bring under British rule. It must have been galling for Kakungulu that the junior European official (W. R. Walker), to whom he was made subordinate, even took over his followers as administrative agents directly responsible to the Protectorate government and not, as before, to Kakungulu. As if all this was not enough, even the estates which Kakungulu had given to his followers were disallowed by the Protectorate administration. This was final proof, if any was needed, that the regal ideas that Kakungulu had entertained about himself had finally evaporated under his very nose and by an administration he had helped to gain a foothold in the erea. While Kakungulu nursed his grievances, an orderly and firm administration was gradually established over the segmentary societies of eastern Uganda—a process which was rendered much easier by the fact that these societies possessed no sense of political cohesion. As they did not act in unison against British presence—as indeed they had not done in the days of Kakungulu —it was not difficult to "persuade" them, one by one, to accept British rule.

British interest in western Uganda had been exhibited as early as the period of Lugard's sojourn in Uganda as we have seen. So far as Bunyoro is concerned, we have already seen that that kingdom, subsequent to its conquest in1893/4, continued to be treated as hostile territory and was occupied, not so much for the purpose of its annexation to the protectorate as for ensuring that Kabarega's influence was exterminated, root and branch, from Bunyoro. Bunyoro was ravaged by war as we have seen and her economy was effectively shattered in addition to which she suffered loss of territory both to the expanded kingdom of Toro and to Buganda—the latter kingdom having been the principal British ally, especially in the conquest of Bunyoro. Bunyoro's territory which came to be known as the "lost counties" was transferred to Buganda by Commissioner Berkeley in November, 1896. That Bunyoro's resistance had posed a serious obstacle to the advance of colonialism in this region of Africa cannot be gainsaid. Matson, for example, tells us that the opportunity to mount punitive expeditions against the "Mau tribes" of Kenya arose because:

". . . . Bunyoro, which had tied down the bulk of the Protectorate forces for many years was quiet (in 1897). It was largely because of the Government's pre-occupation with Kabarega in the past that the pacification of Eastern Province had been deferred, apart from the inconclusive attempt to conquer the Nandi in 1895."[4]

Bunyoro itself was declared part of the protectorate on 30th June 1896 and this fact was published in the London Gazette of the following month.

It was not until the Kyanyangire rebellion of 1907, whose immediate target was the removal of Baganda chiefs from Bunyoro,[5] that the British attitude towards Bunyoro somewhat softened and that some of the harsher aspects of British policy were toned down. But even then the scars were too deep to be healed by half hearted measures which were given grudgingly. The continuous disorganisation and maltreatment of Bunyoro's royal family by the British agents was a constant reminder to the Banyoro that they had fought a war and lost it. Kitehimbwa, the 12 year-old son of Kabarega, who had been installed in 1898 in succession to his fugitive father, was deposed in 1902 allegedly for incompetence. His elder brother, Andereya Bisereko, succeeded Kitehimbwa, taking the title of Duhaga II, and he suffered the mortification of being treated with undisguised contempt by the British officials and, as Uzoigwe suggests, he was probably tolerated by the Banyoro quite simply because he was Kabarega's son.[6] He endured this humiliation until his death in 1924 whereupon he was succeeded by Tito Winyi IV. It may be added, in retrospect, that the Banyoro could tolerate the humiliation of their king just as the king tolerated it himself because they did not have the means of removing his tormentors. To all intents and purposes Kabarega remained the spiritual king of the Banyoro until his death in 1923. With the death of the veteran warrior-nationalist-king, the spirit of passive resistance in Bunyoro finally came to an end and ten years later Bunyoro was elevated to the doubtful honour of being granted an "agreement" by the very colonial authorities who had tried so much to destroy her spirit and identity.

In an earlier section of this work we dealt with the kingdom of Toro, one of the three kingdoms of Western Uganda, whose independent existence dated from about 1830. Reference has also been made to its reconquest by Kabarega's Bunyoro and the subsequent reinstatement of Kasagama by the British agents. The formal agreement that constituted the kingdom of Toro as part of Uganda Protectorate was signed in 1900 and by that document Toro accepted the protection of H. M. 's Government. Though far less elaborate than the Buganda agreement, the underlying principles of subordination of Toro to the agents of imperial rule were the same. Kasagama, who in any case was beholden to the agents of that rule for his throne, was a willing collaborator from the word go. Besides being grateful to the British for his throne, Kasagama had more to be thankful for because the 1900 agreement confirmed the expansion of his kingdom by the addition of territories that had not formed part of Toro before. With Kabarega in exile and Bunyoro lying prostrate, the throne of Toro appeared to be finally free from external threat. But this is not to suggest that Toro's independence had been made secure; what had happened was that Toro was relieved of an old form of imperial rule and saddled with a brand new one. Toro's independence had ended just as effectively as if Kabarega had not been defeated and his armies rolled out of Toro, first by the agents of the I.B.E.A. Co. and then by those of the British government. Moreover, by accepting new rulers, Toro was exchanging an old master—and a near relation for Toro and Bunyoro had very close dynastic and historical ties as we have seen—for a new and alien one. But as this was the order of the day, it seemed natural and even desirable—some even said the step was "progressive".

To the south of Toro lay the kingdom of Ankole to which reference has been made. The news of the Toro agreement had found its way into Ankole and when the Special Commissioner passed through Ankole on his way from Toro during the early part of 1900, the king and chiefs of Ankole promptly asked for an agreement also. They had also heard something about the agreement which had been signed in Buganda and in neither case, it can be reasonably assumed, had they any idea about the contents of those agreements although this does not seem to have dampened their enthusiasm in any way. It is to be remembered that in Ankole European agreements were not new because we have seen that Cunningham had signed one with Ntare's representatives as recently as 1894. The Special Commissioner did not think that the Banyankore had reached a sufficient degree of preparation that would justify the bestowal of an agreement upon them and consequently he did not offer them one although technically Ankole, like Toro, was already part and parcel of the protectorate; a legal enactment to that effect having been published in the London Gazette of July 1896.

It has already been pointed out that Ankole was in a state of flux by the time the empire builders arrived and the factors leading to this situation have been indicated. It now needs to be added that by 1900, when the Special Commissioner came to Ankole, the political atmosphere was still confused. This is why it appeared to Johnston that neither the king, Kahaya, nor his chiefs wielded sufficient authority in the country to be able to fulfil the terms of any agreement. But the rulers of Ankole did not give up and their efforts were "rewarded" in the following year when the Ankole agreement was concluded between the Sub-Commissioner for Western Province (representing H. M.'s Government) and Kahaya and his chiefs. Like that of Toro, it was a far less elaborate document than the Buganda one but it was quite as specific on matters of subordinating Ankole to British rule. The signing (or rather thumb-marking in the case of the Banyankore) of the Ankole agreement did not bring political calm immediately and it was to take another ten years before the new order could take root and be acceptable.[7] But Ankole had finally and formally become part of Uganda Protectorate and that is all that seemed to matter for the time being.

To round off the south western limits of the Protectorate, there was the district of Kigezi whose political and social systems, owing to the nature of their complexity and diversity, were something of a Chinese puzzle. Kigezi was of interest to the British not so much because of the people who inhabited it—indeed we are told by Denoon that the British knew little and cared even less about the people—but because it bordered on the Belgian and German territories. Because of that factor, the boundaries of that district assumed some importance in the minds of the British agents and from 1911 its geographical limits were determined and attempts to establish a viable administration were made. But the problems encountered by the British agents in Kigezi were legion. In Rujumbura, for instance, there existed a hereditary ruler (Makobore at the time) who elected to have his territory included in Kigezi rather than in Ankole. But Makobore was advanced in age and he resented the importation of Baganda agents into his territory. He was even opposed to the presence of the British themselves and he took every opportunity to frustrate the work of the protectorate administration in his new capacity as a county chief of the territory he had ruled as a king.[8] In Kinkizi county the nascent Administration struggled to contain the rivalry of the petty hereditary chiefs who had been absorbed in the new administrative structure as sub-county chiefs. In central Kigezi, where the majority of the population lived, the Bakiga were a segmentary society and the Administration initially failed to locate anyone with sufficient authority to be appointed chief and also clan rivalries had to be contained before an orderly administration could be established. The solution to the problem of chiefs seemed to lie in extensive use of Baganda agents and this was done. Finally, in Bufumbira county, there were a variety of chiefs and the British appointed one Nyindo and styled him "Paramount chief" of Bufumbira—a step that did not lessen the problems of the British officials since Nyindo's new "subjects" scarcely recognised his authority. All these cross-currents found their outlet in frequent uprisings centred around the cult of *Nyabingi*. This cult had originated in Karagwe and had found its way into Rwanda and by the beginning of this century it had reached Kigezi. The elements opposed to the presence of Europeans and their corrupt Baganda agents rallied behind the cult and this cult was to play a very important part in Kigezi's political life until well into the 1920s. By this latter period there was a general resentment against the Baganda agents all over Kigezi and the district did not settle down to the new order until these were replaced by indigenous chiefs—a policy that was vigorously persued from April 1929.

Finally, in order to round off our survey we may turn our attention to the methods by which the northern province of Uganda was incorporated into the Protectorate.[9] In so far as it could be said that the British officials had any policy relating to what became the northern province of Uganda, this ranged from complete confusion to the bizarre. The only point that aroused British interest in this region was the possibility that the French had ambitions of advancing upon the Nile through that direction. The British obsession with the security of the Nile and of the Indian Empire has been indicated so that we do not need to retell the story. It was with the object of forestalling this possibility that Macdonald had been ordered by the British government to lead an exploratory expedition northwards but then this expedition had been held up by the Sudanese mutiny and it did not set out until May 1898. Leading one column, Macdonald travelled through Karamoja, but failed to reach the Nile. Capt. Austin, at the head of another column, managed to advance as far north as Lake Rudolf. Both of these officers signed "treaties" of friendship and protection with the communities they encountered on their way. Before the return of these two parties, Berkeley, the Commissioner, sent yet another party by Major Martyr with instructions to get into contact with General Kitchener who, at the head of Anglo-Egyptian troops, was confronting the French at Fashoda. Martyr, too, was instructed to sign treaties of protection and friendship with the peoples he encountered along the route up to Fashoda. Martyr's expedition followed the course of the Nile from Bunyoro, signing treaties and setting up military posts as they advanced, but the Sudd prevented the expedition from reaching Fashoda and joining up with General Kitchener. It was Martyr's treaties and posts that were ratified by London and the area he had traversed was styled Nile military province. This, however, had only paper value since these stations remained isolated outposts from which no attempt was made to establish anything like administrative control over the surrounding peoples.

This was the situation when Johnston arrived in 1899. One of his instructions was to consider the future of the territory between the Sudan and what was then the Uganda protectorate—an awkward instruction in that there was no definite boundary between Uganda and the Sudan and nothing was known of the people who inhabited the area. But then Johnston was not the man to be deterred by such obstacles and he accordingly instructed his military Commander, Delme-Radcliffe, to extend British authority in the region. Delme-Radcliffe, was to be constantly on the move, signing treaties and fighting skirmishes, but these activities made very little impression upon the small-scale political communities of northern Uganda. And very soon the Foreign Office got cold feet about pushing British influence in the outlying districts about whose commercial potential nothing was known and Col. Hayes-Sadler, the new Commissioner, accordingly discouraged British incursion into the area. In fact instead of Uganda being expanded north-eastwards, as had been Johnston's intention all along, a large tract of territory of Uganda's eastern province was transferred to the British East Africa (Kenya) in April 1902. Hence the administration of the truncated Nile province remained nominal and from the posts at Wadelai, Gondokoro and Nimule, British officials carried out occasional tours of the region which tours amounted to nothing much more than fighting a few skirmishes and then hastily withdrawing into the safety of their stations. The Protectorate Administration could comfortably shelve the decision about the occupation of northern Uganda, especially as the area continued to generate revenue from the ivory trade without icnurring administrative expenses—a most satisfactory state of affairs as far as the British officials in Uganda and the Foreign Office were concerned.

With the appointment of Sir Hesketh Bell as Commissioner in 1906 (the title of Commissioner was changed to that of Governor the following year), the chances of incorporating the northern communities into the protectorate grew even dimmer. He considered the region to be a grave economic liability and he downgraded its status from that of a province to a district. He also reasoned that the province could not be fitted into the general structure of the Protectorate administration since it appeared to him that the communities of that region did not have any concept of institutional authority such as was to be found in the Bantu kingdoms of the south. He reasoned that the Kiganda model of administration, to which by then the British were completely sold, would neither be understood nor accepted in northern Uganda. This latter conclusion was based on a wider misunderstanding and this was that what the British officials had understood to be the Kiganda model of government was identical with that of the other kingdoms. This, of course, was not so as we saw earlier, but such minor points of detail did not deter H.M.'s imperial, and often imperious, Commissioners.

Bell therefore decided that the ideal structure of administering the protectorate would never function properly in northern Uganda and would only be costly in men and money without any prospect of a compensatory *quid pro quo*. There were of course two other important considerations besides economic potentiality and one of these considerations was noted by Barber. This was that the Communities of northern Uganda were individually too weak to pose any threat to British interests or to share the burden of colonial expansion such as Bunyoro and Buganda, respectively, had been.[10] The second consideration was a practical one and it arose out of the first one and that was that there was no single individual or group of individuals who could be subdued or treated with so that their respective communities could thereafter automatically accept British rule. It has already been indicated that owing to the small polities and democratic tradition of the societies of northern Uganda, there was no individual who wielded personal authority on anything like the scale required for the clear transition into colonial dependence as the British had experienced in the southern kingdoms. Almost literally every village had to be cajoled, persuaded, threatened or beaten into accepting British presence separately. This was a daunting task requiring patience and resources— the very things that were not forthcoming from the Foreign Office for expenditure in African dependencies, especially those whose economic potential was unknown.

Yet two factors compelled the British government in London and thus the Protectorate government itself to make up their minds about Uganda's northern province. The first of these was the unrestricted killing of elephants for ivory and the attendant gun running in the region. The activities of the Ethiopian traders were so harmful that by 1914 the vast herds of elephants of north-eastern Uganda were virtually exhausted and this, in turn, led to the sharp decline in the revenue the Protectorate had been used to collecting from this source. Additionally, through the same ivory hunters, the peoples of northern Uganda were getting and accumulating large quantities of arms and this worried the Protectorate administration, especially as an increasing number of breach-loaders—considered to be sophisticated weapons by the standards of those days—were finding their way into the region. This was especially true of Acholi. Hitherto the British officials had reasoned that the communities of northern Uganda, armed with a few antiquated weapons, could be subdued as and when it became necessary: that is to say, the Government could choose the time and the occasion for the occupation of northern Uganda at its own leisure. But the increasing supplies of sophisticated weapons made the occupation of the region urgent since the longer the occupation was delayed, the more these communities would learn the effective use of those weapons and hence the more difficult they would be to subdue in the future.

The second factor which compelled the British officials to pursue an active policy in northern Uganda was the old but still powerful bogey of the security of the Nile. Concerning the Macdonald expedition among the peoples north of Mt. Elgon, to which reference was made earlier, James Barber tells us the:

"British had been drawn into the territory, not because they thought it or its inhabitants had any intrinsic value in themselves, but because of British strategic interests."[11]

Although this comment primarily referred to north-east Uganda, it was just as true for the whole of northern Uganda. It is instructive to note that the author, after informing us of the British interests in the region, then lapses into the claptrap of "civilising mission". He states:

"The opinion of Wilson (the Ag. Commissioner pending the arrival of Sir Hesketh Bell) and his fellow officials did not simply rest upon administrative convenience or upon love of "empire building", but a guinine feeling of *obligation and duty* to provide government and order among the frontier tribes, *even if there was no obvious direct advantages for the* government. (*my emphasis*)[12]

This belated realisation of Britain's civilising mission, misplaced as it is, does not tell us why these British officials were so unwilling to share that burden with the French—even among the people who had "no intrinsic value" in themselves, according to the author. But then Victorian enthusiasm—and some call it hypocrisy—knew no bounds.

These factors therefore made the British officials enter northern Uganda with the object of establishing administrative control and once the decision had been taken, the military measures to effect the occupation were set in motion. The first breakthrough was in Lango where British posts had been established at Bululu (1907) and Palango (1909). In 1910 Boyle, the Acting Governor, informed the Foreign Office that the Langi were friendly and that their country was not economically valueless as Bell had claimed. London approved his suggestion that the administration should be extended to Lango district and, on 1st August 1911, the two districts of Bululu and Palango were merged into Lango district.

The force which was deployed in northern Uganda—called the Northern Garrison—continued to patrol the plains of Acholi and Karamoja and to make forays into West Nile. But the task of this force was uphill owing to the nature of the societies among which it carried out its patrols. In Madi villages, for instance, the Madi neither brought their complaints to the British officers for settlement, which would have been an indication that they had been reconciled to British presence, nor did they give battle; they simply melted away when the troops appeared. It was then found necessary to attack them at night with maxim gun fire and noisy rockets, largely for effect of the noise, and these attacks had a demoralising and softening effect. In the rest of the area the Garrison contented itself with settling inter-community disputes which came their way and with capturing livestock and burning down a few huts of the people who appeared most likely to cause trouble.

As a result of these forays the headquarters of the Nile district were transferred from Nimule to Gulu and another station was opened up at Kitgum to be the headquarters of Chua district (East Acholi) so that by 1913 both East and West Acholi were placed under a civil administration. The one major incident of resistance to the new order was the Ramogi Rebellion in West Acholi. Mention has already been made of the huge quantities of firearms in Acholi and one of the objects of the administration was to get these arms registered and, if possible, to get the Acholi disarmed. The people around Kitgum allowed themselves to be disarmed without incident. But in Gulu when the British officials demanded that the guns should be registered, the Acholi concluded that this was a trick by which the British intended to deprive them of their arms. The Ramogi clan rebelled and, fortunately for the nascent British administration, they were not joined by other clans so that it was comparatively easy to isolate them and suppress the rebellion.[13]

For some years Karamoja remained a thorny problem, largely because of the nomadic nature of the society and also because of the raiding propensities of the Karimojong and their neighbours, the Turkana—this latter has remained a problem right into the post-independence period. In 1913 a military station was set up at Moroto for the protection of the Karimojong, but by and large Karamoja remained a closed district under a military administration and it was not until 25th April 1921 that a civilian District Officer for Karamoja was appointed.

Then finally West Nile district was added to Uganda and this rounded off the northern limits of the Protectorate. West Nile used to form part of what was called the Lado Enclave which had been leased by Britain to Belgium's King Leopold II. Leopold died in 1910, the lease lapsed and the Enclave was handed over to the Sudan. Then in January 1914 a boundary readjustment between Uganda and the Sudan was made and West Nile district was handed over to Uganda while Gondokoro and Nimule districts were transferred to the Sudan. Thus by 1918 the British Protectorate of Uganda had attained a definite shape and by 1921 the whole protectorate was under a civil administration.

The methods by which Britain gained control over the various parts of Uganda were for the most part dictated by circumstances obtaining in these societies—in particular by the political and social organisations of the people and also by the degree of preparedness to receive aliens and their ideas. But whether British occupation had been established by elaborate negotiations as in the case of Buganda or by outright military conquest as in the case of Bunyoro or by a mixture of cajolery and threats of the use of force as in most of the other areas of Uganda, the end result was the same: British control over the whole protectorate was established and this fact brooked no argument.

To make virtue of necessity, the British then embarked in implementing what was called indirect rule over the whole protectorate, using what appeared to them to be the Kiganda system of administration. Indirect rule itself was a convenient fiction to cover up the fact that the colonial authority did not have sufficient manpower to man all the hierarchies of administration and that therefore they had to rely on local personnel for the fulfilment of these functions. But the more it seemed to work, the more it was elevated to the level of an administrative science—a science, moreover, patently invented by the Bitish for their African dependencies! And all this in spite of the fact that indirect rule was a contradictory precept. According to Sir Donald Cameron, one-time Governor of mainland Tanzania, indirect rule was "designed to adopt for purposes of local government the tribal institutions which the native people have evolved for themselves, so that the latter may develop in a constitutional manner from their own past, guided and restrained by the traditions and sanctions which they have inherited, moulded or modified as they may be on the advice of British officers, and by the general control of those officers."[14]

This definition is as good as any on this subject. The self-justifying paternalism with which this definition is littered needs no further comment. The first point to note is that indirect rule was nothing new in Uganda for, as we explained earlier, in all these societies there were agencies through which authority was handed down and this was indirect rule if the expression means anything at all. Secondly, the type of indirect rule that subsisted in precolonial Uganda was vastly different from that envisaged by our colonial rulers. And, more importantly, the colonial concept of indirect rule was a mass of contradictions incapable of reconciliation. This is so because to allow indigenous institutions to evolve according to their traditions (even assuming that the British officials understood what these were, which they did not) could not possibly be achieved by an administrative and economic colonialism. We may take two contrasting examples to illustrate this point.

In Buganda, the concepts upon which the governance of the territory was based were swept away by the 1900 agreement. This was achieved in a number of ways. By formally making the Lukiiko into a deliberative assembly, with defined functions, the exercise of which functions was not dependent upon the Kabaka, the agreement had done away with one of the fundamental functions of the Kabakaship—the power to make all laws for all Baganda. Nor can it be said that this step was taken to democratise the Lukiiko or the Buganda government, for these two arms of Buganda government remained oligarchic and autocratic until they were abolished in 1967. Again by creating an independent class of landowners whose ownership of these lands could not be tampered with by the Kabaka, the agreement had swept away, at a stroke, the whole basis of Kiganda social and political organisation and by imposing various limitations, which we have outlined, upon the Kabaka and his government as a whole, Buganda's state structure was changed out of recognition. How, then, could it be said that Buganda institutions were being allowed to evolve according to their inherited traditions?

Secondly we may take the case of Teso where the people lived in small segmentary kinship groupings, each of which was independent of the next one. In Teso a hierarchy of chiefs, at the pinnacle of which was the European District officer, was instituted by the British and a more untraditional and baffling arrangement could hardly have been imposed upon the Iteso. Gone was the traditional concept of the collective leadership of the Elders which had governed Teso society for so long.

These two examples, and they can be multiplied for every single community in Uganda, show that the old order had been overthrown by the new and alien one. To call such fundamental changes in the bases of these societies a "modification" would not only be an understatement, even by English standards, but it would also be a gross falsification. This is not to argue that these changes were undesirable for this is a matter of opinion and everyone can make his value judgements and probably stick to them too. But this is not the point. The point is that in order for colonial rule to be effective it had to subvert the existing indigenous centres of authority and not to enhance them. This is almost a truism. The fact that, for instance, the Kabaka continued to be revered by his subjects did not spring from the British presence and encouragement: this had everything to do with the emotional make up of the Baganda in a rapidly changing environment. Indeed the Kabakaship was an institution of emotional appeal because it connected the Baganda with their past but not because it was any longer a centre of political authority in Buganda of the colonial period. I have also argued elsewhere that in Ankole colonial rule transformed the king into an exasperating irrelevance.[15] Had colonialism not achieved these fundamental changes, it would have failed in its primary objective of ruling "native races"—it would not have been colonialism as we understand it.

There was yet another aspect in which indirect rule was a contradictory expedient. This has something to do with the use of African Chiefs as tools of administrative control. In the first place, in those areas where chiefs who had legitimate claims to the exercise of authority could be identified, such as in Busoga for instance, these did not become malleable tools for carrying out administrative instructions from the colonial officials for the simple reason that they were not used to carrying out orders from anyone and in most cases these were removed and replaced with more malleable men whose authority was anything but traditional. This happened in Acholi, Kigezi and Busoga to mention only a few examples. These new-style chiefs, who were created by the colonial government, both in centralised and segmentary societies, could not, by any stretch of imagination and English grammar, be said to be furthering the evolution, less still the preservation of traditional institutions. They were quite simply British puppets (almost in a literal sense) whose chief role in the governance of the protectorate was to transmit orders from the colonial officials to the people. Thus a veteran statesman like Apolo Kagwa of Buganda could be dismissed from office by a junior European official and nobody seemed to see the absurdity of it all. From the foregoing it can be reasonably concluded that British rule was a fact of life in all areas of Uganda whether such an area had been conquered or acquired by agreement. And indirect rule did not give, as it could not give, meaningful or real power to the African rulers or chiefs. This was true of all areas of Uganda.

If the fiction of indirect rule has permeated African historiography, the sanctity of the so-called agreements has endured for even longer and has done so in the face of numerous facts to the contrary. The fact that these "agreements" were an unequal bargain between the British and the Ugandan Africans with whom they were made admits of no debate. That the colonial officials found it necessary or desirable to sign them at all is a mystery for they must have known them for the fraudulent fictions they were. It is perhaps necessary to state that if the African signatories or thumb-markers of these agreements misunderstood their import, this was only to be expected for they were couched in a language too intricate and they embodied ideas too foreign to be understood. In the case of Buganda, for instance, no one could have expected the Kabaka or his chiefs to have grasped the quasi-legal phraseology of the 1900 agreement—the Kabaka was too young to understand much about anything anyway. What is baffling, however, is why this misunderstanding should have been displayed by people who should have known better and several years after the conclusion of these agreements. There are several examples to illustrate this. We find, for instance, that in October 1929, one Yusufu Bamuta, writing to the colonial secretary and "explaining" to him the status of Buganda under the agreement and stating that: "to limit the powers of the Native Government would be *prima facie* contrary to the Agreement, itself, and definitely *ultra vires*." He concluded this baffling treatise by asserting that, "to all practical intents and purposes "the Kabaka is the head of a sovereign state."[16] All that one can say is that, apart from the sprinkling of legal jargon in this extract, the writer must have got his constitutional theory and terminology upside down.

Professor Low, a renowned historian, found it appropriate to state that the Buganda agreement:

> ". . . . unlike so many European agreements with African Chiefs, ... was not of the kind to be shelved by the British, if the Baganda kept to their promises."[17]

The fact that this agreement imposed no "promises" upon the British is not explained. In any event there was absolutely no legal obligation upon the British to keep the terms of the agreement as perhaps Professor Low was well aware.

During the political turbulance of the late 'fifties in Uganda, the Lukiiko of Buganda approved a Memorandum to be sent to the Queen of the United kingdom to the effect that the Lukiiko no longer saw the benefit of remaining in Uganda and under British protection and the Memorandum concluded:

"If we want to terminate the Agreements the British cannot refuse us—just as we could not refuse them if they wanted to terminate the Agreements (referring to the 1894 and 1900 agreements)."[18]

That this statement could have emanated from a Lukiiko which had trained lawyers among its members and almost an unlimited access to legal advice both within and outside Uganda is perhaps the greatest testimony of how ingrained the fiction had become. And as recently as 1966 a graduate student of Political Science flatly stated that,"

"Perhaps one of the greatest mistakes of the colonial government was its failure to define a precise relationship between the Protectorate and the Buganda Governments."[19]

Later on, he poses what appeared to him a momentous question as to whether Britain was bound by such agreements when the chips were down—a question which could only be answered in the negative, whether or not the chips were down, in the light of the existence of the British Foreign Jurisdiction Act of 1890, the existence of which probably the author was unaware. The point is that Buganda was ruled by the agents of the British government and that was all there was to it. All these questions could not have arisen if all these agreements, the Buganda one included, had been seen for what they were: a set of colonial regulations which the colonising power could unilaterally change at its pleasure and quite lawfully too.

Lest the impression is created that such misunderstandings were confined to the Buganda agreement because of its elaborateness, we may take one last example from the western kingdoms of Uganda. With reference to the agreements of Toro, Ankole and Bunyoro, Uzoigwe argues that only the agreement of Bunyoro conferred meaningful power to the Omukama while those of the other areas reduced the power of their respective rulers. He even gets carried away when he states:

".... Kasagama [king of Toro] was never an Omukama in the traditional sense. He was imposed on the Batoro by a foreign power and given little freedom to be a proper king even before the Agreement was signed. In other words, the 1900 [Toro] Agreement did not reduce any actual power that Kasagama possessed."[20]

These statements confuse several issues. In the first place the fact that Kasagama had been defeated and chased out of his kingdom by Kabarega of Bunyoro and was subsequently reinstated by the British, as we have already seen, only shows that Bunyoro was stronger than Toro and that the British were stronger than the Banyoro in military terms. It does not in any sense prove that Kasagama was an illegitimate king. Kasagama was in the royal line that had ruled the Toro kingdom since its foundation and the Batoro had not questioned his legitimacy before Kabarega's invasion or even after it. Indeed he did not acquire legitimacy *because* he was reinstated by the British—he was reinstated *because* this was one of the ways of hampering Kabarega's power since he had already been adjudged to be hostile to British interests. Again the only victory that the Omukama of Bunyoro could have gained from the 1933 agreement could only have been psychological and not politico-psychological because Bunyoro had not had an agreement for so long. The heart of the matter is that in all the agreement areas, as in the non-agreement ones, in Uganda the real power lay with the colonial officials and not with these rulers or the new-style chiefs. To contend otherwise would be superficial. Perhaps we can conclude this part of our argument by quoting Ibingira. With a lawyer's penchant for obscure details, he shows that these agreements did not bind Britain and he cites a series of decided cases to prove this point. He concludes by stating:

"It is beyond dispute, therefore, that within Uganda and in British municipal law, these agreements lacked the force of law and bound the British crown only during its pleasure."[21]

Perhaps all that a layman can add is that a misunderstanding does not become a constitutional truth no matter how many times and by whom it is repeated. Whatever the concessions that the British Government chose to make to Buganda local government or to anyone else, these were given on grounds of political expediency and not beause of any legal or constitutional requirement.

Thus what had, by 1921, happened to Uganda was much more than the establishment of colonial rule for this event set in motion many fundamental and obtrusive changes and these changes affected all the societies in Uganda. Initially these changes were not realised by both the colonisers and the colonised because they were gradual and, for the most part, imperceptible. Uganda had finally been given definite territorial boundaries but not a national identity and this is not surprising because it can scarcely be said that colonialism had come to Africa in order to create nation-states. The societies which made up Uganda were nowhere near becoming homogeneous. In fact it can be said that what was in the process of coalescing was the British rule itself while, at the same time, the African societies were being differentiated or made to drift apart. This will be the subject of our next chapter.

1. Low and Pratt: *Buganda and British Overrule, 1900-1955.* (O.U.P., 1960), p. 24.
2. For a detailed analysis of the 1900 Buganda Agreement, the reader is referred particularly to Law and Pratt: *op. cit.* and D. Apter: *The Political Kingdom in Uganda—A Study in Bureaucratic Nationalism.* (Princeton University Press, 1961).
3. The career of Semei Kakungulu and the establishment of British rule in this region generally may be obtained from: H. B. Thomas: "Capax-Imperii: The story of Semei Kakungulu," *Uganda Journal,* Vol. 6/3/1939.
   J. Barber: *The Imperial Frontier.*
   M. Twaddle: "Political Change in Eastern Uganda During the 19th Century." *M.S.P. 10/70/71.*
4. A. T. Matson: *Nandi Resistance to British Rule, 1890-1905,* (E.A.P.H., 1972), p. 239.
5. G. N. Uzoigwe: *Revolution and Revolt in Bunyoro-Kitara,* (Makerere History Papers No. 5) has an erudite and impassioned account of this rebellion.
6. G. N. Uzoigwe: "The Agreement States," (an unpublished manuscript kindly made available to me by the author), p. 24.

7. For the political upheavals in Ankole during this period See: S. R. Karugire: *Mbaguta and the Establishment of British Rule in Ankole* (E.A.L.B., 1973), p. 41-53.
8. For a fuller account of the incorporation of Kigezi into Uganda Protectorate see: D. Denoon (ed.): *A History of Kigezi in South West Uganda,* (Kampala, 1973), p. 200-221.
9. The account that follows is partly based on: Moyse-Bartlett: *History of the King's African Rifles.* J. Barber: *The Imperial Frontier.*
10. J. Barber: *ibid.* p. 88.
11. *Ibid.* p. 18.
12. *Ibid.* p. 55.
13. A. B. Adimola: "The Ramogi Rebellion of 1911-12", *Uganda Journal* Vol. 12 (1948).
14. D. Cameron: *The Principles of Natives Administration and their Application,* (Government Printer, Lagos, 1934).
15. S. R. Karugire: *Mbaguta,* p. 85.
16. Quoted in D. A. Low: *The Mind of Buganda,* p. 83. all emphasis in original.
17. Low and Pratt: *op. cit.* p. 147.
18. *Uganda Argus* 19/12/59 (Kampala), p. 7.
19. A. R. Nsibambi: *Federation in Uganda: Myth or Reality.* (M.A. Thesis for the University of Chicago, 1966—in Makerere University Library).
20. G. N. Uzoigwe: "The Agreement states," p. 13 and 29.
21. G. S. K. Ibingira: *op. cit.* p. 13-19.

CHAPTER FOUR

THE ADMINISTRATIVE FRAMEWORK
(1921-1960)

Once the limits of the Protectorate were ascertained through the measures that we have outlined in the foregoing pages, it remained for the British to establish the actual machinery through which the Protectorate was to be formally administered and, as an incidental bye-product, "developed." Against the background of the diversity of the social and political organisations of Uganda societies this was by no means an easy task. At one extreme there was the comparatively large kingdom of Buganda whose size and history made it look and feel like a state rather than a unit of local government and, at the other extreme, there was Karamoja whose segmentary political organisation was rendered even more complex by the nomadic life of its population. In between these extremes fell the rest of the components of the Protectorate and these themselves were far from being uniform. The first challenge to the nascent British administration, therefore, was to establish a uniform system of administration over the whole protectorate and this challenge was not fully resolved throughout the colonial period—and even for some period after independence—because the factors militating against uniformity of administration were to prove intractable.

From the outset the British administrators were convinced that the Kiganda model of local government would be the most viable, and probably the cheapest also, and that therefore this should be "exported" into all the parts of the Protectorate. What this meant was that the form rather than the substance of the Kiganda system of government should be the pattern of local government everywhere in the Protectorate. This was so because we have already argued that the substance of Kiganda government had been effectively undermined by European intrusion and that this fact had been confirmed by the 1900 agreement. It would make no sense, therefore, to speak of promoting a system of local government in the other parts of the Protectorate which had already been basically discarded on its native soil.

The first practical problem arose out of the fact that the Kiganda system of administration was peculiarly fashioned to suit Buganda conditions and that this fashioning had taken well over a century to take a definite shape within Buganda. Outside Buganda, the system was a strange one, even in the kingdom areas. The first formal and concrete steps to establish the Buganda model of administration were taken by the promulgation of the 1919 Native Authority Ordinance.[1] The main purpose of this Ordinance was to formalise and clarify the powers, duties and privileges of African chiefs in all areas of the Protectorate, excepting Buganda. This was an important consideration because the African Chief was to be the principal grassroot instrument by which British control was to be established and consolidated in Uganda. By this law chiefs were given wide-ranging powers to enable them to discharge their new duties. They were to maintain law and order in their respective areas of jurisdiction and they were given all powers necessary to enable them prevent the commission of crimes: powers of arrest of offenders, prohibition of the carrying of arms by Africans, the requisitioning of free labour for public projects and so on. All these powers, needless to say, were only to be exercised over the African population and always subject to the overall direction of the British officials who could countermand any orders issued by any chief and who had power to dismiss any chief.

In their enthusiasm to create the Kiganda system of administration outside Buganda, the British had given the African "chief" extensive powers—powers that were not even exercised by the chiefs of Buganda in the pre-colonial period. But this was a minor consideration, even assuming that the framers of the ordinance bothered about it, in the whole complex and ponderous machinery of colonial rule. The law had been made, but what mattered was how it would work in practice for this is the ultimate test of the effectiveness of any law.

It was naturally in the segmentary and quasi-segmentary societies of Uganda that the Ordinance met its greatest challenges because it was primarily in those areas that the concept of one-man authority was entirely alien. Two examples will illustrate this point. We have already seen that in the small kingdoms of Acholi the kings reigned rather than ruled and that the consensus of all the assembled elders of the particular kingdom was the source of the direction of public policy but decidedly not the opinion of the kings or of any other single person. Russell tells us, particularly in respect of Acholi, that:

"To an astonishing extent it was true that one clan member in opposition could hold up a whole course of action, even though eventually he was almost certain to agree".

He concludes by stating:

"Government by civil servants, as under British rule, was therefore particularly obnoxious to the people of Northern Uganda. Not only were the wrong people governing, they were governing by the wrong method."*[2]

Thus the Rwot of Atyak was deposed in 1927 "because he failed to carry out government orders", and was replaced by one Jakariya Atoyo from Patiko so that the "the rule of Atyak's royal line came to an end at this time". In some instances some humiliating punishments were handed out to these traditional rulers for trivial offences. For instance, the ruler of Pajule, Aliker by name, was put into a latrine pit by the District Commissioner and he died soon thereafter. Lakidi, the ruler of Paimol, was imprisoned and finally hanged in public and in his place was installed one Amet, who was not only from outside the royal house of Paimol, but had also, to the considerable outrage of the Acholi, suffered from leprosy and lost some of his fingers. And this outrage was perpetrated by a European Officer (Postlethwaite) whom the Acholi had nicknamed *gweno* (chicken)—a very unflattering epithet indeed in Acholi.[3] As a result of all these drastic measures government interpreters, clerks and other obsequious people were gradually put into positions of power over a society in which age and proven merit were the criteria for leadership. The system ultimately worked not because it was initially acceptable or understandable but because the British had the physical force to back up their appointees.

We may take the second example from the Karimojong, a pastoral people in northern Uganda. Among these people not only was the concept of collective leadership a time-honoured one, but also the society was a nomadic one, very much unfamiliar with the idea of a settled government such as the British were attempting to impose upon them. The Karimojong knew no chiefs. Their society was regulated by recognised elders of the clans and this was even quickly realised by the first civilian District Officer of Karamoja for in his first annual report he wrote that:

"The influence of the elders is at present the greatest obstacle in the way of progress. As a result of this influence the majority of the chiefs . . . . . are mere puppets, and have no authority. In many cases better men refuse the position of chiefs as they fear the influence of the elders which leads public opinion and makes their position far from enviable."[4]

But according to the Protectorate officials, the Karimojong had to have chiefs just like everyone else in the Protectorate—no glib talk yet of protecting the Karimojong's traditional institutions!

Initially the Karimojong tolerated the presence of British officials in their midst largely because the latter seemed to be preoccupied with matters that did not touch upon their own everyday pursuits—the construction of roads, the occasional collection of tax and so on. To be sure these tasks were sometimes irksome to the Karimojong but they were not oppressive. But then the new Administration began making regulations aimed at restricting cattle movements—and they even tried to enforce them. These new rules made the movement of cattle from permanent settlements to dry season areas dependent on the chiefs' permission. Apparently the regulations were aimed at preventing wholesale emigration of young men during certain periods of the year thereby leaving no labour for government work. Attempts to enforce these rules were greeted with hostility all over Karamoja because, unlike other colonial exactions, these rules impinged directly on the daily lives of the people. It had always been the prerogative of the elders to determine the timing of the movement of livestock according to seasonal requirements and now the government was attempting to abrogate to itself this ancient right of the elders, that is, to give this right to new-style chiefs who, moreover, were universally unpopular.

Matters came to a head in 1923 at Nabilatuk headquarters of Pian county of Karamoja. The chief, named Achia, found that some of the people in his area of jurisdiction had moved their stock without his permission as the new rules required. He then embarked on the exercise of rounding up the herds which had been moved "illegally" and he succeeded in capturing some cattle. But even these were rescued by a hostile crowd and Achia was speared to death so that, in the words of one elder, "everyone can herd his stock where he likes".[5] This violent expression of public opinion had a salutary effect on Government attitude towards Karamoja. Sir Geoffrey Archer, who was the Governor between 1922 and 1926, summoned a meeting of top administrators in December 1923 and a new and sterile policy was adopted for the administration of Karamoja. It was decided, among other things, that although the system of indigenous chiefs would continue, such chiefs would in future be appointed on the advice of elders which elders would continue to be responsible for the administration of clan affairs as in the past. This policy was to make Karamoja the most undeveloped district of Uganda because the Government's overriding concern in Karamoja was "restricted to maintaining the status quo,"[6] unlike anywhere else in the Protectorate. To the present day Karamoja has remained something of a tourist attraction not so much on account of its natural attractions but because of its backwardness in comparison to the other parts of the country.

What all these examples show is that it did not prove possible to establish a uniform system of administration in Uganda. Buganda continued to be the only provincial local government in the Protectorate and in the other districts and kingdoms the policy was usually modified to meet local conditions and this somewhat cumbersome machinery worked after a fashion.

After the war of 1939-45, the British Government realised that she had to develop her colonial dependencies at a faster rate than hitherto and, in particular, to democratise the organs of local government and to give them wider responsibilities. This new policy was conveyed to the colonial governors in the Colonial Secretary's despatch of 25th February 1947. Then in 1949 the Local Government Ordinance was promulgated and this was intended to be the legal instrument by which the new policy was to be implemented. The new Ordinance was to give Corporate powers and responsibilities to the District Councils of those areas where no agreements had been signed. It empowered the Governor to establish a district council in any part of the Protectorate by proclamation and to determine the powers they were to exercise and the functions they were to carry out. The Governor was also empowered to establish Provincial Councils in any part of the Protectorate, which Councils could consider matters affecting their respective provinces. But they were to be consultative bodies since they were not empowered to pass laws or bye laws. For our purposes it is sufficient to note that for the first time District Councils were established by law and the districts were formally recognised as the basic units of administration so that the 1949 Ordinance was the legal instrument by which "tribally"—oriented local governments were established in Uganda. In the process of determining district boundaries much care had been taken to include, wherever possible and practicable, one ethnic group in one district. To a large extent this had been achieved because with the exception of West Nile, Bukedi and Kigezi districts, the rest of the districts of Uganda were virtually inhabited by a single ethnic group each. This, in turn, meant that these District Councils were also "tribal" councils whose main exertions concerned matters affecting their respective communities. This development had far graver consequences for the development of Uganda as a single entity than the apparent smooth functioning of these councils would have one believe. We shall examine these consequences along with the other institutional problems which were brought about by colonial rule.

By these enactments the administration of Uganda was given a final and legal form, but not a democratic one as the Colonial Secretary had intended. But each unit of local government (the district) was treated as if it was an independent entity. The District Council of Acholi, for example, knew little and cared even less about the problems of Kigezi District Council and vice versa. What these districts shared in a tangible form was the Governor whom they saw rarely anyway.

This reluctance to forster the growth of territorial or national organs of government and the promotion of parochial ones does not seem to have been wholly accidental on the part of the colonial Administration. As Ibingira points out, as early as 1898 a suggestion that there should be established a central council for Uganda had been killed by the Protectorate Government and a proposal from the rulers of Uganda's kingdoms and Busoga that they be allowed to hold regular meetings was vetoed by the Governor in 1925.[7] It was by such measures that organs that could have fostered a territory-wide outlook were frustrated and parochial ones flourished as a consequence of official policy. As Burke states:

> "The establishment of districts based wherever possible on tribal residence has contributed to a sense of district nationalism and separatism that in many cases did not exist prior to the arrival of the British . . . ."[8]

Besides administrative separation of the districts, there were other extraneous factors which enhanced this sense of separatism. Earlier in this survey we saw what there had existed a considerable volume of trade between the precolonial communities of Uganda based largely on iron products and salt. The coming of colonial rule also brought in its train foreign manufactures which were far cheaper than the local ones. For instance the Chillington hoe was far cheaper to produce on a large scale in British factories than the local hoe and this is why the local smiths were effectively put out of business by the new wares which were produced by skills far superior to their own. Moreover, the new things looked "better" as one by one the African values were debunked with the help of the ubiquitous missionaries. It was not, for example, considered "progressive" or "civilised" to don the Kiganda barkcloth except for the few exotic traditional ceremonies which in any event were becoming more quaint and rarer day by day. This meant that the Muganda did not need to travel to Bunyoro to purchase a hoe or the Munyoro to travel to Busoga to sell one—each one of these could get a "better" hoe at the local Indian shop and at a cheaper price too. Thus the primary stimulus which had brought several communities together in the past were removed and this in turn promoted the growth of ethnic and insular nationalism because for nearly sixty years no Uganda ethnic group needed its neighbour for anything. This is the sense in which we observed earlier that the consolidation of the Protectorate really meant the coalesence of British rule and the differentiation or separation of the African communities. This differentiation was fundamental despite the fact that it took subtler and sometimes imperceptible forms.

Besides administrative innovations, the energies of the new administration were also engaged in structuring the economy of the country. At an earlier stage of this study it was argued that one of the primary motives for the British occupation of Uganda was economic; that is to say that it was primarily the British quest for tropical raw material for her industries at home which had brought about the British occupation of Uganda. Together with this concern was the consideration that the Protectorate should at the very least generate enough revenue internally to defray the expenses of its occupation. This had been as much a concern for the Chartered Company as it became for the British government when it took over Uganda from the Company. Capt. Lugard and then Johnston after him had all considered a variety of tropical products that could be raised in Uganda and Johnston in particular had been instructed to pay particular regard to this aspect of the Protectorate since the expenses of occupying Uganda had caused Parliamentary concern in Britain as we have seen. Thus at various times tea, cocoa, sugar, rubber and coffee had all been contemplated and dropped. Ultimately, and somewhat accidentally, the choice fell on cotton. This choice was accidental because Johnston, for instance, had grave doubts about the viability of Uganda cotton for he did not think that it could compete with that of the other established cotton producing countries.[9]

Despite the concern for the economic viability of the Protectorate, however, the initial impetus for cotton growing did not come from the government; it came from a private company, the Uganda Company, which was an adjunct of the CMS. Mr. K. Borup of the CMS was supplied with cotton seeds by the British Cotton Growing Association and he brought these to Uganda in 1903. The Association itself had been formed a year earlier with the object of promoting cotton growing in British dependencies in order to free the British textile industry from dependence on the United States cotton. The seeds were distributed to Buganda Chiefs and the rest was left to them. We have already noted the hierarchical structure of Buganda society and the authoritarian nature of her government. Even when the chiefs of Buganda were turned into civil servants by the 1900 agreement, this did not immediately change the obligations of the peasants to their chiefs and one such obligation was the chief's right to the peasants' labour for certain periods of the year or for the completion of a specific project. It was thus normal for the chiefs to turn over the seeds to the peasants for the cultivation of this new crop. It should perhaps also be mentioned in passing that although cotton growing was not initially a government project as such, to the Baganda, chiefs and peasants alike, there was hardly any difference between a government sponsored project and a private European sponsored one—both were demands of the new-style government and as such they were to be carried out just as one had to pay the taxes whose immediate utility to oneself was a mystery. Wringley tells us that from

> "1904 and for the next two or three years official interest in the (cotton) crop was spasmodic and half-hearted, and the main credit for its establishment must remain with the Company."[10]

Thus the cotton experiment in Buganda was such a staggering success that by the 1915/16 financial year the Protectorate dispensed with the imperial grants-in-aid mostly as a result of the export of cotton grown by peasant cultivators and thus a major government objective—the Protectorate paying for itself—was achieved. From Buganda even more spectacular success in cotton production was registered in the Eastern province—especially in Busoga and Teso districts. Then cotton growing was extended to northern Uganda, notable successes being achieved in Acholi and Lango districts.

The importance of the success of cotton as a cash crop did not lie solely in the fact that the Protectorate could now pay for its administration although this was important enough. There was also the further important consideration that this objective had been achieved through the agency of a crop grown entirely by Africans and without European supervision or, as so often in colonial dependencies, coercion. This was important because the official thinking throughout British East Africa was that agricultural development was not possible without European-run plantations or, at the very least, European close supervision of the "natives". In Uganda also some of the colonial officials wanted to encourage white settlement in order to speed up the "development" of the Protectorate—the most outstanding exponents of white settlement were Sir William Morris Carter, Uganda's principal judge, of later Kenya notoriety and Sir Robert Coryndon, a Rhodesian pioneer who became the Governor of Uganda in 1917. By 1920 some 184 square miles of Uganda were in fact under European plantation.

Although the immediate post-war years looked rosy for European planters in Uganda, this was only superficial since even a well-disposed government had no means of overcoming other fundamental obstacles that militated against plantation agriculture in Uganda. To begin with there was the old problem of Uganda's distance from the coast which even the approach of a railway could only mitigate but not do away with altogether so that the benefits or profits to be gained from plantation agriculture would always be reduced considerably by transport costs. Moreover, the colonial office itself was never wholly behind settler enterprise in Uganda and from time to time that office exhibited lukewarm interest when prospects looked good and shelved the problem altogether when they did not. Related to this was the fact that not all the colonial officials welcomed white settlement and in Uganda the Department of Agriculture and the Provincial Commissioners were decidedly hostile to European settlers mostly on paternalistic grounds, [11] but also because European settlers were an unmitigated political nuisance for they would, as they were doing in neighbouring Kenya, disturb the placid administration of the "natives." Wherever they existed, settlers always demanded far too much in the way of social services although they were usually unwilling to be taxed in order to meet the cost of those services. In Bunyoro, for instance, in 1914 the local planters complained against official encouragement of cotton growing by Africans and the District Commissioner acidly informed them that it was

> "neither the wish nor the intention of His Majesty's Government to exploit this country's many advantages for the sole benefit, financial or other, of a white population, numerically small, at the expense of native interests, or at the expense of improving native conditions of livelihood."[12]

This contrasts so sharply with Major Grogan's appeal to the Kenya Governor in the same period to save that country from being a preserve of natives, missionaries and government officials—and no one thought that appeal to be absurd. It was the conflicting views of the men-on-the spot which kept the colonial office unsure of the whole project of white settlement in Uganda and which ultimately turned that office against it. Perhaps the most enduring achievement of British paternalism was the passage of Busulu and Nvujjo law of 1928 for Buganda which not only fixed the dues that the peasants were to pay to their landlords but which also prohibited the eviction of tenant peasants for any other cause save the failure to pay the statutory dues which were not stringent by any standards and which the subsequent fall in the value of money rendered somewhat derisory.

Another intractable problem that faced the Protectorate government as well as the planters was the problem of labour and to this problem there were several dimensions. In the first place the Uganda Africans were proprietors of the small land holdings scattered all over the Protectorate. This may not have been so in written law but it was so in fact because any attempt to effect wholesale movement of population would almost certainly have led to rebellion. Over the various patches of land cultivated by the Africans there was raised enough food for their families so that there was no need to work for wages to pay government dues or for the few luxuries they were beginning to enjoy.

Moreover, with the introduction of cotton and then coffee each family could cultivate its own patch of the cash crop, wherever these crops could be grown, and this was sufficient to meet its demands for cash. There was thus little or no incentive to work for Europeans. Secondly, even the advocates of white settlement were not prepared to go to the extreme of demanding the suppression of African agriculture in order to force out the labour to white plantations and yet this seemed to be the only alternative as the experiments were showing in neighbouring Kenya. This was so because no Uganda government, nor indeed the colonial office, could sanction the suppression of African cash crop farming when this was the principal source of government revenue. There were of course other areas where these crops could not be grown such as most of western province and some parts of eastern and northern provinces, but this fact offered little comfort to the settlers and their supporters. People from such areas did migrate looking for wage-paid work in cotton and coffee producing areas, especially in Buganda. But these never formed a stable labour force for they were always target workers. The men from Kigezi district or West Nile, for instance, would work for wages for a few months in order to raise a specific sum of money for a specific purpose—such as government tax, bridewealth or school fees—and then they would repair to their respective districts and villages. It would then take several months, if at all, for the same persons to look for paid employment. Therefore the supply of labour from such sources was undependable in the extreme and this is the chief explanation for the failure of Trade Unions in Uganda during and after the colonial period. There was quite simply no category of people one could call workers. Since on grounds of practical politics and economics the government could neither force the African to work for European planters nor suppress African production, labour remained an insoluble problem right up to the time white settlement in Uganda became an academic subject.

What finally decided whether or not Uganda would have a plantation economy—a *coup de grace* to white settlement one might say—was the world wide economic slump of the 1920's. This ruined most of the existing planters and discouraged any possible influx of the would-be planters. It is true that the Africans also suffered because they were the principal producers of cash crops, but their losses were nothing compared to the losses sustained by European planters largely because plantation agriculture was both labour and capital intensive while African farming was neither. Besides, the Africans did not engage in cotton or coffee production as a full–time activity. The little cotton or coffee patch, often to be found alongside other food crops, was something of a hobby which was undertaken by a few family members on a part–time basis. Not so for the planters for plantation agriculture was a means of living as well as capital already expended in the hope of realising a profit at some future date. When no such profit was forthcoming and, worse still, when even the cost of production could not be realised, the planters were effectively ruined as many of them could not even pay back the bank loans and they were faced with foreclosures and other ramifications of capitalist finance which inevitably follow the collapse of an enterprise so funded. What is more, the government became considerably jittery in case the Africans gave up cash crop farming in the face of falling prices. This is why the government decided to help the Africans (by buying their produce) rather than planters as a matter of official policy. Any discouragement of African farming would have adverse effect on government revenue since African farming had proved its viability just as plantation agriculture had failed to do so. Just as the human and animal epidemics of the 1890s had aided the British in securing control over Uganda at relatively little cost, in men and money, so also did the world economic slump of the 1920s save Uganda from a white settler population and its attendant evils on the African population. Uganda settled down to an agricultural economy whose principal producers were the African peasant small-holders.

Allied to the promotion of the economic viability of the Protectorate was also the idea of the federation, or closer union as it was called, of Kenya, Uganda and, possibly, mainland Tanzania. The idea was by no means a new one for Johnston had indeed proposed the merger of Kenya and Uganda on economic grounds but nothing had come of his scheme and, instead, as we have seen, the Eastern province of Uganda was transferred to Kenya. In the post war period, the idea was revived with more fervour by Mr. L. S. Amery who was soon to become the Tory Colonial Secretary. That economic benefits would accrue to these territories if they were federated, was undoubted and for Amery:

"Small units should be organised into large states which would be capable of contributing more fully to the needs of the empire"[13]

By which he meant that such larger units of the empire would offset Britain's disadvantages in world trade, especially with respect to trade with the United States. But the political implications of such a Union and the ambitions of the white settlers of Kenya proved to be the undoing of Amery's ideas of imperial economic expansionism.[14] To the white settlers of Kenya, the idea of federation was an attractive one provided the union could be formed and placed under their political control and for this very reason the other European officials in Uganda and mainland Tanzania had grave reservations about the whole scheme or were openly hostile.

The Asian Communities of all the three territories and, more decisively, the African population were opposed to the scheme as they feared that their own interests would be harmed if their connection to the Colonial Office via their respective governors was modified or, worse still, severed by a federal council under the control of Kenya settlers whose baneful influence on the political life of Kenya needed no proof to be believed since it was already common knowledge. For this reason a succession of Commissions—Ormsby-Gore (1924), Hilton-Young (1927) and Sir Samuel Wilson (1927)—achieved nothing more concrete than recommending periodic meetings of the three Governors. Finally, the report of the Joint Select Committee of the British Houses of Parliament put the question into abeyance in 1931 because it was felt that the political climate made the creation of the union undesirable for the time being. The hostility it would provoke in the three territories far exceeded any foreseeable benefits it would bring. Thus in the inter-war period Uganda was saved from a white settler population and close association with settler–dominated Kenya and, to all appearances, the Protectorate could settle down and develop sedately under the guidance of a succession of paternalist and often benevolent Governors who were usually sent out to the Protectorate by Whitehall. Yet all was not as well as appearances suggested and this brings us to the unresolved problems that were basic in Uganda's public life during the colonial period.

The administrative and economic structures that were being fashioned were being built on structures that were basically unhealthy. This was so because within the social fabric and the body politic of the Protectorate there had been created, by the imposition of colonial rule, basic problems which, instead of the Colonial Administration facing them squarely, were merely glossed over.

The first of such problems was that there were several important groups in the country which were denied access to economic and political power by the very nature of the imposition of colonial rule. By far the largest group of such excluded elements were the Catholics in the whole Protectorate. We have already dealt with the manner in which the new religions were introduced into Uganda and we have indicated how quickly these faiths were transformed into political parties. We have also noted that the Protestant victory over the Catholics in 1892 in Buganda established Protestant ascendancy not only in Buganda but also in the whole Protectorate as its boundaries expanded beyond Buganda and as with this expansion also went the spread of Christian missions. Discrimination against the Catholics took the form of denying them public offices or not giving them such number of offices as were commensurate with their numbers. In the political heat of the 1950s an Acholi Catholic newspaper put this grievance bluntly. It stated:

"The dispute concerning religion in Uganda is not over doctrinal differences but about jobs and scholarships. The Catholics feel aggrieved and wonder why such important posts like that of a county chief . . . . . are held by Protestants. For evidence of this unfairness try to find out about the major African officials like Ministers, the Kabaka, the Mukama, the Mugabe and many different grades of chiefs . . . . . . Note the small number of Catholics among them."[15]

The foregoing was an accurate assessment of the situation obtaining in Uganda and this assessment is mild in tone considering that none of the four kingdoms of Uganda had ever been ruled by a Catholic. This same fact is confirmed by Ibingira who points out the obvious imbalance in the distribution of important offices in Buganda since 1900 and also in the other area of Uganda where the heridatary rulers or the Secretaries-General (in areas without heridatary rulers) were always Protestants. But with a characteristic lawyer's instinct for avoiding commitment to a single definite point of view, he offers two explanations for this imbalance. The first is that it could be argued that the Protestants possessed men of the right calibre. Secondly, he says, it was possible to argue that Protestant ascendancy could not have lasted so long unless it was backed by a partial imperial power whose religion was also protestant and, he concludes, "Apart from noting this fact, it is of no value to apportion the blame . . ."[16] But of course what Ibingira does is not merely to avoid apportioning the blame but rather to avoid offering an explanation for such an important development in the national life of Uganda.

Welbourn explains this long-standing injustice in a typical Anglo-Protestant fashion. He says:

"Protestants did not obtain administrative influence in Buganda merely because Lugard had given them political powers. The whole tendency of the Protestant education was to train for leadership. Missionaries established and administered the schools on the pattern of the English public schools"[17].

And so, God help us, here we get the battle of Waterloo being won in Buganda by virtue of the superior educational system of the English public schools! There is nothing new in all this of course because all the Catholic complaints to the Protectorate officials against discrimination were blandly answered by the time-honoured English formula— all appointments were based on individual merit and certainly not on grounds of religious affiliation. It passes belief that anyone could expect a British establishment—and colonial service was part of this—to promote the adherents of a religion that was barely tolerated in their own country. The heart of the matter is that the Protectorate Administration, aided by their Anglican Missionaries, encouraged the Africans in the belief that their religion and their education (hardly distinguishable in those days) were superior to Roman Catholicism and the imbalance in the distribution of public offices was an instinctive reaction to prove that point to the unwitting African converts. To argue, as Welbourn does, that the Protestants had the personnel with the required merits for such offices by virtue of their "education", one would also have to illustrate that the few offices held by the Catholics—such as county chiefships for example—were not as well managed as those held by the Protestants and to even attempt to do this would be an exercise in absurdity. After all, is not the basic problem of Northern Ireland today the unwillingness of the British government to "hand" over Protestants to the control of the Catholics? It would be too much to expect a different policy in Uganda. But that such a policy would sooner or later cause tensions in Uganda's political life was serenely ignored by the Colonial Officials.

Another element of Uganda's population that belonged to the excluded groups were the African Muslims. Reference has already been made to the religious conflicts in Buganda in the 1890s. When the dust settled down, missionary work, especially the spread of missionary education, proceeded apace in the Protectorate. But in all this the Muslims were left out because they had no missionaries of their own to build them schools like their Christian counterparts. The Protectorate did not see anything anomalous in a situation in which a whole religious faith had virtually no access to educational facilities and this despite the fact that the issue was brought to government attention frequently. During the 21st Session of the Legislative Council in 1941, for instance, one member, Mr. Margarch, urged the government to set up non-denominational schools to enable Muslim children to obtain education. He went on:

> "Government does not provide a non-denominational school. What more pressure could be brought on any people than just leaving them without schools, then giving the Missions school sites in such areas? Where is education to be got except by joining one or other of the Missions? I know in theory it is not so, but in practice it is[18].

And characteristically the Director of Education blandly assured the Council that there was no discrimination against Muslims since "there is strict parity of treatment as between a Moslem and one of any agency." To illustrate this "even-handed" policy, he informed members that government had established a school at Masindi intended primarily for Muslims[19]. This of course amounted to no answer since the majority of Muslims were to be found in Buganda and not near Masindi. Besides, the statement about parity of treatment was not quite true since in that year (1941) out of a grant of £6,631 towards education, Muslim education benefitted to the tune of only £252 18s[20] and no one could call this generous. At any rate the solution did not lie, and could not lie, in making equal grants between Christian and Muslim schools since this would only serve to perpetuate the imbalance between them as the Christians had far more schools than the Muslims could hope to get without government support and this was not forthcoming. The Protectorate Government seemed to be content by the fact that the Muslims primarily became the country's petty butchers and taxi-drivers and there seemed to be no compelling reason to change the situation. In the case of the Muslims even the standard excuse of appointment by merit could not be advanced, as it was in the case of the Catholics, because it would be absurd to argue that having denied a section of the community educational opportunities, one could then turn round and accuse that section of failing to obtain the necessary qualifications for this or that position. This deliberate denial of fair openings to a section of the community, albeit a minority one, laid farther grounds for resentment in Uganda's political life.

In Buganda there was yet another group whose influence had been considerable during the pre-colonial times but which influence was wiped out by the new order thereby rendering this group an excluded one in the governance of Buganda. This group was the Bataka or Clanheads. We have already outlined the importance of clan kinship in Buganda and we have commented upon the value the Baganda attached to land. Each clan was attached to some specific piece of land which was its burial ground or Butaka as it was called in Buganda. These clan lands were sacred and were not controlled by the Kabaka or his chiefs but by the clanheads who managed them on behalf of their respective clans. Then came the 1900 agreement which gave freehold land to the leading chiefs and other notables of Buganda as we have outlined. But since the demarcation of these estates was left to the Lukiiko—in effect to the allotees—the clanheads found themselves left out in the cold as their rights were simply brushed aside. This came about for two primary reasons. Firstly, the chiefs who were carving out estates for themselves wanted the most fertile and populous areas and in the pursuit of that objective they were not, and they could not be expected to be, thwarted by the claims of clanheads.

Secondly, and arising out of the foregoing, it was comparatively easy to ride roughshod over the claims of the clanheads because social values had changed. The basis of political association for the exercise of power was the church in which one "read" and anyone falling outside the ambit of this, as most clanheads did, was quite simply left out of the system altogether. Therefore *it did not become* Christian chiefs to respect institutions that were becoming rapidly outmoded; institutions, moreover, which had been branded "pagan" by the very people (missionaries) who had brought them their brand new god (and incidentally unprecedented power).

This disposed group in Buganda was to form itself into a Bataka Party and to petition incessantly for the restoration of their rights at least to their burial grounds. For instance the Bataka of Buganda petitioned the Chief Secretary of Uganda in May 1921 and pointed out that they had been petitioning for the restoration of their rights in vain:

> "Because of the reason that those who are expected to arbitrate are the ones who unlawfully, acquired their fellowmen's butaka lands by reason of the 1900 agreement: which provided that each one should survey his own estates which (sic) held in possession.
> "We have come to realise that the foundation of our country based on 1900 (agreement) tends to develop a smaller section of the country whereas the larger section is on the contrary discontented and petitioning about the preservation of the good customs of Buganda .... without the Bataka, there is not Buganda[21]."

Even the Kabaka of the day agreed that many Bataka had been dispossessed by the 1900 land allocation and that some of the graves of their ancestors had been destroyed[22]—and in Buganda a greater abomination could hardly be imagined. Yet both the Kabaka and the Protectorate Officials agreed that it would not be possible to undo the land allocation and thus the Bataka nursed their grievances without any hope of redress. But these long-nursed and unremedied grievances gave good material to those who masterminded the civil disturbances in Buganda in 1945 and 1949 and also, to some extent, in the trade boycott of 1959. There were of course other causes behind these disorders but the fact remains that some of the major causes of these outbreaks were due to the cavalier fashion in which the colonial agents had tampered with some of the fundamental institutions of Buganda way back in 1900.

One more example remains to be given of yet another excluded group within the Protectorate. This was the Bairu agriculturalists of the kingdom of Ankole in Western Uganda. The inhabitants of that kingdom had always been divided into two distinct social classes which were traditionally engaged in distinct economic occupations. The Bairu were entirely agriculturalists from which activity they provided for their needs. The other class were the Bahima who were cattle keepers and who did not engage in any other activity unrelated to their cattle on which they depended for their living. For centuries these classes had lived side by side and shared a great many customs as they spoke a common language. Over this period of time cattle had come to be regarded as the yardstick of national wealth. But the environmental conditions were such that cattle keeping could not be carried on simultaneously with the cultivation of crops and this is why these two occupations were mutually exclusive. It was from the cattle-owning Bahima that a majority of the office holders of the kingdom were drawn.[23] But during the pre-colonial period, there had always been an upward and downward mobility within this political and social system. Then the introduction of a cash-oriented economy and the new concepts of government and new social values of colonial rule effectively froze the mobility between these classes without introducing an adequate substitute mechanism of social control. And this was not all. The British officials had been deeply impressed by the Bahima's physical features which, for some reason, they associated with intelligence.[24] Thus while introducing new concepts of government, the British continued to appoint local officials from the wealthy Bahima families thereby leaving the Bairu on the periphery of the management of public affairs in the kingdom. And on being questioned on why this was so, the British officials could always give the self-implementing excuse that appointments were made on individual merit. This was true enough because the Bairu were given very little opportunity to prove their merits or demerits. But then the Bairu had embraced the new education system with greater vigour and in greater numbers than their Bahima counterparts and by the 1940s they began to question the injustice of excluding them from public office when those who were being appointed did not seem to have any better qualifications than themselves for those positions. In turn this resentment was to make the governance of that kingdom very difficult in the 1950s and much more so during the Obote Administration after independence.

The disillusionment which was shared by all these excluded elements was the realisation that the basis of their exclusion was becoming an endless circle of self-justifying excuses—privilege begetting more privilege. It had ceased to make sense that these particular groups should be permanently excluded from avenues of self-advancement on any other grounds than individual merit. British Officials' obsessi with chiefs and their sons and daughters could no longer be acceptable

as a cornerstone of social policy. In the fullness of time this disillusionment was bound to have unsettling consequences on the political
life of Uganda, and it did. In the meantime, however, the machinery
of colonialism ground ponderously on.

It was indicated earlier on that the Northern Province of Uganda
had been included in the Protectorate with a certain amount of reluctance on the part of the British officials and that even then this was done
in order to preclude other European powers from acquiring the area
rather than from a desire to acquire the area for its own sake. Once the
province had been acquired, however, it was left very much to its own
devices so far as economic and social development was concerned.
Thus, for instance, although cotton was found to thrive in some of the
districts of northern Uganda, such districts did not derive as much
benefits from cotton growing as the districts of Eastern and Buganda
Provinces since for a long time cotton cultivation was uneconomic
owing to lack of transportation facilities. This was so because these
districts were not served by a railway and they were far from the lake
ports that would have rendered it comparatively cheap for their produce to reach the coast and thence the market. For this reason the
northern districts found it cheaper to send their able–bodied young men
to the south to look for paid employment rather than engaging in
cash crop farming themselves.

In the field of education the Northern Province was even more
neglected even long after the Protectorate government had taken an
interest in the field of African education and the excuse for letting this
province lag behind in the extension of social services was always the
same: its stage of development was not yet of the order to make full
use of such facilities. This was the kind of excuse that could and did
perpetuate undevelopment since if the people are not given facilities to
improve their condition, they are likely to stagnate or even deteriorate.
Thus the Director of Education ecstatically informed the Legislative
Council of granting six African secondary schools and two Teacher
Training Colleges self governing status and "of these institutions,
four are in Buganda, two in the Eastern and two in the Western
Province". No mention was made of the Northern Province although
he promised that in the plans of educational expansion:

".. . every district will share, from the West Nile and Karamoja
to our more privileged Buganda[25]".

For one thing no date of such expansion was indicated. Secondly
the tone in which this announcement was made indicates that the very
idea of extending educational facilities to Northern Uganda was

nothing short of a revolution— and this after nearly half a century of colonial rule!

When the Colonial administration decided to admit some Africans to the Legislative Council, the Governor informed that Council that three African representatives would be chosen to represent Buganda, Western and Eastern Provinces and, he explained:

> "It will not have escaped the notice of Honourable Members the system of nomination which I have just described will leave Nilotic districts in the north without direct representation. Their tribal and administrative organizations have not yet in all districts advanced to the stage requiring the creation of centralised native executives and thus of appointments similar to that of Secretary-General."[27]

The Protectorate Government did not lack warnings about the dangers of such lopsided development of the country. For instance during the Sixth meeting of the Legislative Council in 1956 a considerable time of the Council was spent on this theme. One Member warned:

> "If self-rule is going to be ultimately the object, can we have these backward provinces kept always backward so that in the future there will be retardment of self-rule or troubles as in the Sudan in this unitary state [?] we have to educate these backward people and bring them up so that some kind of homogenity is achieved between the backward and the advanced people of Uganda. It is our duty to see that these backward people are educated . . . . . . so that the future of this country is not put in jeopardy"[27]

So far as the Protectorate Government was concerned, the northern districts of Uganda remained to be a good source of labour and, much more importantly, the biggest source of recruitment into the army and the police forces of the Protectorate. The denial to Northern Uganda of such bounties of social advancement as the colonial administration chose to bestow upon the Protectorate made that region distinctively backward even by Ugandan standards. And the full cost of this neglect has yet to be paid, not by the colonial officials, but by Ugandans themselves.

All these underlying sources of instability did not look as menacing as they were because there was hardly any national forum in which they could be aired. We have already referred to the 1919 and 1949 Ordinances which were the basic laws by which the routine administration of the Protectorate was to be carried out. When these were found not to work satisfactorily, suitable amendments were carried out such as those which were embodied in the District Administration (District Councils) Ordinance of 1955 whose main aim was to get the District Councils more involved in the administration of their respective districts and to give those councils considerable control over the chiefs. When these measures proved unsatisfactory, the 1955 Ordinance was amended in 1959 primarily in order to insulate chiefs from the pressures of the politicians who by then formed the majorities on the District Councils. But then the concern of the Protectorate government, even as late as the 1950s, was to ensure the proper functioning of the local governments under the progressive control of the Africans and under the overall guidance of the European officials. No comparable efforts were made to involve the Africans in the functions of the Legislative Council which had existed since the 1920s. Ever since its establishment, the Legislative Council remained an isolated and exotic institution which was of interest to Europeans and some Asians. So far as the Africans were concerned, the Legislative Council had little or nothing to do with them while their local governments had everything to do with their political aspirations and ambitions. In fact the Legislative Council did not even sit in Kampala until towards the end of 1945—it had enjoyed its glorious oblivion in the equally glorious surroundings of Entebbe until then. In some of the advanced areas of Uganda, notably in Buganda, the Legislative Council was viewed with misgivings and sometimes hostility, but for the rest of the Protectorate, in so far as anything was known about it all, the Legislative Council was an irrelevant institution and it was so to remain until the 1950s. In other words the Uganda Protectorate continued to exist on the law–books and maps of the Land Office but hardly in the minds of the Ugandan Africans for whom the Protectorate was supposed to exist. It is not reasonable to assume that the Protectorate government was unaware of some or all of these problems but that no attempt was made to grapple with them is a fact of history. It was in fact during the colonial period that Uganda acquired a technique, which has since become something of a national habit, of "solving" thorny problems by simply ignoring the fact that such problems existed. All these internal fissures were, at different times, to rock the stability of the Protectorate and nearly to wreck the country under an African government. But this is to anticipate events for our attention must now revert to the stages by which the colonial government almost literally frog-marched Uganda into independence and the nature of the problems that had to be surmounted along this route.

1. This ordinance and the subsequent ones have already been discussed in detail by other writers: See for instance: F. G. Burke: *Local Government and Politics in Uganda.* (Syracuse, 1964), p. 34–48. G. S. K. Ibingira: *The Forging of an African Nation,* p. 22–5. We shall only summarise the substance of these Ordinances and estimate their effect on the general governance of Uganda.
2. J. K. Russell: *Men Without God? A Study of the Impact of the Christian Message in the North of Uganda,* (The Highway Press, London, 1966), p. 41.
3. R. S. Anywar: *Acoli Ki Ker Megi,* (Eagle Press, Kampala, 1954), an English translation by N. E. Odyomo, p. 109–129.
4. Quoted in J. Barber: *The Imperial Frontier,* p. 204.
5. J. Barber: *Ibid.* p. 206.
6. J. Barber: *Ibid.* p. 208.
7. G. S. K. Ibingira *op. cit.* p. 27.
8. F. G. Burke: *op. cit.* p. 14.
9. For the history of cash crops in Uganda see a brilliant paper by C. C. Wrigley: *Crops and Wealth in Uganda,* (East African Institute of Social Research, 1959).
11. *Ibid.* p. 32.
12. *Ibid.* p. 35.
13. Ingham: *A History of East Africa,* (Longman, 1962), p. 311.
14. See also: K. Ingham: *ibid.* p. 310–19. G. Bennet: *Kenya: A Political History.* (London, 1963), p. 53–61.
15. Lobo Mewa of March 15, 1958 quoted in D. A. Low: *Political Parties in Uganda; 1949–1962,* (Athlone Press, 1962).
16. G. S. K. Ibingira: *op. cit.* p. 81.
17. F. B. Welbourn: *Religion and Politics in Uganda, 1952–62,* (E.A.P.H., 1965), p. 9.
18. *Proceedings of the Legislative Council, Official report, 21st Session,* 1941, p. 35.
19. *Ibid.* p. 52.
20. *Ibid.* p. 32.
21. D. A. Low: *The Mind of Buganda,* p. 62–3.
22. *Ibid.* p. 65.
23. S. R. Karugire: *A History of the Kingdom of Nkore,* Chapter 1.
24. Accounts of this bias exist in the accounts of the early travellers in Uganda. See for example J. F. Cunningham: *Uganda and its Peoples,* (London, 1905), p. 20. Sir Harry Johnston: "A Survey of the Ethnography of Africa," *Journal of the Royal Anthropological Institute,* Vol. 43. 1913, p. 375–442.
25. *Proceedings of the Legislative Council, Official Record,* December, 1945, p. 50.
26. *Ibid.* October 1945, p. 3.
27. *Ibid.* January 1956, p. 41.

CHAPTER FIVE

A HOUSE DIVIDED AGAINST ITSELF
(1945-1960)

In this part of our survey we shall primarily be concerned with the growth of political parties in Uganda and, more importantly, with the basic parameters of disunity which became clearer and clearer as the British determination to get out of Uganda became a matter of time only. It is to be borne in mind that when we are talking of leaders of political parties and other party functionaries, we are referring almost exclusively to those Ugandans who were educated or semi-educated. We have already indicated that the introduction of western education and values had effectively disenfranchised those who, for one reason or another, did not get that education so that for the uneducated populace—something in the region of 80% or so of the population— were largely spectators rather than active participants in the events leading to the granting of independence. It is perhaps necessary to explain that for the illiterate peasants this development was not initially seen as being disadvantageous to themselves and this itself was due to the great premium that every family had come to put on education, which was literally the key to everything. For every African family the education of even a single member of the family was both an investment and an insurance for the benefit of that family. Initially, therefore, the illiterate peasants had almost unquestioning trust in the good intentions of their educated leaders-to-be until they found out that they were short-changed at every turn. But this realisation came after independence. As Davidson says:

> ". . . . we shall review a mass of slogans, solutions, arguments, debates, decisions, and types of political behaviour. Behind them all it will be well to keep in mind the unseen audience, the village audience weighing and deciding for itself, often waved this way or that by audacious oratory or skillful manouvre, but still preserving, if sometimes awkwardly and sometimes curiously, a firm and final notion of what is good for ordinary folk and what is not."[1]

This indeed is true enough, but the realisation did the illiterate peasants no good as they did not known how to redress the imbalance in their favour. But this is to anticipate our story.

By and large Uganda, unlike her two mainland neighbours, Kenya and Tanzania, had a different colonial experience largely because of the absence of European settlers. That there were no European settlers in Uganda was due, as we have indicated, to a combination of circumstances which were beyond the control of the Protectorate administration. In other words, it was not solely or even largely because of official policy that Europeans did not settle in Uganda. We have already indicated that the structures of local government which were fashioned by the colonial administration in Uganda had the effect of making district councils self-contained units of administration and that although these were under the overall supervision of the Provincial and District Commissioners, they were nevertheless overwhelmingly African in membership. It has also been observed that within these units or districts, the Councillors and chiefs were usually concerned with matters affecting their respective districts and that rarely, if ever, was any attempt made to relate the problems of one district to those of another district, however similar these might be. So far as the colonial administration was concerned, this was a satisfactory arrangement because it limited the scale of any disorder that might errupt in any part of the Protectorate to the particular unit of local government. It might be pointed out that this arrangement was also satisfactory to the Africans themselves since within each district administration there were ample openings for advancement and self expression because notwithstanding the fact that the range of subjects falling under the purview of district councils were very limited, there was nothing to prevent any District council discussing any subject under the sun and with as much heat as they chose.

Although it can be said that this pattern of administration and liberalism—by colonial standards at any rate this was liberalism—facilitated the establishment of a stable and placid government, it is nevertheless true that this hindered the growth of nationwide political parties. This was not only due to the fact that there was political contentment in the different compartments of the Protectorate, but also to the fact that there was hardly any alien provocation to induce the formation of such parties. In Kenya, for instance, the existence of the notorious Convention of Associations through the 1920s provoked, among other things, the formation of the Young Kikuyu Association to oppose the extreme demands of the white settlers, especially to resist the proposal to reduce African wages by one-third (in the 1920s this stood at the impressive level of Sh. 10/- per month). Again, because of White settlers the Asians of Kenya formed the Indian National Congress to fight for equal rights with the Europeans. These alien parties prompted the formation of African organisations not only to counteract the demands of the alien population, but also to press for their own betterment. This stimulus was lacking in Uganda because of the small number of settlers, still fewer of whom looked upon Uganda as their permanent home and consequently had very little interest in the kind of supremacist politics of their Kenyan counterparts. The substantial number of Asians in Uganda were largely apolitical and were engaged in commerce and because the colonial government bestowed upon them such overwhelming favours in that field by way of discriminatory licencing, trading credits and so on, the Asians were quite content to live in their closed communities and to eschew anything that smacked of politics being made the concern of any of their respective communities. Thus because of these circumstances neither of the alien communities in Uganda posed a tangible political threat to the Africans as they did in Kenya or mainland Tanzania.

The political climate, however, was not as serene as the foregoing account might suggest because from time to time there flared up some contentious issues, especially in the cotton and coffee growing regions of the Protectorate. British policy with regard to these two principal cash crops of the Protectorate has been briefly indicated and this was that although the Africans were the primary producers, it was the European and Asian firms which were to handle the processing and the marketing of those crops. This had, for a considerable length of time, been a sore point with the African farmers—especially the enlightened and ambitions ones most of whom were to be found in Buganda and, to a lesser extent, in Bugisu. These farmers felt quite rightly that all the African farmers were being paid far less than a fair price for their produce while the prices on the world markets were high so that a high proportion of what they regarded as their rightful earnings was being pocketed by the very foreigners who were frustrating their efforts in gaining a foothold in the processing and marketing business. Besides this, the cotton ginneries and the coffee curing works were owned almost entirely by Asian companies and it was virtually impossible for the Africans to break into this side of cash crop production and this state of affairs was facilitated by Protectorate legislation which discriminated against Africans acquiring ginneries.

It is important to note that although these economic malpractices affected all the African producers of cash crops, especially in Buganda and the Eastern Province, no attempt was made on the part of the Africans to join forces and bring pressure to bear on the Protectorate administration with the view of securing some remedial measures. Thus, for instance, from the 1940s there existed in Buganda the

Uganda African Farmers' Union whose concern, among other things, was the Protectorate government's policy with regard to the processing and marketing of cash crops. But, despite its name, it limited its activities to Buganda and decidedly did not attempt to make common cause with Busoga, for example, which was one of the most important cotton-producing areas. Alongside the Farmers' Union, there also existed the Bataka Party (or Union as it sometimes called itself) since the 1920s and this somewhat amorphous organisation came into existence as a result of Buganda's land settlement—or perhaps unsettlement—of 1900 which had, as we have indicated dispossessed so many of the clan leaders. The link between the Bataka Party and the Farmers' Union is not easy to pin down, but it is clear that these two organisations overlapped both in leadership, membership and objectives—Ignatius Musazi, for example, was the most outspoken leader of both organisations at various times. It would not be too much of a simplification to say that these two organisations had two principal objectives, namely to fight against the Asian monopoly in the processing and marketing of cotton and coffee and, secondly, to struggle against the ruling oligarchy which had seized control of Buganda since the 1890s and whose position had been confirmed by the 1900 Buganda agreement. It was in the furtherance of these aims that these two organisations were the principal instruments which masterminded the civil disturbances which occurred in Buganda in 1945 and 1949.[2]

The outcome of these disturbances was very unsatisfactory in the sense that hardly any of the demands of the rioters were met and none of their fundamental causes was tackled by government. In 1949 the demands put to the Kabaka were:

(1) Your Highness should open the rule of democracy to start giving people power to choose their own chiefs.

(2) We want the number of sixty unofficials to be completed (i.e. sixty representatives to the Lukiiko).

(3) We demand the abolition of the present government.

(4) We want to gin our own cotton.

(5) We want to sell our own cotton in outside countries, that is free trade (Low and Pratt p. 28).

The reports of the Commissions of inquiry into these disturbances were themselves masterpieces of irrelevance and the "reforms" based upon these reports were "of little more than book-keeping significance."[3] These disorders were quickly suppressed and the ringleaders arrested and incarcerated. What is more, these disturbances were largely Buganda affairs. But then there was an increasing number of educated Baganda who were largely outside the governing hierarchy at Mengo (Kabaka's seat of government), and who were feeling frustrated by the failure of the 1949 disorders to produce meaningful reforms both in the economic field and in the democratisation of the Lukiiko. It was these elements, under the leadership of Ignatius Musazi, veteran of the Farmers' Union, who were to provide Uganda with the first political party which sought to organise support on a country-wide basis. This was the Uganda National Congress which was founded in 1952 with Musazi as its first President-General.[4]

The history of the UNC has been ably dealt with by such writers as Law and Welbourn and we may here restate the problems which they adduce and which were to lead to the disintegration of the party within a decade of its founding. As Welbourn points out, the UNC had a very inauspicious beginning to put it midly. For one thing the party leadership was overwhelmingly Protestant — especially composed of the Old Boys of Budo — the then bastion of Protestant education in Uganda—who formed nearly 70% of the Governing Council of the new Party. For another thing, in the initial stages, the leadership and the most active supporters of the new Party were Baganda; a fact that did not go down well with the other regions of Uganda since for a long time the other provinces of Uganda believed, not without justification, that the colonial authorities favoured Buganda at their expense. That the party had been formed in Kampala, Uganda's capital, was natural enough because it was in and around Kampala that many of the literate Africans were to be found. The handicap was not therefore that the Party had been formed in Buganda but that the composition of its leadership could have reflected a more even distribution of Uganda's diverse population. It has already been stated that from 1892 Protestant domination had been established in Buganda and then in the rest of the Protectorate as British rule was extended beyond Buganda Kingdom. It was therefore an unfortunate beginning for a party which aspired to be the vehicle of African political opinion to reflect the established Protestant domination in a country in which the Roman Catholics so obviously outnumbered the Protestants. Thus it can be stated that the first national party in Uganda started with two fundamental weaknesses: its Protestant–dominated leadership and also the preponderance of the Baganda in the upper echelons of the party.

When the Congress started getting out of Buganda to open up branches and mobilise support, it was immediately faced with the grim reality of Uganda history and this was that there were no country-wide issues on which it could base its appeal or generate interest in its activities. Against the background of what we have discussed, this was only to be expected because each of the administrative divisions into which Uganda had been divided had been run as if it were an independent entity and this had naturally fostered the growth of excessive and exclusive concern with parochial matters. It has also been noted that even where similar or identical problems existed, as in the case of the marketing of cash crops for instance, such discontent as was expressed was never co-ordinated on a protectorate-wide basis—it being usually deemed sufficient for the farmers of the locality to complain to their local District officer and there the matter usually rested. What, in turn, this meant for the new Party was that it of necessity became a party of local grievances and not of national mobilisation or action. In districts where no such grievances existed, the Congress received indifferent hearing or worse. Thus, as Low points out, when the Congress opened up its campaign in Toro, it found initial support because of land grievances there which had been in existence for quite some time. There had been "loss" of land by the creation of European-run tea plantations and this had been resented by the Toro government. Then in 1951 Kasese was granted township status and thus passed out of the control of the Toro kingdom government since all urban authorities were run by the Protectorate government—Kasese was the prospective terminus of the western extension of the railway which was to facilitate the exploitation of Kilembe copper mines (themselves in Toro kingdom). In the following year there was even "greater loss" of land when the Queen Elizabeth National Park was created as most of it was in Toro kingdom. National parks, like urban authorities, were also administered by the Protectorate government.

In these circumstances, the Congress found willing listeners when its campaigns brought it to Toro. But when it subsequently became evident that the Protectorate government would not do away with tea-plantations, the Queen Elizabeth National Park or the town of Kasese, whatever the pressure could be brought to bear upon it, even the Toro government gave up the "lost land" as a lost cause. When land ceased to be an issue, the Congress found itself without a viable cause in Toro and its support there dwindled correspondingly. The example of the fortunes of the Congress in Toro can be matched in several other districts of Uganda and what such examples would uniformly show is that where there was no particular local grievance the Congress did not get off the ground and vice versa.

Despite these vicissitudinous beginnings in most areas of Uganda, however, the Congress achieved remarkable success in the Northern province, especially in Acholi and Lango districts. The circumstances favouring the success of the Congress in the north were varied and, as in the other regions of Uganda, parochial. In Acholi, for instance, the chiefs were considerably unpopular—as indeed they had always been since the beginning of colonial rule in that area as we have indicated. The Acholi saw the chiefs as mere tools of an oppressive and alien regime so that the elements opposed to the chiefs rallied to the Congress and Musazi's frequent visits to Acholi were a rousing success and for some years the Acholi branch of the Congress was to remain the strongest branch of the Party outside Buganda.

In contrast to Acholi, the chiefs in Lango were not unpopular and the District Council was responsive to public opinion. But the chief grievance of the Langi was the absence of educational facilities —more especially the absence of a secondary school. Since the district council itself could not build and maintain a secondary school on its own resources, many educated Langi felt that their problems would best be solved by a country-wide organisation. But the Langi's initial reaction to the formation of the Congress was cautious as some of their leaders suspected that the Congress might be yet another device by which northern Uganda could be left behind other regions of the country as the following letter to the *Uganda Herald* of 24th April 1952 illustrates:

> "I shall be highly obliged if you would allow me space .... to express the feelings of young enlightened Semi-Hamites and Nilotes about some of the aims of the Congress. Not long ago, Mr. Fenner Brockway, M.P. came to Uganda and concentrated his activities in and around Kampala. He returned to England and gave his version of the "Unification of all Tribes in Uganda" .... his version .... is a direct negation of the established traditions of the Semi-Hamites and the Norsemen (Nilotes) and ... we are worried about it. It will, therefore, be of great interest to us if the Uganda National Congress will point out exactly what they mean by the "Unification of all Tribes in Uganda" .... Co-operation with the Government is also recommended *but we Semi-Hamites and Norsemen of Uganda who have had no educational opportunity as the rest of Uganda,* feel that the Congress is aiming at "Self-Government in Uganda," is hastening and thereby leaving us behind. Because of our present inability to aim so high ... it must be pointed out to the Congress here and now that with us, *the question of questions lies in education and rapid development of African Local Governments.* .... the height of folly [on the Congress's part] is the apparent omission .... of a definite aim to the slogan of "immediate Local Self-Government in Uganda."[5] (emphasis added).

After these initial misgivings, however, the Congress made substantial progress in Lango and A. Milton Obote, the author of the letter just quoted, became one of its most prominent members. What can we make of all this? It is reasonable to state that right from the beginning the Congress was a coalition of parochial and isolationist elements and in this state it was to remain without formulating a coherent national programme right to the end of its days.

Before the UNC could settle down to its organisational and ideological problems, there descended upon Uganda a political crisis of great magnitude. This was the deportation of the Kabaka of Buganda or the Kabaka crisis as it is more commonly termed. This crisis is an important landmark in the history of Uganda and, more especially for our immediate purposes, for the history of Uganda national movements for it set patterns of the conduct of public affairs that were to persist well into the post-independence period. For this reason, if for no other, it is necessary to give a brief outline of the Crisis itself.

In January 1952 there arrived as Governor of Uganda Sir Andrew Cohen. Sir Andrew was possessed of political acumen and energy not normally associated with colonial governors and their subordinates.[6] One of the cardinal points of Sir Andrew's policy was to involve the Africans in all fields of government activity and at all levels of government and also to democratise local governments. The obvious starting point was Buganda where a self-appointed and self-perpetuating oligarchy had ruled the kingdom for half a century. By March 1953 the Governor and the Kabaka had agreed and publicly announced the constitutional reforms that were to be made in Buganda. These principally were to make Buganda's Lukiiko more representative by having a majority of its members elected and by making Kabaka's ministers accountable to the Lukiiko. It may be remarked in passing that since the 1900 agreement, the Kabaka's ministers had been partially accountable to the Governor and the Kabaka but principally to God and to themselves. Other reforms of a financial and administrative nature were proposed and agreed upon. Alongside these reforms, some modification of the Legislative Council was undertaken to increase the number of African representatives. It was earlier stated that Buganda had at times been indifferent and at times hostile to the existence of the "Legco" largely because Buganda's leadership regarded that Council as a challenge to their own Lukiiko. Then in June 1953 the Colonial Secretary, Mr. Oliver Lyttleton made a speech in London in which he implied that the federation of the East African Territories was being contemplated by the British Government. As Low and Pratt put it:

"Few pronouncemen could cause a sharper and more unanimously adverse public reaction."

Buganda government protested to the Governor as indeed did the Toro Government, but the latter lost interest in the matter when assurances were given that federation was not being contemplated at

the time. The Buganda Government went on and soon the Kabaka
himself entered the controversy with abandon.

There ensued a hot exchange of correspondence between the
Governor and the Kabaka, the latter demanding not only more solid
assurances against Buganda ever being included in any federation
of East Africa but also the transfer of Buganda's affairs from the
Colonial to the Foreign Office and the formulation of a time-table
for Buganda's independence. These new demands opened up a whole
new range of visitas to new misunderstandings. It is necessary to
quote some of this correspondence in order to get this crisis in its
proper perspective. In a lengthy letter to the Governor, on 6th August,
1953, the Kabaka requested the transfer of Buganda's affairs to the
Foreign Office on the strength of the following arguments:

> "As it is well known, and according to the framing of the 1900
> Agreement, and all other agreements prior to it, the kingdom of
> Buganda is a protected state .... and consequently, the said
> Agreements were ratified by the Foreign Office under whose
> jurisdiction the affairs of Uganda lay since it was clear from
> the beginning that Uganda could not be treated as a colony.
> The status which is now accorded to Buganda is an indication of
> the direct result of Uganda's transfer to the colonial office."[8]

The Governor's reply to the letter just quoted amounted to nothing
less than a patient lecture on the efficacy of colonial rule and statutes.
He informed the Kabaka that assurances about federation, which had
been accepted in the past, had not ruled out federation for all time.
He went on:

> "The Secretary of State has asked me to say that your request for
> transfer of responsibility for the affairs of Buganda to the Foreign
> Office is evidently based on a misunderstanding. The Foreign
> Office is responsible for the relations of Her Majesty's Government
> with foreign countries outside the British Commonwealth. The
> Colonial Office deals with the affairs of territories inside the
> British Commonwealth for which Her Majesty's Government
> is responsible, whether they be colonies, Protectorate, Protected
> States or Trust Territories .... Under the terms of the 1900
> Agreement Buganda is clearly stated to rank as province forming
> part of Uganda Protectorate (Article 3) ...... In these circum-
> stances there could have been no alternative but to transfer
> responsibility to the Colonial Office, a step which in any case
> logically followed once Buganda came under the Protection of
> H.M. Government."

In conclusion the Governor pointed out an obvious truth that has
nevertheless always eluded our leaders and this was that breaking
up the Protectorate would be to everyone's disadvantage. He said:

"A strong and united protectorate rather than weak separate units must therefore be the aim of all our efforts in the interests both present and future of the people of the Protectorate."[10]

What is astonishing from this correspondence is the extent of the misunderstanding, on the part of the Kabaka, of Buganda's legal position within the Protectorate and this inspite of the fact that Buganda government and monarch had an ample supply of constitutional lawyers both locally and abroad.

Arising from this correspondence, and from a great deal more that has not been cited (for Buganda's leaders were assidious in the art of assembling memoranda), it became clear that a confrontation between the Kabaka and the Governor had arrived and, for our immediate purposes, that the proposed reforms were imperilled. This latter was the case because the implementation of the proposed reforms would greatly depend on the co-operation of the Kabaka and the Lukiiko and both of these were clearly hostile to anything emanating from Government House. The Kabaka would not persuade the Lukiiko to accept the reforms and would not even undertake to be silent when they were to be introduced to the Lukiiko for debate as the Governor requested him to do. Further meetings between the Governor and the Kabaka bore no fruit and on the 30th November, 1953, Cohen withdrew recognition from Mutesa II on the grounds that he had refused to co-operate loyally with the British Government as the 1900 Agreement required him to do and on the further grounds that he had sought to separate Buganda from Uganda. That same day Mutesa was whisked off to Britain into exile and, so as to contain any eventualities, a state of public emergency was declared. Mutesa's understanding of this crisis is somewhat baffling for he believed that what was at stake was Buganda's integrity, whatever the expression meant to him. He was to write:

"Buganda's integrity had become an issue during these talks [i.e. between him and the Governor], and to accept the rest and forget it would have been to betray that integrity."[11]

The point was that the integrity of Buganda as a state had been compromised beyond recall since the acceptance of the 1900 Agreement so that to revive this as an issue in the 1950s was, at best, misleading.

What has all this to do with Uganda political parties, one may ask? A great deal. As soon as the deportation for the Kabaka was known, Musazi, the Congress President, fled to the Sudan because he feared that he would be arrested. The General Secretary of the Party was out of the country studying in England. This meant that in the ensuing battle of wits and nerves between the British and Buganda governments, the Congress played no conspicuous role. It was, for example, a delegation of the Lukiiko, not of the Congress, that carried out the cumbersome negotiations for the Kabaka's return. In fact the Kabaka's deportation dealt the Congress the first stunning blow and this came about as follows: The irreverent manner in which the Kabaka had been packed off into exile had provoked the most intense and insular nationalism among the Baganda—a determination to defend and venerate anything Kiganda as never before. One of the manifestations of this determination was the extreme demands that began to flow from Mengo to the Protectorate Government, the Colonial office and the press. Demands such as the abolition of the Legco, the recognition of Luganda as the second national language of Uganda, the recognition of the precedence of the Kabaka over everyone in Uganda save the Governor and so on were endlessly and daily issuing from the Mengo establishment. In order for the Congress to get a hearing at all in Buganda, it had to espouse the cause of Buganda nationalism and champion courses of action that could not possibly be acceptable to the other Congress members or followers outside Buganda. In fact this led to the division of the Congress both within and outside Buganda because this excessive concern with Buganda affairs was not shared by all the Baganda Congress members. For example, Luyimbazi Zake protested against the Party's increasing concern with Buganda rather than with Uganda affairs and he resigned from the Party in September, 1954. It would not altogether be just to accuse the Baganda Congress leaders of being short sighted in espous—ing Buganda's inward-looking demands. This was necessary for their physical safety within the boundaries of Buganda because that kingdom was so extravagantly endowed with hot-headed mobs, which could easily become violent, that any attempt to understand Buganda's political behaviour without taking this factor into account, is not worth the effort.

The second major consequence of the deportation of the Kabaka was the formation of another party in January, 1955. This party was again formed by the Protestants, many of them Old Boys of Budo—the very men who had dominated the Namirembe Conference of 1954 which worked out the terms under which the Kabaka was to return from exile. These were led by Eridadi Mulira and the new Party styled itself the Progressive Party, not on account of its being progressive but rather because it was conspicuously conservative. The Progressive Party, unlike the Congress, did not succeed in establishing itself outside Buganda and it blighted its little chances of success by adopting a Luganda Motto, a fact which made it suspect outside Buganda. By 1958 the PP had practically ceased to exist even within Buganda.

The PP merits mention in our narrative not because of its short span of life nor indeed because it made any significant contribution to the political development of the country, but because its formation and its lacklustre existence represents one of the recurring ironies of Uganda history. This is so because the deportation of the Kabaka presented Uganda with the first real opportunity of forming a genuinely national party, or, at the very least, an opportunity of revamping the existing national party in such a way that it became a genuinely national one. In turn this was so because the deportation was deplored by every district up and down the country and nearly all district Councils passed strong resolutions condemning the British and the Protectorate governments for this deed. But no political capital was made out of this general and genuine sentiment on a countrywide basis and it was soon to evaporate in the face of other developments. Instead of forming a political party with country-wide appeal, Buganda became inward-looking as we have seen and very soon the other regions of the country began to think that the deportation of the Kabaka might not have been such a bad thing after all, largely because of Mengo's arrogant bellicosity to which reference has just been made. The Congress, instead of benefitting from the crisis by increasing its following and influence, began the process of falling apart—being largely impotent in Buganda and divided outside. The only Party to emerge out of the crisis before the tumultous return of the Kabaka in October, 1955, was the Progressive Party which, as we have observed, was neither national nor progressive and even this soon passed into the oblivion from whence it had emerged. Thus by October, 1955, when the Kabaka triumphantly returned to his palace at Mengo, the compartments of which the Protectorate was made were just as secure as before—secure from co-operating with each other and there had not emerged anyone to play the role of nation-builder to break down these compartments or, at least, to induce some osmotic pressure between their walls. And it is certainly not a "questionable assumption that a strong nationalist movement would have developed in Uganda while the British were still in effective control."[12] The whole history of decolonisation, be it of British or of any other dependencies, attests to the validity of that assumption. To argue otherwise is to put the cart before the horse for it can scarcely be maintained that strong national movements developed *after* the colonising power had lost effective control.

Now we return to the Kabaka and the general political atmosphere in Buganda. Soon after the deportation, there settled over Buganda an ominous lull—the kind of eerie lull that precedes a storm. Neither the Protectorate nor the Buganda governments seemed to be sure of what to do next. The colonial Secretary announced, on 22nd December, that Mutesa would never be allowed to return to Buganda. By this announcement, the Colonial Secretary had put himself and the Protectorate in a political quagmire. This was so because in Buganda, the public agitation for the return of the Kabaka had become almost unanimous and the work of ordinary administration had equally become well-nigh impossible as neither the Baganda chiefs nor the populace would have anything to do with the British officials. Yet the Governor saw quite rightly that there was nothing to be gained by forcing the situation to a point where violence would have erupted in Buganda so that his attempts to get the Lukiiko to choose a new Kabaka or even to approve a Regency of ministers—attempts which were entirely fruitless—were at best made half-heartedly. And this constituted only one half of the dilemma. On the other hand, to allow Mutesa to return; that is to reverse a major policy statement in the face of Baganda's sullen protest, would undermine the authority of government in Uganda generally and in Buganda particularly. There was also the attendant risk that to give in to such political protest, or "agitation" as it was termed in colonial parlance, would create a dangerous procedent and hamper government policy in the future.

In the face of this seemingly insoluble dilemma, Cohen's determination and shrewdness did not desert him. He proposed a constitutional conference under the chairmanship of Professor Keith Hancock on which the Lukiiko would be effectively represented and, after some delays and bargains, this was accepted by the now deeply suspicious and hostile Lukiiko. This was in itself a notable achievement because to the masses of the Baganda what was amiss was not the constitution of Buganda as it then was, but rather the Kabaka's exile. The single issue before the Baganda and their leaders was the return of Mutesa and this was the issue to the total exclusion of other issues.

The Committee finally got off ground and pursued its deliberations with patience and diligence at Namirembe and this is what is known as the Namirembe Conference of 1954. The Committee made extensive recommendations for the reform of Buganda government and, as part and parcel of the same deal, important reforms of the Legislative Council and the Executive Council, were also proposed and agreed. This was important because a major source of Buganda's intransigence stemmed from her hostility to the Legco and the Executive Council and her refusal to take part therein. After the completion of the Committees's work, the next step was to get the proposals accepted by the Lukiiko. This was the crux of the whole proceedings for without an express undertaking that the Kabaka would return, the whole of the Hancock proposals would have been heavily defeated in the Lukiiko and everything else would have gone back to square one or worse. The Colonial Secretary found a way out of his political problem through the ever-helpful English Casuistry. If the Lukiiko accepted *all* the Hancock proposals, then the Lukiiko could either select a new Kabaka or Mutesa would be allowed to return. This, of course, he assured the House of Commons without batting an eyelid, was not a change of policy but of circumstances. Since the Hancock proposals were to form the basis of a new Buganda agreement upon the acceptance of which the Kabaka's return would be assured, from this point onwards there were no real obstacles. On 17th October, 1955, the Kabaka returned to Buganda through throngs of hysterically rejoicing subjects, the like of which few had seen within living memory and on the following day, the new Buganda Agreement (1955) was signed between the Governor and the Kabaka at Mengo. These happenings in Buganda had a marked effect on the political tempo in the whole Protectorate and it is to this subject that we must now turn our attention.

The point has been made that the deportation of the Kabaka had been widely condemned throughout the Protectorate. But the return of the Kabaka was not equally widely acclaimed, at least not with equal zeal everywhere. Outside Buganda, as indeed inside Buganda, it was seen as a victory of Mengo over the Protectorate administration. This alone would not have occasioned uneasiness, but since Buganda had always been accorded special privileges in the Protectorate, many outside Buganda fearfully wondered what new concessions were about to be given to Buganda in the wake of her astounding victory and to what extent such concessions would be at the expense of their own interests.

Before these matters could be resolved one way or another, it was necessary to have a new Buganda government under the new agreement and it was the constitution of the new Buganda government that partly led to the formation of a new nationwide political party in Uganda. For this reason a brief outline of the main events leading to the formation of this party is called for.

For the purpose of constituting a Buganda government, the Lukiiko functioned as the Electoral College and this, since 1900, had been made up of 89 members and by 1955 these were divided up as follows: 3 Ministers, 20 county chiefs, 6 nominees of the Kabaka and 60 elected members. For the post of the Katikiro, there were three candidates, namely Kavuma, the outgoing holder of the post; Matayo Mugwanya, the Chief Judge of the outgoing government; and Kintu, a conversative county chief who had played a prominent role in the Namirembe Conference and the subsequent return of the Kabaka.[13] According to the prevailing forecast before the election, it seemed that Mugwanya would get an absolute majority of the elected members and a small overall majority of the whole Lukiiko. But if this forecast came true, it would change the religious balance of power in Buganda; a balance that had lain undisturbed since 1900. Mugwanya was not merely a Catholic; he was also the grandson of the Stanislaus Mugwanya who had led the Catholic party through the civil wars in Buganda of the 1880's and the 1890's and Buganda had not had a Catholic Katikiro since 1900. Just before the election, the nominees of the Kabaka were changed and Kavuma, who had had enough of politics anyway, was "persuaded" to withdraw from the contest. Kintu was subsequently elected with a majority of 4, three members abstaining from voting and thus Buganda got a Protestant Katikiro once again. Welbourn and Low infer from these manouvres, and the present writer concurs with them, that the Kabaka was not keen on having a Catholic Katikiro. This is a reasonable inference not only because of the change of his nominees with unseemly promptitude, but also because upon his return, the Kabaka's influence over his people generally and his chiefs particularly was immense. If this line of reasoning is accepted, it is not unreasonable to assume that he exerted a great deal of undue influence over all the chiefs (some had been replaced and some were soon to be) and on some of the elected members in order to secure the election of Kintu. In the new enlarged Buganda government, the Protestants were alloted two ministries and the Catholics and Muslims one each. Yet in Buganda the Catholics were greater in number than the Protestants and far greater still than the Muslims with whom they were equated in the allocation of ministries.

In 1956 Mugwanya, the unsuccessful bidder for the Katikiroship of the year before, won a bye-election to the Lukiiko as a member for Mawokota, but he was prevented by the Kabaka himself from taking his seat on the dubious grounds that he was a member of the East African Legislative Assembly. It was against the background of this frustration that the Democratic Party was formed in 1956 with the same Matayo Mugwanya as its first President General.

Before we proceed with the fortunes of his party, it is necessary to pause and consider some of the views that have been expressed about its formation. Welbourn states that it was Mugwanya's defeat for the Katikiroship and his being barred from taking the seat he had won at a Lukiiko bye-election which set the stage "for political action on a specifically Catholic basis,"[14] and hence the formation of the D.P. A concerted effort has been made to stand this sequence of events upon its head. Thus Ibingira tells us:

"The general public and most academics, have usually assumed that the Democratic Party was founded by Matayo Mugwanya in 1956. However, recently compiled Democratic Party documents suggest that Mr. Joseph Kasolo, a retired Makerere-educated civil engineer, was the Founder-President of the Party in 1954. When Matayo Mugwanya, a leading Roman Catholic politician, was rejected by the Kabaka for the post of Katikiro in 1954 (sic), he joined the Democratic Party; in 1956 he succeeded Mr. Kasolo as President-General."[15]

But Ibingira does not indicate what type of documents these are or were and he admits having no personal knowledge of them.[16]

More recently a more concerted attack on associating the DP with the general disillusionment of the Catholics in Uganda and with the frustration of Mugwanya in Buganda has been made by Matiya Kiwanuka. His main contentions are that the DP was formed in 1954 and therefore it had no connections with Matiya Mugwanya's disappointments which the party predates; Mugwanya did not become the President of the Party because he was a Roman Catholic, but because by 1956 he was "the most progressive senior chief in Buganda;" and, finally, Benedicto Kiwanuka did not accede to the leadership of the party in 1958 because he was a Catholic, but because by 1958 Ben Kiwanuka "was the most brilliant and successful lawyer in Uganda . . . ."[17] For all these value judgements we are given no evidence to back them up and, in any event, the reasoning is unconvincing. In the first place the fact that Mugwanya had been the Chief Judge in Buganda government—traditionally the highest office a Catholic could aspire to in Buganda since 1900—proves that he was a recognised leader of the Catholics because, his personal merits apart, *he was quite simply a Catholic*. Additionally, the fact that he was also a grandson of Stanislaus Mugwanya who had led the Catholics through the civil wars cannot easily be discounted in the light of what we have indicated about the nature of religion, politics and family ties in Buganda. These two considerations certainly made him the best choice for the leadership of the party that was unquestionably Catholic in leadership and membership.

So far as Benedicto Kiwanuka's accession to the leadership of the Party in 1958 is concerned, the explanation that this was because by 1958 he "was the most brilliant and successful lawyer in Uganda," is demonstrably inadequate. Kiwanuka, like Mugwanya before him, was also a Catholic. In any case, the acquisition of the skills of a legal practitioner, successful or otherwise, does not automatically qualify one for the leadership of a political party. Moreover, in the light of the fact that Kiwanuka was enrolled as an advocate of the High Court of Uganda on 21st July 1956[18] and also in the light of the fact that by that date there were several Uganda African lawyers at the Bar who were senior to him—in the Chambers of one such African lawyer Mr. Kiwanuka actually served his pupilage—the contention that he was the most brilliant and successful lawyer in the country seems to be more of a statement of personal devotion and not of historical judgement. For to be the most brilliant and successful lawyer at the Bar in a space of less than two years would be the accomplishment of a magician, not of an average lawyer such as Mr. Kiwanuka was.

Dr. Kiwanuka's zeal for disclaiming any connection between the DP and the Catholic Church in Uganda sometimes outruns the bounds of prudence and runs counter to established facts in the same paper just quoted. He castigates Welbourn for emphasizing the Catholic character of the DP and for failing to see that in Ankole where there were "more Protestants than the Catholics," the DP won four of the six seats in the 1961 elections to the National Assembly. He continues:

> "So anxious was he [Welbourn] to "make a case for the Catholic character of the DP" that he ignored the fact that two of the four successful DP candidates in Ankole were protestants."[19]

These two criticisms are based on a misunderstanding of ascertainable facts. In the first place in Ankole the Catholics outnumber Protestants by a wide margin and this fact is admitted by Ibingira in the following terms with reference to the 1958 elections:

> "Ankole had declined to hold direct elections because the ruling protestant group heading the local government feared that if they opted for direct elections, the predominantly Catholic electorate would defeat them."[20]

Consequently, the District Council, which was dominated by the Protestant chiefs as everywhere else in the country, nominated two Protestants to represent Ankole in the Legco. And Ibingira should have a first-hand knowledge of these goings-on because he was himself soon nominated to replace Rwetsiba, one of the two nominees on this occasion, upon the latter being made a Junior Minister.

In the second place, the two protestants in the ranks of the DP successful candidates after the 1961 elections, do not reflect the non-religiousness of the DP but rather the complexity of electoral alliances within Ankole. It was pointed out earlier that during most of the colonial period, the colonial administration had favoured the Bahima over the Bairu in the apportionment of public offices. But with the introduction of elections to the District Council, the Bairu became increasingly dominant because of their numbers. From 1955 they began definitely to ease the Bahima out of chiefly offices. But these were Bairu protestants who were ousting the Bahima who were and are also almost entirely protestant by faith. The Bairu Catholics, as most catholics everywhere in the Protectorate, were excluded from positions of power as we indicated earlier. The rivalry between the protestant groups in Ankole is to be explained in terms of the history of that kingdom and this has been indicated briefly. The introduction of western religions in Ankole therefore had opened up another venue of social cleavage and by an ironic twist of fate the Bahima and the Bairu Catholics found themselves in the same camp in the 1950s— the camp of being excluded from power, an experience by no means novel to the Catholics of Ankole and of the whole Protectorate. What happened therefore was that with the introduction of direct elections in 1961 in Ankole, the Bahima were allied with the Bairu Catholics in the DP against the Bairu Protestants of the Uganda People's Congress. The two protestant candidates in the DP ranks were Bahima who had been selected by the Party to stand in those constituencies where the combination of the Bahima and Bairu Catholics' vote was overwhelming —and these were South West and North East Ankole constituencies.

Kiwanuka then concludes his paper with a true statement which appears to contradict the essence of the whole paper. He says:

> "For a period of over seventy years, religion became the spring-board to power, privilege and influence in Uganda. All hereditary rulers, all Secretaries—General, all District Heads, all District Chief Ministers were Protestant. (p. 33)"

This being the case, it would be a slur upon the Catholics of the country to be content to accept the position of second-class citizens in their own country indefinitely when party organisation and numbers could enable them to redress the balance in their favour. This is precisely what DP was formed to achieve and the fact that should surprise us is not that the DP was overwhelmingly Catholic in inception and following but that it took so long to be formed since the genuine grievances of the Catholics were of longstanding over the whole Protectorate. Since the basis of their exclusion from power was their religious faith, it makes sense that their collective political action to better their position should have been their church.

In so far as the date of DP's formation is concerned, there are two pieces of evidence which tend to support 1956 as the date when in fact the Party was formed. It is said that during 1954 when Benedicto Kiwanuka was still pursuing his studies in Britain, he used to tell his fellow Uganda students that upon his return to Uganda, he, together with a number of sympathisers, would form a party which would be more democratic and more representative of Uganda than the Congress.[21] Now, we have already remarked that the DP was over-whelmingly Catholic, especially in leadership. If such a party had been formed or was about to be formed before Kiwanuka's return—and he returned in 1955—he should perhaps have known something about it because as a lawyer-in-training, he was definitely high ranking among Catholic Counsels.

The second piece of evidence concerns the address Benedicto Kiwanuka himself delivered to the students of St. Mary's College, Kisubi, in 1959—i.e. after he had become the President of the Party. He told his audience that the UNC had been the first party to be formed and that some of the DP members had also been members of UNC, but that the UNC accepted foreigners in their ranks and that therefore one could not fight imperialism with imperialists in one's ranks. He continued to say that the DP was founded in 1956 with the intention of telling the people the truth and being a nationalist "in a true sense."[22] So far as I can ascertain, the accuracy of this report was not questioned, either by the Party President or by the Party's propaganda machine. Assuming that this was so, would it not be very strange indeed, if the President of the Party was ignorant of the date of its foundation—a party, moreover, which had been in existence for less than ten years?

Owing to these considerations, and in the absence of convincing evidence to the contrary, I feel inclined to accept that the DP was founded, as a party known and open to the public, in 1956 and for the purpose of mitigating the discrimination that the Catholics had endured in Uganda for over half-a-century. To criticise Welbourn, Low and others for labelling DP Catholic and for not attributing protestant motivation to the UNC, for instance, as Dr. Kiwanuka does, seems to me to be beside the point. This is so because the protestants had no interests to promote that were not already catered for by all the existing hierarchies all over the Protectorate. Yet the contrary was true for the Catholics as we have illustrated.

We have already observed that the formation of the UNC did not bring the country together and that that party was completely disorganised in the wake of the events following upon the deportation of the Kabaka. Similarly the formation of the DP was not a step towards uniting the country under the umbrella of a single national, less still nationalist, party; it was a step towards conforming to the religious polarities that had existed in Uganda's public life since the turn of the 19th century. Religious faith and ethnic boundaries still counted for a great deal and Uganda for little or less.

To complicate this already confounded political situation, control of the kingdom of Buganda was seized by a very reactionary team of leaders upon the return of the Kabaka. The importance of this development cannot be overemphasized because Buganda was the political nerve-centre of the country so that any adverse political developments in Buganda had profound effects upon the rest of the country. The point may also be made that although the 1955 Buganda agreement had vested the control of Buganda government in the hands of the Protectorate government, this was largely on paper. This was because the return of Mutesa II had made the Protectorate government very nervous in its dealings with Buganda. Similarly, the Kabaka had been ostensibly made a constitutional monarch by the same agreement, but in fact he retained a great deal of power over his ministers so that it would be right to say that the 1955 agreement had achieved quite the opposite of what it had intended: it had left the Kabaka's real power intact while at the same time relieving him of the responsibility for the actions of his ministers.

> "This enabled Mutesa and his associates upon his return to bring pressure upon "disloyal" chiefs to resign and to appoint "loyal" ones in their place. . ."[23]

It could thus be rightly said that, like the Bourbons of old, Mutesa had learnt nothing and forgotten nothing. In these circumstances, the Kabaka and his ministers could literally get away with anything and they often did. What Low describes as the "advent of pupulism in Buganda,"[24] was in fact a much more complex development than he presents it to be for it was not merely an alliance between the Kabaka and the people against overmighty chiefs. It had been this but it had ceased to be so after the populace had secured the resignation af Kulubya way back in 1945. After the return of the Kabaka from exile, ond at the highest point of his popularity within his kingdom, what developed in Buganda was a terrifying and insular kind of nationalism at the spiritual head of which was the Kabaka himself. In this movement, if one may so term it, the Kabaka, his chiefs and most of his subjects were one and their main object was to protect the institutions of Buganda against all kinds of threat, mostly imaginary, from whichever source these might emanate.

The government of Buganda which took office after the signing of the 1955 agreement had identified two "threats" to itself, and, for propaganda purposes, to the Kabakaship as an institution. These were the Legco and the Uganda-wide political parties. Against these Mengo was to wage an unremitting war right up to independence and even afterwards. The point has already been made that the Buganda government had always been indifferent and, by the 1950s hostile to the Legco. This had been one of the causes of the Kabaka Crisis. But because Buganda's participation in the Legco had been one of the conditions of the Kabaka's return, the Mengo negotiators had been compelled to accept it. Ironically, having accepted representation in Legco, it had been the Buganda delegation which had insisted and been granted the right for Buganda representatives to the Legco to be directly elected—a right that was extended to other districts on condition that in each case the district council concerned gave its approval. But that was way back during the Namirembe negotiations so that by the time the elections were to be held in 1958, Buganda government had changed its mind about direct elections and about participating—Buganda's representatives to the Legco having been withdrawn the year before. Buganda had executed this *volte-face* in a space of less than three years.

As part of the planned consitutional advance of the Protectorate, it had been decided to increase the number of African representatives to 18 of whom 5 would represent Buganda and all these were to be directly elected in October, 1958. But then by 1958 Buganda had changed her mind about participating in the Legco by whatever method of selecting representatives. Buganda in fact went even father and instituted a suit against the Uganda government in order to block direct elections—the case of The Katikiro of Buganda versus The Attorney General of Uganda (1959). Buganda lost the case as they were to lose numerous others subsequently even after independence. In fact this was a curtain raiser for Buganda government henceforth became something of a vexatious litigant against the Protectorate government and then against the Obote administration after independence. Ankole's District council, as we have seen, also objected to having direct elections for fear of being defeated in a predominantly Catholic electorate, but it nominated two representatives. Toro and Bugisu District Councils also refused to have direct elections on grounds that were similar. Toro argued that the number of African representatives should have been increased to more than 18 and that an assembly of all districts should have convened to discuss the future constitution of Uganda before any direct elections could be held. The real reason, however, seems to have been that the District Council had concluded that Toro, on her own, could not secure for herself the same advantages as Buganda, but could do so with the assistance of other districts. Bugisu, the other district abstaining from direct elections, argued that there should first be created provincial assemblies—a step that would raise the other three provinces of the protectorate to the negotiating status of Buganda which was the fourth province. Of these abstentions, it was Buganda's which was the most important because it prevented the national parties from building up support for themselves by mounting electoral campaigns—precisely the kind of outcome the

Lukiiko had hoped for when it informed the Protectorate government that there would be no direct elections in Buganda.

Not content with hamstringing the national parties in this way, Mengo government inaugurated and stepped up a harassment campaign against the leaders and supporters of the national parties lest they secured a foothold in Buganda and then threaten their own monopoly of power. This harassment took the form of frequently imprisoning the leaders of the parties on trumped up charges and encouraging arson directed against the party leaders and supporters alike. This was comparatively easy to achieve by the use of the chiefly hierarchy which had recently been purged of "disloyal elements" as we observed. This harassment, it should be noted, went on simultaneously with the various demands that the Buganda government was making to the Protectorate government. As was pointed out earlier, these demands were not well-received by the rest of the country. It was this political atmosphere that the Munster Commission had in mind when it recommended that Buganda should not be allowed to control an armed police force in the following terms:

"As we have made clear, Buganda's present government is tribally minded and politically backward. It would be most dangerous to place a powerful police force in her hands."[25]

It will have become obvious why this hostile campaign, which was directed against the national parties by a backward regime at Mengo, was crippling to these parties. Kampala and Entebbe, respectively the commercial and administrative capitals of the country, were located in Buganda so that a great number of literate Africans were to be found in and around these towns and this is where the newspapers had the greatest circulation. Yet the national parties were almost entirely precluded from exploiting these factors by the Mengo government. And the Protectorate government helplessly looked on.

In October 1958 direct elections were duly held in the remaining parts of Uganda for the African representatives. In these elections, the Congress won 5 seats, the DP 1 seat and 4 seats were won by independent candidates but as the nominated member for Bugisu and the two indirectly elected members for Ankole counted as independents, this brought the number of Independent members to 7. As soon as the new Legco met, a new political party was formed and so a new chapter in the chequered political history of Uganda was opened. This was Uganda Peoples' Union. In fact the UPU was hardly a party in the accepted sense of the term since it had no existence outside the walls of the Legco—all its membership comprising of the majority of the African representatives. Upon the formation of the UPU, therefore,

the state of the parties altered as follows: UPU 7, UNC 3, DP 1
Independent 1 with one seat still vacant. The main strength of the
UPU lay not so much in the fact that it had a majority of the African
representatives, but in the fact that its founders were also established
leaders of their respective districts—men like Nadiope of Busoga and
Magezi of Bunyoro to mention only two. Just like the parties that had
been formed before, the UPU was also founded on a negative motivation—largely to oppose the concessions that Buganda was demanding
from the Protectorate government. But, more important than this, the
UPU was the first party to be formed and to be led by non-Baganda,
a fact that was not lost on the leaders of Buganda as Mutesa was
to confirm.[26] To the chagrin of Mengo government what had always
seemed to be a remote possibility, and an undesirable one at that,
looked like it had materialised with the formation of the UPU—i.e.
the possibility that the rest of the Protectorate would "gang" together
to strike Buganda down from her pedestral of eminence. Mengo looked
around for a suitable response and was soon furnished with an excuse,
by the Protectorate government, to make such a response.

Before he concluded his term of office, Sir Andrew Cohen had
announced that following on the elections of 1958, a constitutional
committee would be set up to draw up plans for a general election
on a common roll in 1961 and that that Committee would be drawn
largely from the Legco itself. On 4th February, 1959, Sir Frederick
Crawford, who had succeeded Cohen towards the end of 1956,
announced the composition of the Constitutional Committee, the
majority of whose members were African representatives. Before this
announcement, however, another ominous development had taken
place and this was the split of the Congress in January 1959. The
party split into two Congresses, each of which claimed to be the "true
Congress". One wing was under the leadership of Obote and the other
wing under Musazi. I regard this development as being ominous
because it was a farther step in the polarisation between Buganda
and the rest of Uganda. The Obote wing of the Congress was virtually
the non-Baganda congress and the one which remained under Musazi
was the Baganda one. Buganda was thus being increasingly isolated
largely as a result of her shortsighted leadership in this period but also
because of the intemperate public utterances of the politicians from
outside Buganda.

Thus, when the composition of the Constitutional Committee was
announced, the Kabaka's government refused to nominate any
representatives to it and even to give evidence before it. The ostensible
reason for this attitude, so the Kabaka's government argued, was
that one of the terms of reference of the Committee was to devise some

method of securing Legco representation for non-African minorities and the Buganda government insisted that this was concerned with the question of citizenship which only an African government could deal with. The assurances of the Governor that the question of citizenship was not involved did not make Buganda relent—in fact it could not relent because this was merely an excuse to avoid being involved in the affairs of the Legco except on their own terms. Then the Uganda National Movement (UNM) was formed under the leadership of Augustine Kamya, a Kampala cobbler of considerable demagogic talents. Despite its name, this was a Buganda movement and to its ranks it attracted all the leaders of the Buganda–based perties— Musazi of one of the wings of the UNC, Mulira of the PP and Binaisa of the United Congress Party—the last named was one of the off-shoots of the original Congress which was formed in 1957 but which had never really got off the ground.

The UNM soon declared a trade boycott of non-African goods and enforced that declaration by intimidation and actual violence against persons and property. This aspect of the UNM caused great embarassment to the Kabaka's government which, though approving of the boycott, could not publicly endorse lawlessness and violence. For a period the boycott was a success in Buganda and although the UNM was primarily an instrument by which the Buganda government sought to embarass the national parties generally and the members of the Constitutional Committee in particular, its success was due to long-standing economic grievances, some of which we indicated earlier. To the ordinary Baganda, who were terrorising each other to ensure the success of the boycott, what was at stake was not the Kabaka's position or Buganda's constitutional relationship with the rest of Uganda—it was the possession of ginneries and the marketing of cash crops. The stranglehold that the Asians had established over the economy of Uganda was real and that is why the target of the boycott was the Asian businesses. When the UNM resorted to violence, it was proscribed and many of its leaders were arrested and detained in various parts of the Protectorate. Soon the violence was contained and the movement fizzled out. It is not true to say, as the Kabaka says:

"Though many Indians managed to survive by employing Africans as a front, their monopolly was broken. [27]"

The boycott did not last long enough to make any impact on the Asian monopoly of commerce that merits mention.

As a result of the upheavals in Buganda, the leaders of UPU and of Obote's wing of the Congress merged their parties in March 1960 and formed the Uganda Peoples Congress (UPC) with Obote as the leader. In fact, as Low says, Obote's Congress and the UPU had worked as complementaries rather than as rivals so that it seems most probable that if the Congress had split earlier, the UPU might not have been formed at all. The new party had an overwhelming majority of the African representatives in the Legco who were also the most well-known leaders of the various district councils in the Protectorate. The UPC was essentially an anti-Buganda party and the point may be made here that up to the eve of independence, Uganda politics had revolved around local issues and there had not emerged a political party which had purely national aims nor indeed national leaders—these were parties and leaders aiming at striking down some section of the country or uplifting some other section but always at the expense of someone else in the country. In other words, Uganda had parties founded on negative motivations and were geared to achieving parochial objectives. Regrettable as this no doubt was, it was nevertheless a logical development consistent with Uganda history. Dr. Akiiki-Mujaju has neatly summed up the formation of the UPC thus:

> "It is difficult to see how the established Legislative Council Members from outside Buganda such as Obwangor (Teso), Obote (Lango), Magezi (Bunyoro), Babiiha (Toro) could have acquired their commanding status in political parties already led by a historically powerful Buganda protestant core. Since they knew this to be difficult, they organised outside [i.e. outside Buganda-based parties]."[28]

It might also be added that few people, especially in Africa, join politics if there is no prospect of exercising power so that since these non-Baganda politicians did not see any prospect of gaining power by working together with their Baganda counterparts, they sought to achieve the same objective by competing with them. As the British threatened to give independence to Uganda, the Ugandan leaders did not close their ranks—mutual recriminations intensified instead.

1. B. Davidson: *Which Way Africa? The Search for a new Society* (Penguin Books, 1964), p. 15.
2. Excellent accounts of these disturbances are contained in: Low and Pratt: *op. cit.* p. 275–285.
3. ibid. p. 284.
4. There is wealth of literature on Uganda political parties, the best of which are probably: D. A. Low: *Political Parties in Uganda, 1949–62.* F. B. Welbourn: *Religion and Politics in Uganda, 1952–62.* (E.A.P.H., 1965).
5. Quoted in D. A. Low: *Buganda in Modern History,* p. 254. The writer of the letter was A. M. Obote, ten years later the Prime Minister and thereafter the President of Uganda not of Lango as his ealier views would have led one to expect

6. The crisis is covered in Low and Pratt: *op. cit.* p. 317–49. Although the authors term their analysis "tentative", it is remarkably accurate.

7. *Ibid.* p. 323.

8. D. A. Low: *The Mind of Buganda*, p. 164.

9. *Ibid.* p. 169.

10. *Ibid.* p. 173.

11. The Kabaka of Buganda: *Descretion of My Kingdom* (Constable, 1967), p. 120.

12. Low and Pratt: *op. cit.* p. 332.

13. See F. B. Welbourn: *Religion and Politics in Uganda,* Chapter 4.

14. *Ibid.* p. 18.

15. G. S. K. Ibingira: *op. cit.* p. 49 (in a footnote).

16. G. S. K. Ibingira: personal communication, New York City, U.S.A., May 1974.

17. M. S. M. Kiwanuka: "Political Science in Africa: Is it a hard academic discipline or High School Journalism," *M.S.P.* 2/72/73, pp.10, 12, and 13.

18. Advocates' Roll, High Court of Uganda, Kampala. I am indebted to Mr. J. A. Kateera, LLM, (Harvard) of Hunter and Greig (Advocates) who procured this piece of information for me.

19. M. S. M. Kiwanuka: *Loc. cit.* p. 22.

20. G. S. K. Ibingira: *op. cit.* p. 46.

21. W. W. Rwetsiba: personal communication, New York City, U.S.A., May 1974. Rwetsiba was studying with Kiwanuka in U.K. that year.

22. *Uganda Argus,* (Kampala), 6th Nov., 1959, p. 5.

23. D. A. Low: "The Buganda Mission, 1954." *Historical Studies,* Vol. 13/51/Oct. 1968, p. 379.

24. D. A. Low: *Buganda in Modern History,* p. 44–53.

25. Lord Munster: *Report of the Uganda Relationship Commission,* (Government Printer, Entebbe, 1961), p. 69.

26. The Kabaka of Buganda: *op. cit.* p. 154.

27. *Ibid.* p. 155.

28. A. B. Mujaju: "The Religio-Regional Factor in Uganda Politics," *M.S.P.* 8/1973/74, p. 19.

CHAPTER SIX

TRIUMPH OF HOPE OVER EXPERIENCE?
(1960-1971)

The period between the beginning of 1960 and the granting of independence in 1962 was the crucial period in Uganda politics. When the Wild Report—the Constitutional Committee Chairman was Mr. J. V. Wild—was published, it was greeted with a large measure of agreement by the political parties. The Governor accepted the report in February 1960. But the Mengo government rejected it out of hand and thereafter Buganda government started negotiations with the Governor about "Buganda's position," as it was called. The non-Baganda politicians warned the Governor and the Colonial Office not to discuss matters concerning Uganda with Buganda delegations. Definite suggestions began to be heard at Mengo that Buganda should have separate independence if her terms of staying in Uganda were not acceptable to the Colonial office. This started off a hail of hostile correspondence in the press and in addresses to public meetings. The dispute—for so it seemed—was whether the Colonial Office would grant Buganda concessions that would be unacceptable to the rest of the country and to the political parties. Mr. Obote, in his capacity as the Secretary of the Elected Members Organisation of the Legco, publicly stated that "African nationalism hates small states because this is emergent Africa . . . . it will crush Buganda,"[1] referring to Buganda's secession. Subsequently, this statement was given wide publicity by the Buganda government as it was interpreted to mean that Obote and his party would crush Buganda. Mr. Chango Machyo, writing from London, condemned Buganda government in the following terms:

> "And because their leaders [Buganda] lack wisdom, foresight and sense of responsibility the most well meaning and innocent Baganda have suffered. However, we the non-Baganda are beginning to appreciate this and are quickly becoming aware of the difference between Mengo and Buganda."[2]

By the standards of that period, this was a mild letter for when it came to denying Buganda anything or everything, then every non-Muganda politician became an instant nationalist. In fact during this period Buganda provided for non-Baganda politicians the same kind of rallying point that the Republic of South Africa provides for the

Organisation of African Unity since whenever it came to condemning Buganda's separatism, there was almost a unanimity of views but this unanimity was hardly achieved on any other subject as we shall see.

In June of 1960, by way of implementing the Wild Report, the Colonial Secretary announced that there would be direct elections throughout Uganda to the Legco in 1961 and that these would be the elections which would precede the granting of self-government to the Protectorate. This announcement was a prelude to pandemonium in the political life of the Protectorate. As expected Buganda vehemently opposed the holding of the proposed elections and a delegation, led by the Kabaka himself, went off to London to persuade the Colonial Secretary to postpone the elections until federal status was granted to Buganda in a self-governing Uganda. This in turn raised a storm of protest in the rest of the country. The Legco members, for example, protested against British favourism of Buganda for having borne the expense of Buganda's delegation to London when that delegation was only going to deal with Buganda affairs while, at the same time, a West Nile constitutional delegation which had gone to Entebbe to see the Governor was required to pay its own bus fares.[3] Some district councils, such as Acholi, for example, passed resolutions urging the Protectorate Government not to meet the expenses of the Buganda delegation which was pursuing selfish motives.[4]

While the Kabaka and his delegation cooled their heels in London, the Colonial Secretary visited Uganda to open the new buildings of the National Assembly (as the Legco was to be styled) and on 20th September, 1960, the three rulers of the kingdoms of Western Uganda presented to him a memorandamum in which they endorsed Buganda's position that the general elections be postponed until the future form of government for Uganda was worked out.[5] But these rulers were promptly embarassed by their district councils which disassociated themselves from such a view. The General Purposes Committee of the Bunyoro District Council disagreed with the views of the Mukama on 22nd September, 1960 as did the Ankole District Council a few days later. These rulers had in fact taken a political risk because their district councils were already controlled by the political parties as the Lukiiko of Buganda was not and this is why it was not wise of them to adopt the intransigence of Mengo without the express sanction of their councils.

It should not be supposed that it was Buganda alone which was causing all the difficulties: this appears to be so because she was given the greatest facilities to make the most noise. In this period, for example, Toro government did everything to outdo Buganda in making excessive demands upon the Protectorate government. On hearing a rumour to the effect that the Protectorate government was considering making the Kabaka the head of state, for instance, Toro District Council threatened to secede and join their kinsmen in the Congo "to avoid Uganda's internal quarrels."[6]

Meantime the press war for and against Buganda was stepped up. One Paul Tebandeke, for instance, wrote to the *Uganda Argus* to inform the leader of the UPC of a few home truth in the following terms:

> "Mr. Obote seems to have been misled or misinformed that the Baganda will accept a commoner to rule this country when the British go. The truth is Buganda will use all its available forces to see that the Kabaka becomes head of state of Uganda or Buganda secession [sic] when independence is attained."[7]

The writer left it to the leader of the UPC to gauge the extent of Buganda's "all available forces" as he did not indicate this. A few days earlier another correspondent to the same paper had challenged Buganda to secede provided the following conditions were fulfilled: (a) all Baganda serving in various capacities in the other provinces be repatriated, (b) all means of communication be diverted from Jinja via Hoima to Kasese (thereby bypassing Buganda), (c) Buganda compensate the rest of the Protectorate for the collective social capital invested in Buganda by the Protectorate government and (d) the lost counties issue be settled unconditionally. If she could not meet all these conditions, she should join the rest of the country and stop frustrating Uganda's political progress.[8] It should be said that not all the Baganda were insular nationalists of Paul Tebandeke's type for we find a Mr. Sebana-Kizito writing to the *Argus* in the same period and condemning his fellow Baganda for wanting to secede and for insisting on their Kabaka being Head of State of Uganda. He concluded by stating that:

> "Buganda cannot just run away with all the property developed for the good of the whole country."[9]

And he was one of the many Baganda who felt this way but then these sane voices were powerless against the separatist and reactionary forces at Mengo.

One could go on multiplying these examples *ad infinitum* and all they would show is that most districts, and especially kingdoms, wanted everything at the expense of whatever form of government would be evolved for Uganda. The national parties gained nothing from these disputes because the more they denounced the separatist tendencies of Buganda, the more the Mengo government seemed to get popular within Buganda and the more unpopular did the parties get. In order to underscore the multitude and magnitude of the political problems facing the Protectorate which was reluctantly being prodded into independence, it is necessary to note that neither Buganda nor the other Kingdoms were the only obstacles hampering a smooth transition into independence. These other problems were of such an emotional nature that the British government was being urged to settle them before independence. Owing to the absence of goodwill, patience and understanding among the emerging African leaders, it did not even occur to these same leaders to close their ranks and ask for independence and then try and sort out these problems afterwards—a request that Britain would have readily and happily granted if only because of her desire to wash her hands off the whole mess. What then were these problems?

The first of these problems was that most of the district councils were becoming impossible to operate because of factionalism based on religion. In January 1960, for about a week, there was extensive rioting in Bukedi district and in the Nakaloke subcounty of Bugisu district. The chief cause of these disturbances was the method of tax assessment and collection and also the fact that some chiefs belonging to the "wrong" religion were posted in areas where they should not have been posted. These civil disorders did not abate until the units of the KAR were deployed to rescue and protect the chiefs in the affected areas.[10] This left a nasty taste in the mouth in the affected districts.

In Bugisu district, factions grouped around Mr. Wakholi (the Chairman of the district council) and Mr. Wanyoto (the Secretary General), each of these factions seeking to oust the other from the district administration. The tension generated by these factions was such that the functioning of the district administration was greatly impeded. In a stormy council meeting of 14th March 1960, a "resolution" was passed dismissing the Secretary General with effect from that day and the advice of the District Commissioner that the proceedings had been improperly conducted and that therefore the resolution had no legal effect and was null and void did not deter the vigour of the faction which was opposed to the Secretary General. The Protectorate government found it necessary to appoint another Commission of Inquiry to look into the working of that Council.[11]

In Ankole the DP had won the majority of seats in the district council, but the Protectorate government denied the party the right of selecting the Enganzi or Ankole's Prime Minister from among themselves on the curious grounds that the officers of the Ankole government were appointed by an independent Appointments Board and that therefore the Enganzi should be similarly appointed on a non-political basis.[12] This decision was resented by the DP, especially as in neighbouring Bunyoro where the UPC had won the majority, that Party had been allowed to select the Katikiro. Thereupon the Ankole DP petitioned the Governor who, even before he replied to their petition, confirmed Mr. Nganwa, the outgoing Enganzi and a known UPC supporter, as the Enganzi for another term. Then the DP, the majority party in the Council, boycotted the proceedings of the council for the next eight months. It is not necessary to repeat this tale of woes in respect of the other district councils because, during this period, there was hardly any district council which was not wracked by division of one sort or another.[13] These troubles dissipated the energies of the political parties at a time when more coherent national policies could have been formulated.

The other major problem facing the protectorate was the existence of boundary disputes, the most well-known of which was that of the lost counties between Bunyoro and Buganda. It was indicated earlier that by 1893 the British officials in Uganda had decided to invade Bunyoro in force and to bring Kabarega's resistance to their influence to an end. This was done and in November 1894 Kabarega was already a refugee in northern Uganda. Although Colvile, the Commissioner, had been instructed by the Foreign office to restrict his military activities only to measures necessary for the defence of Buganda and that "any temporary and partial occupation of Unyoro must be for purely defensive purposes," the Commissioner nevertheless gave a verbal undertaking to the Baganda chiefs that "all Bunyoro territory south of the Kafu river would be incorporated in Buganda and divided equally between Protestant and Catholic chiefs."[14] This undertaking was given without consulting the Foreign office and it was subsequently "honoured" by Berkeley, who succeeded Colvile, and two British officers who were serving in Bunyoro at the time, Messrs Pulteney and Foster, were so outraged by this decision that they resigned their posts in protest. The Banyoro were even more outraged and were never reconciled to this loss of territory. In 1921 the "Mubende Bunyoro Committee" was formed by those Banyoro living in the territory excised from Bunyoro with the express purpose of fighting for the return of that territory to Bunyoro. The territory, moreover, was of great historical importance to Bunyoro kingdom in that within the counties of Buyaga and Bugangaizi there were to be found most of the tombs of the former kings of Bunyoro.

Thus the Omukama of Bunyoro petitioned the Colonial Secretary in 1943, 1945, 1948, 1949 and 1954 and the Mubende Bunyoro Committee did the same in 1951, 1953 and 1955—all for the return of the excised territory.[15] To all these petitions there was always the same stock reply: the Secretary of State could not alter a decision:

"Which had been reaffirmed on many occasions and ... the boundaries laid down in the 1900 Agreement could not be changed in favour of Bunyoro."[16]

With the approach of independence, the dispute became hotter and the incidence of violence and counter violence increased in the lost counties and this is what led to the appointment of the Molson Commission, on 20th December, 1961, to look into the dispute.

This commission recommended that Buyaga and Bugangaizi be returned to Bunyoro simultaneously with the granting of independence because, they pointed out, as Buganda had been granted the right to nominate her representatives to the National Assembly, a Prime Minister of independent Uganda would find it difficult to support any concession to Bunyoro if he were dependent on the Buganda block for staying in office.[17] As it turned out, this was a very accurate forecast. As one would expect, the Buganda government was adamant and Buganda ministers were in the habit of assuring their approving Baganda audiences that the only way that those counties could be transferred to Bunyoro would be if a flood (*Mukoka* in Luganda) physically carried them into Bunyoro.[18] The political parties were wary of taking any stand on this issue—finding it safe to say that this was a problem between the British Government, Buganda and Bunyoro, which in a way it was.

The dispute between Buganda and Bunyoro was by no means the only boundary dispute in Uganda. There was also a boundary dispute between Bugisu and Bukedi districts in Eastern Uganda and this primarily concerned the ownership of the town of Mbale. This dispute also had a history as long as but more complicated than the dispute between Bunyoro and Buganda which we have just described. In the early years of the Protectorate administration in eastern Uganda, Bukedi district comprised of modern Bukedi (excluding Samia-Bugwe), Bugisu, Teso and Sebei districts. Owing to the size and diversity of the peoples included in this vast area, the district became too unwieldy for smooth administration. In 1909 Teso was made a separate district and in 1923 the remainder of Bukedi district, to which Semia-Bugwe had been added, was split into three districts of Bugisu, Bugwere and Budama with headquarters at Bubulo, Nakaloke and Tororo, respectively. But Bugwere district also included Mbale county and town and this displeased the Bagisu who felt that they had been robbed of their land by the new arrangement. Then in 1937 farther changes were made for Bugwere and Bugisu districts were combined and named the Central district with the headquarters at Mbale. To compound this confusion further, the central district had two local governments, not one, for in 1941 Budama was added to the central district and in the same year the local administrations of Budama and Bugwere were combined and termed Bukedi native administration and their jurisdiction included Mbale. Then there was also Bugisu native administration. In order to defuse the Mbale issue, that town was granted a neutral status with a subcounty chief directly responsible to the District Commissioner, and not to any of the Local administrations. This compromise satisfied neither party since both of them regarded the neutralisation of Mbale as unjust. There were occasional local fights over this issue in the two districts and, with the approach of independence, the dispute was revived with vigour and it became a subject of yet another commission of inquiry.[19]

There were other boundary disputes—the Sebei wanted a separate district to avoid being a permanent minority in Bugisu district and, in order to remind everyone of their grievance, they occasionally blocked the only road leading to their mountain home. East Acholi felt neglected by the local administration based in Gulu and they wanted their own based in Kitgum. Then there were the Bamba and Bakonjo grievances in Toro against the rule of the Batoro and this was to cause an embarassing guerilla war after independence. The list is almost inexhaustible. It will have become clear that for a country of the size of Uganda, all this was more than a fair share of boundary disputes as illustrated by the appointment of numerous commissions of inquiry on the eve of independence. The appointment of these commissions was itself a fair indication of just how much trouble was being shored up for the African government that was about to take over the administration of Uganda. All these affrays and disputes lead the present writer to agree with Welbourn when he says:

"Despite the claim of the new political parties to be nation-wide in their membership, to be working for an independent Uganda, there is—except among the small percentage of intellectuals— very little true nationalism among the Baganda as such. If they think in terms of independent Uganda, it is of a kingdom united under the Kabaka as an undisputed head—a concept wholly unacceptable to the other tribes of the protectorate."[20]

This statement needs the important qualification that it was not merely the Baganda who were not nationalists but also the rest of Ugandans were not nationalists either: Buganda only made more extreme demands and commanded the hearing of the colonial officials more than anyone else in the protectorate. Our attention must now turn to the implementation of the Wild Committee Report which implimentation, in a very significant way, was an important landmark in the political history of Uganda.

The Kabaka's delegation to London seeking the postponement of direct elections until his kingdom had been granted a federal status was very unsuccessful as the Colonial Secretary would not budge. He insisted that he would only discuss constitutional matters affecting Uganda with the members of the Legislative Council and not with delegations from different parts of the country. Returning empty handed from London, the Kabaka and his government decided to boycott the elections. The Lukiiko began a series of Memoranda to the British Government setting out their case for Buganda's separate independence. One such memorandum to the Queen was presented to and adopted by the Lukiiko sitting on 4th October, 1960, setting our arrangements for Buganda's independence. In conclusion this document stated:

"Buganda cannot sell her heritage for the purchase of Uganda's independence. That heritage is much more precious in the long run. Nor is Buganda prepared to sacrifice everything at the altar of Uganda's unity."[21]

The colonial Secretary's passionate appeal to the Kabaka, in reply to the memorandum of separate independence, in the following terms:

"I therefore call upon Your Highness to join with us and with His Excellency the Governor in an Urgent effort to restore co-operation and goodwill before it is too late."[22]

This call fell upon deaf ears at Mengo.

Buganda duly declared her independence to fall due on 31st December 1960, but not before four members of the Lukiiko's sub-committee which had drawn up the declaration of independence had resigned because they disagreed with it. The declaration itself was signed by Kintu and his ministers (Mayanja being the only Buganda minister who declined to be a party to this futile gesture). In fact the declaration of independence was a quixotic gesture because nothing happened and within a few days even the police patrols within Buganda were reduced to normal strength. It should perhaps be noted in passing that such intemperate resolutions of the Lukiiko could not be opposed within the chambers of that body for fear of the rowdy crowds which were to be found in the public gallery and outside the Chambers of the Lukiiko. Those who of a mind—and they were quite a number —to point out the futility of such gestures to their fellow members would certainly have run the risk of being manhandled or worse. Prudence dictated that they keep their opinions to themselves.

But if Buganda government's declaration of independence was an empty gesture, its boycott of the 1961 elections was not. Just as in 1958 they had lost a court case and blocked the holding of elections in

178   A POLITICAL HISTORY OF UGANDA

Buganda all the same, so also in 1961 their boycott of those elections was effective despite a determined attempt by the Protectorate government to hold them. The Colonial Secretary had not only refused Buganda's request to postpone the elections, but he had also ordered that the registration of voters be started forthwith. Mengo government, in the words of the Kabaka:

".... decided to boycott the election. Our strength would be shown by the number of people who did not vote."[23]

Thereupon the Kabaka's government embarked on a fierce and successful campaign to prevent the Baganda from registering and thereafter from voting. For the achievement of that objective Mengo was excellently equipped. The Kabaka's prestige among his people, since his return from exile, was high and it was known that he was opposed to these elections. But, it seems to me, that this alone would not have given Buganda government the success that it achieved because the DP, then the only party with sufficient organisational strength to stand up to Mengo, and the recently formed UPC, which was not so strong in Buganda, were on the side of the Protectorate government. The decisive factor was that the fearsome machinery of the Kabaka's government was thrown behind the campaign against the registration of voters which was declared to be an act of disloyalty to the Kabaka and to Buganda. It was also noted earlier that upon the return of the Kabaka, the chiefly hierarchy had been purged of all progressive, or "disloyal" elements as Mengo termed it, so that at his disposal the Kabaka had a powerful and malleable instrument to ensure that his wishes could not be flouted with impunity.

To counteract this furious campaign, the Protectorate government passed the Elections, 1961 (Prevention of Intimidation) Bill of 1960 which gave the Governor sweeping powers of detention of anyone guilty of an offence under that law.[24] This Bill was voted for unanimously by the African representatives in the Legco. It was to be in operation only during the period of registration and polling. It was aimed at protecting those Baganda who wished to register and vote against intimidation and arson that had been unleashed upon the Kingdom by Mengo government. Thus in Uganda one had the rare, if not unique, spectacle of a colonial government framing a law *to protect African voters against the violence of their fellow Africans seeking to prevent them from exercising a democratic right that colonial government usually granted most reluctantly*. This is one of the saddest commentaries on Uganda's political development.

Severe though the law was, its severity was on paper because the Protectorate government was ill-equipped to enforce it as Buganda government was well-equipped to defy it. In this trial of strength between Mengo and Entebbe, the latter had no chance from the beginning and this statement merits some explanation. In the villages of Uganda, where the vast majority of the people live, law and order was and is not normally enforced by the Police but by the chiefs assisted by the people themselves. Only when the chiefs encountered situations beyond their means to control, and only then, would they call upon the Police for help. It is beyond the capacity of the Police to even attempt a token patrol of the rural areas and consequently such patrols were and are limited to the towns and, until after independence, they did not even extend to trading centres of sizeable populations.

It has been stated that in Buganda, more than elsewhere in Uganda, the chiefs wielded tremendous power and influence over the people under their jurisdiction. Thus when this powerful agency of the chiefs, instead of being agents of law and order, became the chief instigators of arson and various forms of intimidation, the Protectorate government quite simply could not do much about it. Even if all the police force of the Protectorate had been put on patrol duty in Buganda alone, this could not have prevented crop slashing, house burning, livestock maiming and various acts of arson which were normally perpetrated at night against those adjudged to be "disloyal" to the Kabaka—i.e. sympathisers of national parties who dared register to vote. Against these fearsome odds, the majority of Buganda's electorate judged it prudent to keep clear of registration centres and polling stations and who could blame them? Thus between 3 and 4 per cent of the estimated qualified votes in Buganda actually braved these odds to register and vote and these were mostly DP supporters; its only rival that merits mention, the UPC, having had no opportunity to organise viable support in Buganda since it had only recently been formed and by elements from outside Buganda as we saw. Because of these factors the DP won 19 seats in Buganda and a farther 24 outside, making a total of 43 to UPC's 35 seats. But in popular vote, the UPC had secured the greatest number of votes—UPC's 488,332 to DP's 407,816 votes.[25] There are two explanations for this outcome. The first one was that in Buganda the turn out at voting had been extremely low owing to the circumstances that we have explained. An example may be given to indicate the seriousness of the Buganda government's campaign against registration and voting. In the constituency of North East Kyaggwe, the estimated population was 90,502 and only 188 voters registered. Of this L. Sebalu, the DP candidate secured 119 votes to UNC's S. Sebaduka's 13 votes.[26] The second explanation was hinted on earlier and this is that outside Buganda, the UPC was the more powerful of the two parties largely because its leaders were also the leaders of their respective districts. Obwangor, for example, in Teso East obtained a majority of 15,037 in a three-cornered fight and Nadiope in Busoga West obtained a majority of 10,424 also in a three-cornered fight.[27] These individual huge majorities soared UPC's popular vote just as the poor turn up in Buganda diminished that of the DP. Soon after these elections, Mr. Kiwanuka formed a government and was styled Chief Minister in July 1961, becoming Prime Minister on the granting of self government to Uganda on 1st March 1962. The fact of Mr. Kiwanuka becoming the first Prime Minister of Uganda led to the re-alignment of political forces within the country along the traditional lines with which we are by now familiar and it is to this re-alignment that we may now turn our attention.

It has been stressed in the preceding pages, at the risk of being tedious, that since the establishment of British rule in Uganda, the Protestants had been dominant in all spheres of public life in the Protectorate and, as with practices of longstanding, it was almost taken for granted that this was the natural order of things. We have noted that the formation of the DP was the first real challenge to the ascendancy of the Protestants in the country. At first this challenge was not taken seriously for the Protestant establishment was confident of their ability to nullify it. The victory of the DP and the accession of Kiwanuka to power as the first Prime Minister of Uganda woke the protestant hierarchies to the possibility that on the departure of the British, they might be left under the control of a Catholic-dominated government—a government, moreover, that might even temper with the *status quo*—i.e. introduce reforms which would wipe away the Protestant ascendency thereby altering a system of conducting public affairs that had subsisted undisturbed for some sixty years. This possibility was of greater concern to the Mengo establishment than elsewhere in Uganda because it was at Mengo that the Protestant ascendency, both political and economic, had been most remarkable, oppressive and enduring owing to Buganda's considerable internal autonomy which was not equally enjoyed by any other district or kingdom's local government.

The foregoing was one of the factors leading to the realignment of political forces in Uganda following on the DP electoral victory in 1961. It was by no means the only one because so long as colonial rule persisted, the stability of the country was ensured by the presence of colonial rulers—the Governor and his European subordinates—so that the various divisions we have indicated did not seriously jeopardise the orderly administration of the country. This was because in a fundamental sense the colonial rulers were not only alien but were also remote from centres and issues of conflict in a way that an African Government could not conceivably be. And this attitude was not confined to political institutions for it extended to social ones as well. For example, when Rev. Eric Sabiti was appointed as Assistant Bishop of Toro, Bunyoro and Mboga some 60 Batoro Protestants wrote a letter of protest to the Archibishop of Canterbury (Dr. Fisher) the substance of which was that Rev. Sabiti:

> ". . . . who is a Munyankore, is a person likely to cause a division in their church."

They called for an appointment, instead, of:

> "an impartial European Bishop of exemplary character."[28]

It is to be noted that these "Christians" did not even request for the appointment of a fellow Mutoro; the implication being that an African could not be trusted to be impartial. In the political sphere of course the misgivings about being ruled by an African government were far more intense. This then means that whereas Buganda could clamour for cast iron guarantees about its position in a self governing Uganda and whereas the national parties could condemn Buganda for doing so, it was realised all round that the situation would materially change once an African government replaced the colonial one. It was therefore necessary for all interest groups to find accommodation before an African government assumed full control of Uganda.

The victory of the DP, moreover, illustrated two realities of Uganda politics. The first one was that the Mengo government had the means to frustrate the conduct of elections within Buganda whatever the wishes of the Protectorate government or of the political parties might be. The second reality was that although the UPC had gathered the majority of popular vote, it could not hope to come to power without somehow getting support in Buganda. The point has been made that the DP was primarily a Catholic party and the UPC primarily a protestant one. This was really a matter of simple arithmetic because it was around these two faiths that the political parties had rallied to gain a following. The Muslims were a tiny minority and their vote could be attracted by either party according to the particular circumstances obtaining in the different constituencies where substantial Muslim voters were to be found. The greatest number of voters were the unconverted ones—called "pagans" in Christian and Islamic literature. But these voters, as it has been pointed out, had been relegated to the position of the permanently governed. Thus it came to pass that the contenders for leadership were Catholics and Protestants or, to say the same thing in different words, the DP and the UPC respectively.

There was therefore every reason for the UPC and Mengo government, recent antagonists, to take stock of their positions for a Catholic-dominated government was equally distasteful to both representative groups of Protestant ascendency in Uganda. Moreover, another home truth had dawned upon the rulers of Buganda and this was that since secession was no longer, as it had never really been, practical politics, it was necessary, and urgently so, to forge an alliance within the existing political forces in order to ensure their future accommodation in a country they could no longer hope to dominate on their own terms. Apparently the initiative to establish a *modus operandi* between the UPC and Mengo government was taken by the UPC after the general elections of 1961. This task was entrusted to Mr. Ibingira, assisted by Mr. Kirya.[29] The choice of Ibingira to approach a deeply suspicious and haughty Kabaka was a tactical one since Ibingira was not only a shrewd politician, but also a member of the royal family of Ankole who was also known personally to the Kabaka. Exactly what transpired during the meetings between Mengo and UPC representatives is not yet known but that certain bargains and counter bargains were made is fairly certain. These bargains concerned the positions the two parties would take in the negotiations leading to the framing of the internal self-government constitution for Uganda.

The conference for this purpose opened in London on 18th September, 1961, and ended on the 9th of the following month. Shortly before proceeding to the conference, however, it was announced in Kampala that an "understanding" between Mengo and the UPC had been reached in points that divided Mengo and the national parties and that the two parties to the "understanding" would take a similar stand on those points during the conference. This was the beginning of the alliance between Mengo and the UPC which, although historically natural in the Uganda context, was nevertheless surprising owing to UPC's public utterances since its formation. Ibingira may well be excused for stating ecstatically that this alliance was:

> ". . . . the outstanding achievement of nationalists pacifying sceptical traditionalists but also a basic turning point in the political and constitutional history of Uganda,"[30]

As we have observed, he was deeply involved in its formulation. But, whatever else this alliance was, it was not an act of statesmanship as the statement just quoted above would have us believe. The coalition between the UPC and Mengo government was a cynic's delight because the two parties had divergent views on almost every conceivable subject. Additionally, Mengo did not have, and could not have been expected to have had, anything by way of a national policy. The only point of congruence between the two parties was their common desire to oust the DP from office. This being the case, it would be absurd to argue that turning out the DP was an act conceived in the national interest. And whereas the desire to acquire power was legitimate— all political parties aim just at that—yet the means employed by the UPC to get into power were not justifiable because such political opportunism and unconstructive motivation could scarcely be a basis for political stability in the country and they were not. This was one of those instances where the end cannot possibly justify the means. And when all is said and done, it remains to record the lamentable fact that this pattern of political expediency run true to form: the coalition, like the other parties before it, had limited objectives and no national programme.

The conference itself and the constitution it framed need not detain us here as their technicalities and problems have been fully treated by Ibingira.[31] There are, however, three decisions of this conference which need elaboration because their consequences on the final general elections before independence were far-reaching. The first of these was the decision by the Colonial Secretary, at the instance of Buganda and UPC delegations, that in the final elections, Buganda would have the option to decide whether her representative to the National Assembly would be directly or indirectly elected. This was a concession of the greatest magnitude and that is why the Buganda delegation insisted on it being written in the constitution. The accompanying proviso that the Lukiiko which would act as an electoral college should it opt for indirect elections (as if there was any doubt about it) would itself be composed of directly elected representatives was of little value since the Lukiiko elections were to be managed by the Kabaka's government. Kiwanuka and his delegation protested very strongly that the concession would lead to instability in the country since it would enable Buganda to hold the country at ransom if neither of the two parties won a clear overall majority in the constituencies outside Buganda—as in fact it turned out to be the case. Obote, for his delegation, insisted that the price was worth paying if it meant that Buganda would be integrated with the rest of the Protectorate.[32] Ibingira admits that Kiwanuka had a legitimate complaint against this concession because the Buganda delegation never gave reasons for demanding indirect elections and, flying off at a tangent to find the reasons that Buganda did not give, he says:

"There was no doubt that this demand was motivated by an acute desire to maintain the effective loyalty of their people to their traditional legislature, the Great Lukiiko. Direct elections to the National Assembly . . . . would have diminished or destroyed the distinctiveness and autonomous character of Buganda."[33]

The justifications given by Obote and his legal adviser, Ibingira, are of course contradictory and somewhat specious. They are contradictory because one could not simply integrate Buganda with Uganda by making Buganda distinctively autonomous. They are specious because to maintain the "effective loyalty" of the people by denying them a direct say about who their representatives in the National Assembly would be is usually called muzzling them and this is what it was. Moreover, this concession was a fraud perpetrated upon the Baganda by their reactionary rulers with the help of the UPC and a pliable Colonial Secretary. The Wild Report of 1959 had most emphatically recommended that from 1961 and on subsequent occasions direct elections should be held all over the country and that no option of indirect elections should be offered to any part of the country.[34] And the majority of the members of the Wild Committee were the same leaders of UPC attending this same London Conference. In 1958, as on subsequent occasions, the fear of direct elections in Buganda sprung from the same source and that was that if the Buganda populace was given a free hand in choosing their representatives to the Lukiiko and to the National Assembly, they would have unquestionably removed the backwoodsmen who had ruled them by bullying and intimidation for so long. The vindictive predilection of Mengo government was well known as had only too recently been demonstrated in the 1961 elections. Thus the UPC and the Colonial Secretary knew, or should have known, that Mengo government would so rig the elections to the Lukiiko in order to return malleable people who could be bent to their will. In turn this is why the DP opposed this concession vehemently since it was clear to Kiwanuka and his delegation that the vindictive power of Mengo, now aided and abetted by the Uganda Constitution, would be used to destroy their party, at least in Buganda. It is not even reasonable to suppose that this probability had not occurred to the Colonial Secretary and the UPC. *Thus the Baganda were carefully shielded from expressing their loyalty so directly.*

The second concession that was granted to Buganda also had a direct bearing on the one we have just discussed. This was that Buganda was granted the right to control her local civil service without supervisory interference from the Uganda government.[35] We have already noted how powerful the hierarchy of chiefs in Buganda was. We also noted that after the return of the Kabaka from exile, this hierarchy had been purged of "disloyal" elements so that the reactionary rulers of Mengo had a powerful instrument of political and social control at their disposal. This concession was to prove, as Buganda and UPC delegations had expected it to prove, of inestimable value in the Lukiiko elections of 1962.

Thirdly, and finally, the control of the Protectorate police during the period of internal self-government was vested in the Governor and not in the Prime Minister. This was because, according to Ibingira,[36] it was feared that if the Prime Minister was given power over internal security, he might be tempted to use it against his political opponents and the UPC delegation, which originally wanted this power to be vested in the Prime Minister, changed its mind and supported Buganda, that this power be vested in the Governor. Yet this was not as fair as it looks at first sight because it has already been stated in these pages that the Protectorate government was partial to the Protestant groups in the country. It would appear therefore that the Mengo and UPC delegations, in insisting on this provision, were hoping not for fairness but for unfairness—that this power might be used against the DP. At least this was so in Buganda as is evident when Ibingira says, with his tongue in his cheek one feels, that:

> "There were bitter DP protests that the chiefs were arbitrarily arresting their leaders and supporters in the villages. Kiwanuka must have felt great frustration—considering that he had all the Protectorate's forces at his command—when he could not, under the constitution, intervene effectively to redress alleged injustices or regain the political initiative."[37]

Precisely the kind of handicap that surely Mengo and UPC delegations could not have overlooked when they insisted on these provisions.

It is not contended, by pointing out these shortcomings, that Buganda posed no problem. Indeed many of the problems facing Uganda at this time were complex as we have endeavoured to show. But it is contended that the opportunity to deal with Buganda firmly and fairly was lost at this conference and not in the interests of national unity as the UPC leaders contended. Buganda leadership was not interested in national unity; it was interested in privileges at the expense of their own people and at the expense of the rest of Uganda. I believe this to have been the opportune moment because by 1961 even Buganda government had given up hope and talk of secession. If the two national parties had united in refusing these concessions and with the knowledge that independence was a mere matter of months away, it is difficult to see what Buganda could have done about it. It was possible for Buganda to frustrate the 1961 elections since it was conducted by a colonial administration the end to whose political authority was not immediate—a colonial administration, moreover, that Buganda had succeeded to work up into a state of nerves. There was another chance but it was the last one. It would not have been equally easy to frustrate the 1962 elections and it would not have been in Mengo's interests to do so for fear of the consequences after independence which was to follow shortly thereafter. A self perpetuating oligarchy, such as Buganda government was, is not necessarily a blind one when it comes to seeing the writing on the wall. By the time of the London conference the writing was on the wall, but the opportunity was sacrificed at the altar of political expediency. Within five years, and with much bloodshed, these concessions were cancelled by the same UPC government for much the same reasons as the DP had opposed them in 1961. Truth had at last caught up with the UPC government as it was bound to do.

At the conclusion of the London conference, the politicians came back to prepare for the elections that were to precede the granting of independence. The battle lines were already clearly drawn. The Kabaka was to appoint the boundary Commission which was to demarcate the constituencies for the elections to the Lukiiko and the Kabaka's government, not the Central Government, was to supervise the elections—all this was perfectly legal according to the constitution. The UPC agreed with Mengo that it would not contest the Lukiiko elections—actually it is doubtful whether the UPC could have gained anything by entering this contest since her organisational strength and short span of life would probably have meant that the party would not have won any seats in Buganda. More than this, however, a new Buganda party, which called itself a movement as distinct from a party, was born soon after the London conference. This was the Kabaka Yekka (or Kabaka Alone). The name itself was an ingenious contrivance because the Kabakaship had great emotional appeal among the Baganda so that by using the Kabaka's name and by posing as the champions of the dignity of the Kabaka and of the cultural heritage of Buganda, the movement's propaganda was assured of success right from the start. The movement, moreover, had the vast resources, by Uganda standards, of Mengo government behind it both in terms of manpower and money.

The primary target of the KY and hence of Mengo government was to ensure that the DP was removed from office before independence and in the pursuit of that objective no holds were barred. In an electioneering pamphlet of 1962 addressed to the Baganda voters, the KY attacked the DP and its leader, Kiwanuka, in virulent terms and posed the rhetoric question:

"What kind of Muganda are you to allow Benedicto Kiwanuka
or any other person to "sit over" the 'Lion', His Highness, the
Kabaka of Buganda, as the DP are proposing . . .?"38

To vote for the DP was declared to be an act of disloyalty to the
Kabaka. This emotional propaganda had a considerable impact upon
the population, the more so because the whole powerful machinery of
the Kabaka's government was deeply involved in its dissemination
and was backing it with acts of arson and intimidation against known
or suspected DP sympathisers. It was 1961 all over again but this time
the enemy (the DP) was sharply in focus and, not unlike the Protectorate government in 1961, the DP was ill-equipped to counteract this
style of campaign and intimidation.

The Roman Catholic church in Uganda and its Luganda daily
paper, *Munno*, were the principal instruments available to the DP
but these instruments were demonstrably inadequate to deal with
Mengo government. In a pastoral letter in November, 1961, the Most
Rev. J. Kiwanuka, the Catholic Archbishop of Rubaga, explained to
his flock the desirability of a constitutional monarchy and its insulation
from politics. The letter was highly critical of the Kabaka's involvement
in politics and it concluded:

"That is why I do not like these slogans of Kabaka Yekka (the
Kabaka Alone) . . . . . . Among the parties already established
there is not a single one that has done anything on which could be
based the accusation "Now it is evident that such a party wants to
destroy the Throne! . . . ."39

This letter was read to the faithful all over the country in the Catholic
churches. But what His Grace got for his pains was the arrest of his
assistant, Monsignor Joseph Sebayigga, on the orders of the Kabaka.
The Archbishop himself had just left the country to attend a conference
in Canada and he would presumably have been arrested had he been
present.

The fearsome machinery of the Kabaka's government stepped up
its virulent campaign and many complaints of the violence of the chiefs
and of the other KY supporters against the DP leaders and their
followers were voiced, but the Protectorate government looked on
with benign disinterest. As expected the KY swept the board—winning
65 to DP's 3 seats to the Lukiiko in February 1962. In a lengthy
pamphlet Kiwanuka, who had himself lost the seat he had contested,
catalogues a long list of malpractices which led to the defeat of his
party. These range from candidates who were also the Returning
Officers; candidates who were returned with majorities which were

larger than the number of registered voters to polling booths which were constructed in such a way that the voters could be seen by the KY youth wingers as they cast their votes[40]—i.e. voters would be intimidated because the ballots for the KY and the DP were cast into two different and clearly labelled boxes. Although some of these allegations may be exaggerated, there can be little doubt that the Kabaka's government was guilty of at least many of them. The whole history of Mengo government since the return of the Kabaka from exile had shown nothing but vindictiveness and high-handedness in the pursuit of its chosen objectives. The extent to which the Protectorate government was a silent party to these malpractices is a matter for conjecture for it is difficult to establish with direct evidence. May be such evidence will one day see the light of day. Again, as expected, the new Lukiiko "decided" to act as an electoral college for Buganda's 21 representatives to the National Assembly.

From this point onwards there was no doubt as to who would form the government that would rule Uganda after independence because outside Buganda, for reasons we indicated, the UPC was stronger than the DP. This latter tried desperately to have the general elections postponed beyond April 1962 but even in this the DP was unsuccessful because the Colonial Office passed an Ordinance which enabled the Governor to issue a writ for holding elections in April 1962 without the advice of the Prime Minister. In these elections, as in the preceding ones, the UPC beat the DP both in the number of seats won (37 to DP's 24) and in popular vote (537,598 to DP's 474,256).[41] Thereupon Obote, the leader of the UPC, was called on to form a government by the Governor—a government which was based on an alliance between the UPC and the KY which now, but not for long afterwards, held the balance of power between the two main parties. The final conference to draw up the independence constitution was opened in London on 12th June 1962 and lasted for nearly a month. With a few modifications, the independence constitution was modelled on the internal self-government one. Thus on 9th October, 1962, Uganda became an independent state. Finally an aggregation of divergent interests had assumed control of a new nation and this time without a colonial administration to act as umpire. It can also be said that the coalition of UPC and KY was a collection of individuals who had come together for a single purpose as an end in itself: to get into power. But they had not had time to even think of what they were going to do with that power. The underlying problems and conflicts in Uganda were still there and these were papered over, perhaps too hastily, and also perhaps in the hope that these would melt away with time. If this was not a triumph of hope over experience, what was it then?

By way of providing a postcript to this survey, it maybe of some value to make a few comments on the Obote administration. But because the life of that administration is so recent and the leaders involved are still eminent persons albeit in different roles, and, for some, in different countries, such comments must of necessity be of a tentative nature and even then they can only be made at the risk of being superficial in some respects.

Much has already been said in the preceding pages to show that Uganda, even perhaps more than most other new nations in Africa and elsewhere, was very difficult to administer. It must therefore be stated from the outset that Obote had a most unenviable task to perform when he assumed powers of government from the British officials. It was the practice of British colonial legislatures that the African representatives, by whatever method they were chosen, always functioned as an opposition to the colonial administration and, unlike opposition parties in parliamentary democracies, the African representatives had no hope of exercising powers of government because, among other things, colonial administrations were not parliamentary democracies and were never meant to be. Consequently, when Obote and his ministers assumed powers of government, they had, among their ranks, several eminent men who had considerable experience in berating the Protectorate administration in the Legislative Council but not of exercising actual powers of government or superintending over an orderly administration. And this was by no means the only practical handicap.

Like other leaders of other newly created artificial countries, Obote had inherited power from the colonial governor but he had not inherited the authority that had gone with that power. This was because there were other centres of institutional authority in the various components of Uganda and these centres commanded loyalty and conferred authority to a far greater extent than any new African government could ever hope to do. Thus, for instance, an Obote who had by then become the President of Uganda, found it necessary to pass a stringent law to make it an offence for anyone to even throw a tomato at him and if convicted, one would be liable to imprisonment for life without an option of a fine.[42] Yet a Kabaka of Buganda, who had been deposed by the same Obote, would not have needed such a protection to his dignity within his kingdom. In other words, whereas the Kabaka commanded natural respect and obedience from his subjects, President Obote needed a punitive piece of legislation to exact the same from his countrymen over whom he ruled.

Along with this factor, one has also to consider the fact that Obote had become a leader of the party of leaders. We have already examined the circumstances in which the UPC was formed and we have made the observation that the strength of that party did not lie in the coherence of its organs, for these hardly existed, but in the fact that most of its leaders had also been leaders of their own districts. The party had many heavyweights over whom Obote himself had no particular advantage so that his choice had largely been a matter of chance. It was not on account of his longer experience in politics, proven qualities of statesmanship or charismatic characteristics that he was chosen. Men like Nadiope, Obwangor, Kirya and several others did not need the services of the party organisation, less still the presence of the Party President in their constituencies, to get elected. Obote therefore, through no fault of his, had to be content with being a leader of leaders or the first among equals. In these circumstances, therefore, it was impossible to build a coherent party whose machinery could impose discipline on all and sundry. Party organisation became a matter of securing sinecure positions for this or that leader's followers. In fact by 1965, for the UPC as well as for the DP, the only evidence that political parties had existed in 1962 were the old battered party flags which had braved the elements and were to be found fluttering for only over some buildings which had functioned as party offices during the electoral campaigns of 1961 and 1962. Having achieved that purpose— i.e. fighting the elections—party organisation had gone to seed and with it any hope of formulating a party ideology or indeed of imposing discipline in the party ranks. The UPC had remained a coalition of powerful individuals and its leader was by no means the most powerful individual in this lamentable set-up.

These problems of leadership and authority were farther compounded by other equally Uganda-wide problems. Of these we may single out one problem, which was as old as Uganda itself, for purposes of illustration. This was the problem of religious antagonism about which the Obote administration could have probably done little anyway but in fact did less. Over the duration of colonial rule, this rivalry had slowly but surely percolated to the schools which, as we have observed, were run by missionary societies. In a speech in Parliament, for example, Mr. Sempa said that the source of disunity existed in the country and he quoted the example of the hatred hat existed between the pupils of Budo and Kisubi (respectively the Protestant and Catholic High schools near Kampala). He pointed out that this hatred did not abate until these students came to Makerere University only to find that they could get along well.[43] This antagonism, needless to say, was not confined to the two schools referred to by Mr. Sempa. Owing to the peculiar nature of the expansion of western education over the various parts of Uganda, it so happened that wherever one found a Catholic school, of whatever standard or level, there was to be found a Protestant one of the same standard or level nearby and these institutions were virtually hostile camps. This writer remembers vividly some interschool football matches in the late fifties in the Western province of Uganda. These invariably ended in pitched battles if the opposing teams belonged to different Christian denominational schools or colleges.

Reference has just been made to the antagonism that existed between the Christian faiths. Not content with this cleavage, the UPC government went ahead and created division among the Muslims. Thus we find Badru Kakungulu, who was the leader of the Uganda Muslim Community, condemning Nekyon (a senior cabinet minister and cousin of Obote) for creating divisions among Muslims by forming the National Association for the Advancement of Muslims (Naam) in order to advance his political interests. The Naam, although with far less following than the UMC, enjoyed government bounties much to the annoyance of many Muslims. Kakungulu in fact ordered all his followers that the followers of Naam should be denied access to mosques and schools belonging to the UMC.[44] The point is that for a government which had inherited so many divisions in the country to create more divisions, as was the case with the Muslims, was the very height of short sightedness. But then by 1965 the voices of moderation in the conduct of public affairs in Uganda had long gone the way of Algebra and Chemical valencies.

Yet some of the policies pursued by government after independence tended to show that this antagonism was being intensified rather than abated. For instance, through the same medium of parliamentary debate, Mr Barisigara pointed out instances of discrimination. He stated that qualified Catholic teachers were being transferred to remote areas and were being replaced by unqualified (licenced) protestant ones simply because they were Catholic. He also argued that the policy of the Ministry of Education with respect to the upgrading of schools from primary 6 to primary 7 was based on religious discrimination. He cited Ankole where of the 18 schools upgraded, only 5 were Catholic schools and Kigezi where of the 15 upgraded schools, only 3 were Catholic.[35] These statements were not denied by the government because in fact the statistics were right. What, in turn, this meant was that national government increasingly resembled the colonial one in buttressing protestant domination but differed from it in one important respect: it was far less tolerant of criticism than the colonial administration. This of course is largely true of all African governments all over the continent and one sometimes wonders what those African politicians, whose misfortune it was to find themselves on opposition benches, must feel when they recall their vociferous berating of imperialists in the period before independence.

Whereas it must be freely admitted that the problems of governing Uganda after independence were truly daunting, it must be equally emphasised that the way the Obote administration went about solving or mitigating those problems was the wrong one. In order to enhance his personal authority over his ministers particularly and over the party generally, Obote engaged in the manipulation of the political system in a manner that must be acknowledged to have been imprudent at best. The best examples of this tendency can be seen in the management of the civil service and of the local governments.

So far as the Civil Service is concerned, it has been said that Uganda inherited a viable and reasonably impartial civil service at the time of independence and this, to a large extent, was attributed to the independence of the Public Civil Service Commission which was responsible for the appointment and discipline of the civil servants. This changed after independence and, in the same Parliamentary debate to which we have just referred, an Opposition member accused the Prime Minister of undermining the morale of the civil service by depriving the Public Service Commission of its executive power and making it merely advisory to him. He cited an example of an occasion when the Prime Minister had abused this power by marching into the offices of the Ministry of Information and dismissing a civil servant (named as Livingstone Kamulegeya) for having called Mr. Latim the leader of the Opposition on the radio. He also referred to the frequent arbitrary transfer of civil servants by telegram and at short notice at the whim of ministers and other UPC politicians. He informed the House that that civil servants who were related to ministers were misappropriating public funds with impunity while public officers deserving of promotion were being bye-passed in favour of those most underserving.[46] All these accusations, and many more besides, were justified and the existence of libel and defamation laws restrains one from giving specific examples in respect of each accusation. The once-dignified civil service was filled with obsequious mediocrities as were the parastatal bodies—the only sure qualification for holding these positions was undoubted loyalty to the leader. The Uganda Club (in Kampala), where Obote and his trusted ministers used to hold all-night parties, came close to resembling the court of the Czars during the decline of imperial Russia when cranks like Rasputin could hold sway over the Czar and the Court. By undermining the integrity and the morale of the civil service Obote and his advisers created a following of fawning placemen but they undermined the stability of their own administration because when promotion does not depend on proven merit but on other political factors, then intrigues for position and deposition multiply and this was the case with Obote's administration in the late sixties.

It was stated earlier that the success of the political parties in gaining control of the district councils had sharply underscored the various divisions that existed in the various parts of the country to an extent that seriously impeded their functioning. After independence, this problem was intensified, especially in those districts where the DP had more supporters than the ruling party. Several examples can be adduced to illustrate this point, but a few will be sufficient. In 1964 there were elections for the urban authorities of Kampala, Jinja and Mbale but in the first two, the DP won the majority and thereupon the elections were disallowed by the minister responsible for the local governments who then went ahead to appoint councillors and mayors of those towns.[47] In districts like Ankole, where the DP had won the majority in National Assembly and district council elections, the boundaries of the district council constituencies were redrawn in such a way that many of the DP supporters found it impossible to travel to their new polling stations to vote and the UPC thereupon gained control of that council. The point about these manipulations is that although the government gained the short term aim of planting their supporters where they had no right to be, the government nevertheless did irreparable harm to itself by destroying the faith of the people (supporters and opponents alike) in government's impartiality and capacity to administer the country justly. In the judgement of politicians this may well be dismissed as idle talk from one who is wholly inexperienced in the art of running governments, but it is nevertheless true because, as one Obote's senior ministers ruefully admitted: "You cannot govern a country without some principles."[48] It may well be that this realisation had dawned upon him late in the day for this statement was made shortly before he, together with four other senior cabinet colleagues, were arrested in the middle of a cabinet meeting.

It is not to be supposed that these instances of unprincipled management of public affairs was confined to the Civil Service and the local governments for it extended into other institutions such as the Trade Unions, for example. It has already been noted that Uganda was peculiarly unsuited to the growth of genuine Trade Unions largely because of the absence of a settled working and urbanised African population. Even the Uganda Trades Union Congress which was formed in the 1950's remained to be an ineffective organisation, largely led by railway workers from Kenya. After independence, the government did not get on well with this Union, and especially with its leader who was also a UPC member of Parliament and therefore a government-inspired Trade Union was formed in competition with the existing one: this was the Federation of Uganda Trade Union. But this, even more than TUC, enjoyed superficial existence and its finances were mismanaged by its officials (UPC bright boys) and the fact that it was there at all was due to its being sponsored by government. It is true, as Scott has observed, that "one of the major failures of colonial Trade Unions is attributable to their financial weakness and the consequence that they attract as officers men who are themselves unstable, either crooks or idealists and very few of the latter."[49] This was true of Uganda Trade Unions. This writer was told, in a conversation, by one of the Union officials, who must remain nameless, who attended some Union conference in London and stayed at the Russell Hotel—which he imagined to be the most luxurious in London—of the great sums of money he spent on drink, women and hiring expensive cars. He said this in a tone which was meant to impress one that he had done the workers he was supposed to represent the greatest possible good. And, to the best of my knowledge, this official was never reprimanded either by government or by his "Union".

It has been said by an eminent jurist that:

"... . the wellbeing of a people depends not only on the form of government they have but also on the ordinary laws of the land."[50]

In the fluid situations that new African countries find themselves in, the one sure foundation of stability is the impartial law and the equally impartial administration of justice by the country's courts. From the early days of independence, the Uganda government showed the dangerous tendency of changing the country's laws in order to promote specific political interests in complete disregard of the dictates of justice. Two examples will illustrate this point. On 10th August 1962, the district council of Busoga passed a resolution to the effect that it would be composed of 84 members of whom 67 would be directly elected, 6 specially elected and 11 hereditary chiefs inspite of the fact that the Uganda-Order-in-Council prescribed that the membership of any district council should at least be 9/10ths directly elected (Section 72 subsection (2)). The Council dissolved itself on that day. Then on September 26th, 1962, elections to the council were held and two days later the new council met for the purpose of selecting the 6 specially elected members and this inspite of the fact that the council regulations provided that such a meeting should take place after seven days' notice. The following day the Council also elected Nadiope as the Kyabazinga of Busoga. Subsequently some members of the Council filed a suit in the High Court of Uganda seeking a declaration of the Court that the 6 specially elected members and Nadiope were respectively not members of the Council and the Kyabazinga should be restrained from acting in those capacities. The declaration was granted as sought on 2nd February 1963.[51] On 1st March 1963 the Parliament of Uganda passed the Busoga (Validation) Act (1963) which reversed the decision of the Court and reinstated the 6 specially elected members of the Council and Nadiope as Kyabazinga. The point is that to tamper with the country's judicial system for the purpose of pleasing a political colleague—even a powerful one such as Nadiope was in the UPC—was to breed contempt for the judicial system and it cannot be said that this was a wise policy on the part of this or of any other government.

Prior to independence there were provisions in the Police Ordinance to enable the police to control assemblies and processions. These provisions gave the Police the power to apply for a permit from any magistrate to stop such assemblies or processions if they were satisfied that they were likely to lead to a breach of the peace. But the organisers of such assemblies or processions were entitled to be heard in court before such permits of cancellation could be granted to the Police. The Obote administration found such a liberal law inadequate for the suppression of anyone who might hold views opposed to the government. By 1965 moreover, the UPC itself had fallen apart and divided itself into two factions, not unlike the split of the original congress. This time one wing was under Obote and the other under Ibingira. By the Police Ordinance (Amendment) Act of 1965, the Police, without reference to any magistrate, were empowered to stop any assembly or procession summarily. The point of this amendment was that the Police, which is directly under the minister of Internal Affairs, was much easier to order about than the magistrates' courts. And the first public meeting which was dispersed under this amended law was that convened by Mr. Ibingira, the Secretary General of the UPC, who had played a big role in piloting the amendment through Parliament!

The examples which show that the government was bending laws to suit or hurt individual citizens are legion. And yet the ever gullible (or perhaps more accurately helpless) Uganda public was, at one and the same time, being constantly assured that the government had the profoundest respect for the laws of the country. Witness, for example, this passage, in the President's speech from the Chair (which was of course a government major statement of policy) which was read to Parliament on 15th December, 1965:

"In the field of Administration of justice the Government remains firm in its belief that efficient and impartial administration of justice is the chief cornerstone of any state and that all forms of development rest upon a foundation of an orderly government where the security of the individual is not lost and the rule of law is not overridden."[52]

But then by 1965 the declared intentions of the government and their actual practices were no longer within shouting distance of each other and, what is more, the general public knew all about these confidence tricks.

What, however, led to the fall of Obote's government was its involvement in the disorganisation of the army. The army, like the other institutions to which reference has been made, was not to be left intact. But on this subject it is difficult to decide which allegations and counter-allegations to believe as one has as yet no means of verifying them. What one can ascertain is that by 1965 all the politicians had given up even the pretence of appealing to the electorate and it was clear that it woud be the army which would be decisive in the power struggle that was raging within the ruling party. Exactly how the divisions were caused in the army is not yet known but the two factions into which the ruling party had divided each hoped to get support of some section of the army and in the end, in May 1966, it was the Obote faction which won. From that date it could be said that Uganda had a quasi-military government because the basis of Obote's abrogation of the 1962 constitution, the abolition of the post of constitutional president and the assumption of the office of executive President by Obote himself was based on nothing but force-force provided by the army. Even some of our leaders talked glibly of the impossibility of maintaining a constitutional democracy in Africa because it was so alien to the African conception of government. This argument, if it can be so termed, was of course always advanced by those who stood to benefit by the forcible abolition of all forms of opposition. Could it then be said that by concentrating so much power in the hands of one man and by riding roughshod over all centres of legitimate opposition, Uganda was reverting to the well-tested efficacy of the traditional tyranny of the Chief? To argue thus would be to advance an unsupportable falsehood. We saw earlier that in precolonial times there were even societies in Uganda which knew no rule of one man—the segmentary societies—and we also saw that even where kings ruled, there were always effective checks against the kings' wanton use of political power. The point must be made, and this cannot be overemphasised, that the capacity of modern African governments to oppress their citizens, who for the most part are illiterate, is far greater than anything that could have been devised by an African polity during precolonial times.

The period between May 1966 and January 1971 was a very uneasy one indeed in Uganda for then the country had a civilian administration which employed military methods and means to implement whatever policies they chose. In that period the country had two unconstitutional constitutions rammed down its throat and the kingdoms were abolished—in fact Buganda (the old bogey) ceased to exist on the map because it was divided up in such a way that none of the divisions bore the name Buganda. As so often in the game of power politics, the man who had helped Obote to beat his opponents into submission and into jail in 1966, General Amin, fell out with Obote. This was widely known around the capital but the manner in which this rift came about was the subject of many rumours—rumours that are not easily translated into fact and for this reason it would be unprofitable to go into this subject at this time. During the night of 24th/25th January 1971 gunfire was heard in various parts of the capital (Kampala) and just before 4 p.m. (East African Time) a ponderous voice of an NCO announced on the radio that the army had taken over the government and read a list of 18 points in justification of the army taking this step.[53] Within a few minutes of this announcement, the streets of Kampala were full of hysterical crowds rejoicing at the fall of Obote. Whether or not the army would right the injustices listed in the 18th points and whether or not the rejoicing at the fall of Obote was yet another premature triumph of hope over experience, only time would tell.

1. *Uganda Argus* (Kampala) 3/2/60, p. 3.
2. *Ibid.* 17/2/60, p. 4.
3. G. S. K. Ibingira: *op. cit.* p. 104–1.
4. *Uganda Argus*, 22/9/60, p. 5.
5. *Ibid.* 20/9/60, p.1.
6. *Ibid.* 28/7/60, p. 5.
7. *Ibid.* 20/8/60, p. 2.
8. *Ibid.* 17/8/60, p. 5.
9. *Ibid.* 6/8/60, p. 2.
10. *Report of the Commission of Inquiry into the Disturbances in the Eastern Province, 1960* (Government Printer, Entebbe, 1960).
11. *Report of the Commission of Inquiry into the Affairs of Bugisu District Council, October, 1960,* (Government Printer, Entebbe, 1960).
12. *Uganda Argus*, 23/11/60, p.1.
13. See also Appendix 3, p. 226.
14. Lord Molson: *Uganda: Report of a Commission of Privy Counsellors in a Dispute between Buganda and Bunyoro* (HMSO, London, C.M.D. 1717), p. 3.
15. See also *Appendices 1 and 2*.
16. Lord Molson: *op. cit.* p. 5.
17. *Ibid.* p. 16.
18. See also Appendix 2D, p. 225.

19. *Report of the Commission appointed to review the boundary between the districts of Bugisu and Bukedi* (Government Printer, Entebbe, 1962). This summary of the dispute is based on this report.
20. E. B. Welbourn: *East African Rebels,* (London, 1961), p. 29.
21. Quoted in *Uganda Argus,* 5/10/69, p.l.
22. G. S. K. Ibingira: *op. cit.* p. 136.
23. The Kabaka of Buganda: *op. cit.* p. 158.
24. G. S. K. Ibingira: *op. cit.* p. 60–61.
25. *Uganda Argus,* 28/3/61, p.l.
26. *Ibid. 27/3/61.*

27. *Ibid. 27/3/61.* p. 4.
28. *Ibid.* 22/12/59, p. 5.
29. G. S. K. Ibingira: *op. cit.* p. 202.
30. *Ibid.* p. 201.
31. *Ibid.* p. 200–234.
32. *Ibid.* p. 208–9.
33. *Ibid.* p. 211.
34. Wild Report, p. 12.
35. G. S. K. Ibingira, *loc. cit.* p. 222.
36. *Ibid.* p. 226.
37. *Ibid.* p. 239.
38. D. A. Low: *The Mind of Buganda,* p. 214.
39. *Ibid.* p. 211–3.
40. B. K. Kiwanuka: *Uganda Elections—1962* (Kampala, n.d.—Duplicated typescript in Makerere University Library).
41. G. S. K. Ibingira: *op. cit.* p. 244.
42. The Penal Code (Amendment) Act, 1970, Section 2b.
43. *The Hansard: December 1965—February 1966,* p. 109.
44. *Sekanyolya,* (Kampala), 14/9/65, p. 8.
45. Hansard p. 492.
46. *Ibid.* p. 331–4.
47. *Ibid.* p. 430.
48. *Ibid.* p. 500.
49. R. Scott: *The Development of Trade Unions in Uganda,* (E.A.P.H., 1966), p. 26.
50. Lord Denning quoted in: A. N. Allot (ed.): *The Future of Law in Africa,* (London, 1960) in Introduction.
51. This information is contained in Civil Case No. 101 of 1962: Jowett Lyagoba vs Bakasonga and others in *The East African Law Reports,* (London, 1963), p. 57–65.
    I am indebted to Mr. J. A. Kateera, Ll.M. (Harvard) who gave me access to this literature in his chambers.
52. *The Hansard, December 1965–February 1966,* para. 61.
53. See Appendix IV, p. 238.

APPENDICES

For Appendices 1–2, I am deeply obliged to Dr. Mbabi-Katana, of Makerere University, who obtained them for me from the successors of the late Mr. Kwebiha and also to the same successors for allowing me to make use of these documents.

APPENDIX 1

MEMORANDUM SUBMITTED BY THE MUBENDE BANYORO COMMITTEE TO THE COMMISSION OF PRIVY COUNCILLORS APPOINTED TO INVESTIGATE THE ISSUE OF BUNYORO'S LOST COUNTIES OF BUYAGA, BUGANGAIZI, BUWEKULA, BUGERERE, BURULI AND PORTIONS OF THE COUNTIES OF SINGO AND BULEMEEZI (RUGONJO)

The Right Honourable Sirs,

We, the signatories to this memorandum, for and on behalf of the Banyoro native and other non-Baganda residents of the Lost Counties, have the honour to lay before you our humble submissions for your favourable consideration in the manner most compatible with British justice and with the principles of the United Nations Charter of Human Rights.

We are the Banyoro native of this our homeland comprising the six Lost Counties which formed part of the largest Kingdom of Kitara in Central Africa. These six lost counties, transferred by British Officials from our natural Kingdom to Buganda, are the very core of Bunyoro-Kitara containing the traditions, royal hills and other regalia which we cherish to this day.

The territories we claim to be restored to Bunyoro Kingdom without any shadow of doubt or any hesitation about their boundaries are those declared by Mr. E. J. L. Berkeley in his despatch of 19th November, 1896, to the Marquis of Salisbury as follows:

"It is revealed in R.A. Omukama of Bunyoro's Petition to H.M. The Queen on the Lost Counties issue that on 19th November, 1896 Mr. E. J. L. Berkeley reported the following to the Marquis of Salisbury in a despatch numbered 113: "I proceeded to explain the distribution of these territories between two relegious parties as made by Col. Colvile, would be maintained, namely, the district (marked as South Unyoro) bounded to the North by Ngusi river, to the west by the south-east shore of Lake Albert, to the south by Muzizi river and to the east by Kitumbwi river, would go to the Catholics and the territory lying to the east thereof, viz bounded to the North by the Kafu River to the east by the Nile and to the south by Buganda (as therefore) would go to the Protestants."

The aforesaid was the despatch that sealed off the freedom of many hundreds of thousands of Bunyoro, the inhabitants of the Lost Counties from year 1896 to the present date.

Such gross injustice did not escape the notice of Mr. Pulteny, the Bunyoro District Commissioner of the time who tendered the following resignation to Mr. Berkeley:

"If you decide that South Unyoro is to be handed over to the Roman Catholics, particularly under Lwekula, I regret to be obliged under these circumstances to request you to accept my entire resignation of all civil administation in Unyoro and appoint some officer to relieve me of these duties."

The British administrators in Uganda further sealed off the freedom of Banyoro the inhabitants of the Lost Counties by concluding the 1900 Agreement with Buganda and inserting the lost counties within Buganda boundary without any special regard for the Banyoro.

Confirming our claim stated earlier in this memorandum, we wish to quote a statement by Mr. J. E. P. Postlethwaite, formerly Provincial Commissioner, Buganda, in his Book *I Look Back* which reads as follows:

"In any case, it seemed impossible to make up for the loss to the unfortunate Banyoro of what was in fact their Holy of Holies and the real centre of their Kingdom. It was only an accident, after all, at the time of agreement the Baganda were temporarily in the ascendancey. Incidentally, the caves of the rocky hills near Kakumiro had been standing place of the Banyoro from which, as far as I know, the Baganda had never successfully dislodged them, while in Buyaga, lie the graves of the Banyoro Bakama, where every creature, hill rock and blade of grass cries aloud to those interested that they are Banyoro and can never be anything else!"

It is the same author and Buganda Provincial Commissioner who points out the following in the same book:

> "The inclusion of Mubende District in Buganda Kingdom is considered by many to have been one of the greatest blunders we committed in the past."

We wish to show the Commission here some of our history and traditions, maintained to this day, traditions which will continue to exist even in future, as confirmed in the new Constitution of Uganda which safeguards the traditions and customs of each and every kingdom including the Kingdom of Bunyoro-Kitara. The following are a few notes on each of the six Lost Counties:

BUGANGAIZI:

This was a county of Bunyoro ruled (at the coming of the first Europeans) by Kikukule living at Kasaka (at present Bukumi R.C.H.). This County contains: Bunyoro's royal tombs of our former Kings and Princes: 2 tombs of King Duhaga I at Irangarra in Sabagabo sub-county, one tomb of Queen Masamba d/o Winyi at Rwembuba in Sabaddu sub-county, and another place of Bunyoro's royal drum: Kanumi. At the said former county headquarters (Bukumi R.C.M.) we still find the drum of office presented to Chief Kikukule of Bugangaizi by the Omukama of Bunyoro-Kitara. There is also an important cave, Semwema, near Kakumiro which was Bunyoro's army's stronghold as confirmed by Mr. Postlethwaite formerly Provincial Commissioner, Buganda, as quoted above.

BUHEKURA:

This was Bunyoro's most important territory where all coronation functions were performed. In this county is situated the Coronation Hill of MUBENDE where Queen Nyakahuma resided and was in charge of Bunyoro's ancient palace of King Ndahura. Traditional coronation functions were always performed there throughout our long history down to the coronation of King Cwa II Kabalega. On the same spot are the royal fountain and the coronation tree known today as the Witch Tree (which we always call Nyakahuma's Tree) that can still be seen near the Protectorate Agent's house. Queen Nyakahuma, the said keeper of Bunyoro's ancient coronation palace, was dismissed from her official residence on Mubende hill in 1907 by the British so as to build the present District Headquarters. With the kind permission of R. A. Omukama of Bunyoro-Kitara, Sir Tito Winyi IV, K.B.C., C.B.E., some of Bunyoro's regalia, formerly kept by Nyakahuma on Mubende hill, were taken to the Uganda Museum where a fine portrait and display of Nyakahuma may be seen. When the Protectorate Government officials dismissed Nyakahuma from Mubende, they destroyed Bunyoro's royal residence, filled up the royal fountain, and left only the Coronation Tree which is the only sign left of our cherished traditional site.

When Nyakahuma died, after she had been dismissed from her official residence on Mubende hill, she was buried at Kyakatabarwa near Mubende where members of her family still live looking after some of Bunyoro's regalia and still hoping for the day when they will be permitted to return to their residence up the hill and to resume their traditional functions of the Kingdom of Bunyoro-Kitara.

EBUURU

After the opening coronation ceremonies at Mubende, the new Omukama is then taken to *Habuuru* at the northern side of Butoroogo hills, in Sabaddu sub-county of Buwekula, where the coronation ceremonies are continued. This site is in fact the ancient palace of King Rukidi Mpuuga the ancestor of Bunyoro's Babiito Kings who have ruled the Kingdom to this day. In the same area, the British built Fort Grant when they invaded our Kingdom and fought with Chief Kikukule who ruled the district.

BUYAGA

The importance of this county to the Kingdom of Bunyoro-Kitara cannot be overstressed. The county Chief at that time was Rusebe s/o Rukumba Rukirabanyoro grandson of Omukama Kyebambe Nyamutukura. The County headquarters were at Nkeirwe (Kitemba), Pachwa in Sabaawali sub-county. This county contains very many of the royal tombs of our former kings, namely: Kyebambe IV Kamurasi at Ngangi, Nyabongo at Bukonda and Kinogozi, Olimi IV Rwakabale at Kitoonya, Winyi I at Kicunda near Mugalama, Kyabambe III Nyamutukura at Kibeeḍi and Bujogoro, Isansa III at Kiguhyo, Kabagonza at Kasimbi, Olimi Kabagungu at Buziba, and many other of Bunyoro's princes and princesses.

There are in this county several important people, who were heads of our traditions in this area, such as Mihinga/Kyanku of Rucoma (Buyaga), Mutuba first sub-county, and Bwemi who live at Bwema, Sabaddu sub-county in the extreme west of Buyaga.

RUGONJO (NORTH SINGO/BULEMEEZI)

This is another territory of Bunyoro Kingdom which was ruled (at the time of the arrival of the British) by Chief Mutengesa. His Headquarters were at Kicucu. This county also contains traditional places of importance to the kingdom of Bunyoro-Kitara, namely: The royal tombs of King Winyi I at Kiburara, Mutuba four sub-county (Bukomero), Singo; King Olimi Rwitamahanga at Kalimbi, Mutuba II sub-county (Kadoma), and other burial grounds of our princes. This district was alloted by the Omukama to several princes who owned private estates here and there. One of Bunyoro's most important heads of our royal traditions, *Omukonda* lived at *Kikonda* in the same Mutuba II sub-county, and whenever the Coronation (Empango) ceremonies took place at the palace headquarters, the royal drummers and other regalia heads and all people used to travel to the Omukonda's residence in North Singo (Kikonda) to continue the ceremonies there according to tradition.

BURULI

This county of Bunyoro Kingdom was ruled by an important traditional royal Chief, Princess Nyangoma, whose headquarters were at Kyaruhweza, (Mumyoka sub-county, Buruli).

Today, the successor of Princess Nyangoma, Chief of Buruli, *Warwo* by name, lives at Nyakatoma, Sabaddu sub-county. The actual administration of the territory was the responsibility of Chief *Kadyebo* who lived at Kamuniina, Kigweri (sub-county of Sabaddu). There was also in this county Bunyoro's admiral *Rubanga rwa Kyagwire* who was in charge of the Omukama's canoes and boats on Lake Kioga and River Nile. In the same area is the burial ground of Prince Jaasi Nyakimoso (son of Kabaleega) who died shortly after the capture of his father. Kabaleega's mother, Queen Nyamutahingurwa was buried also in this county at Kaguhyo village. Kabagambe rwa-Iteera and Ibanda were important sub-chiefs who ruled the area.

BUGERERE (Bunyara)

This is again an important county of Bunyoro-Kitara, ruled by royal hereditary chief, *Nyamunyonjo*, first hereditary chieftainship was maintained up to the time of the transfer of the said counties to Buganda, but the successor of Nyamuyongo still lives in the area.

Prince Yusufu Rwadeba of Bunyoro was buried in this county at Galilaya. There is a Munyoro notable, Kibandwa Ntimba who lived at Kizinga, Kalenge, Bugerere. Nyamuyonjo was responsible for the Omukama's canoes on Rivers Sezibwa and Nile. This was witnessed by Speke the explorer who was told by Nyamuyonjo that he could not use Bunyoro's boats to travel northward into Kitara until the Omukama gave orders.

All the named six counties belonged definitely to Bunyoro, but were simply transferred to Buganda by the early British for reasons as yet unknown to all the Banyoro race.

At the present time, the following Baganda Chiefs are ruling the said six counties:

County	Chief's name
Buyaga	Emmanuel Kayemba
Bugangaizi	Simon Kiruruta
Buhekura	Joseph Kiggundu
Buruli	Marko Lwanga
Bugerere	Mr. Kigozi
North Singo	James Lutaya
North Bulemeezi	Latima Sebanakitta.

And all the Gombolola Chiefs administering the six lost counties are Baganda and their Banyoro subordinates who accepted to *become* Baganda in pursuance of Mr. J. L. Berkeley's instructions, as contained in his despatch to the Marquis of Salisbury, dated 19th November, 1896:

"At the same time, however, that these Provinces became part of the Kingdom of Uganda so would their native inhabitants become *Waganda*..."

All the Magistrates in the Lost Counties are Baganda, and for the past sixty-one years, all the Chiefs who administer the Lost Counties have always been sent here from Buganda.

VIRTUAL ENSLAVEMENT

Despite the established fact that "slavery" long before the discussion and eventual signing of "The Atlantic Charter" by the great Nations of the world after the last War, it is to be deplored to find that Buganda Kingdom alone appears to be the only country among the many British Dependencies, that still cherishes and revives the vestiges of "slavery" and "exploitation".

At the time when the terms of the 1900 Agreement was signed, after careful mutual friendly discussions, residents in these 6 counties, were not informed, much less officially represented. This is 61 years ago. We were similarly left out of all consideration quite recently at the time of the discussion and signing of the 1955 Buganda Agreement. Our cable to the Secretary of State for the Colonies copied to His Excellency the Governor of Uganda, on this subject, refers.

Our continual bitter experience of "virtual enslavement" under the Buganda Government even at the present stage of our vaunted advancement in modern civilisation has, certainly, to some extent, caused us to revise our hitherto high opinion about the principles and implications of "British Justice".

As a direct result of the amalgamation of these six counties with Buganda Kingdom some forty-seven original Bunyoro local chiefs were after being got rid of by the new foreign ruling power, replaced by six County and 42 Gombolola Chiefs brought over from among the Baganda. As if not satisfied with such unjustified denial of the hereditary natural rights of the children of the soil over the government of our own undisputed land, these newly imported "alien" rulers soon after resorted to a gradual eviction of a considerable number of our own Banyoro Princes and Princesses from their hereditary estates in these six odd areas.

In pointing out all these matters, however, we would like to make it clear beyond any doubt to your Lordships that it is not our intention to request the Kabaka of Buganda to appoint Banyoro Chiefs and Judges to administer the Lost Counties. We do not ask the Commission to recommend such measures of redress, appointing us Chiefs within the Lost Counties, or asking the Kabaka's Government to remove any causes of our grievances. Our greatest fundamental grievance (which can be redressed in only one way) is to return us and our mother country to our rightful Ruler the Omukama of Bunyoro-Kitara who has our full reverence and trust in every way. We wish to add that the Omukama of Bunyoro is the only one we recognise to be the head and centre of our Clan System, our customs and traditions, our land, our language, and all our culture that distinguishes us from the Baganda and their Kabaka. We would like Commission to know that our patience and tolerance has been taxed for over sixty years and therefore we naturally feel that we can no longer put up with this moral suffering and loss of our rights as subjects of the Omukama Bunyoro-Kitara.

The transfer of these counties from Bunyoro to Buganda (a foreign administration) has retarded the development of our territories in many ways:

1. *Roads*: The whole road system, under the Kabaka's Government, is extremely poor. Most of the roads are quite impassable during the wet seasons. Some roads that lead to Bunyoro Kingdom have been neglected by the Baganda Chiefs for political reasons.

2. *Education and Languages*: The Missionaries deserve a word of thanks for opening and running a good number of primary and Junior Secondary Schools. We have been neglected by both Buganda and the Protectorate Governments for over fifty years, we have not been given bursaries and scholarships which have enabled the Baganda to receive higher education. At present the Buganda Government awards bursaries and scholarships only when our children have renounced their own tribe.

The suppression of our mother tongue, Runyoro, hurts us beyond imagination. Our children are taught in a foreign language in the very first years of their education, and this is, no doubt, a violation and mockery of the Universally established principles of education. Our language has been banned in Court, Offices, Churches in addition to Schools. Quite recently, a Munyoro old woman, Eyengonzi, wife of Isingoma of Bugangazzi, one of the lost counties, failed to give evidence in Luganda and was therefore remanded and later, fined.

3. *Land*: After the British Government annexed our counties to Buganda, the Baganda became the Land Lords with supreme powers in our country, we the Banyoro natives have been overlooked. Some of us have bought land from those favoured Baganda, who in most cases have refused us to buy the land where our grandfathers and fathers lived and even where we were born. This really hurts us beyond imagination, for we have been ill-treated on our own soil which was given to foreigners without our knowledge and acceptance.

4. *Taxation*: In this connection, even the British Government treats us differently from the Baganda. For the Arms Licence Tax, we pay ten Shillings whereas the Baganda pay four shillings. This is a proof beyond doubt that we are classified as foreigners in our own country. Even the present graduated taxation does not take into account our poor conditions of living. We are made to pay relatively higher taxes than the Baganda.

5. *Medical Health Services*: There is only one Hospital in the six lost counties. Whereas there is a reasonable number of dispensaries and Maternity units, we are faced with great difficulties since no Government Ambulances are available to carry the sick to the Central Hospitals, and medicine stocks are extremely small.

POLITICAL AND CONSTITUTIONAL MATTERS

Differences in Political Outlook

We should like to point out, however, that we are different not only traditionally, customarily but also politically to this day. On many occasions when there have been strikes, revolution, boycotts and all sorts of uprisings, namely: the 1945 revolt, the 1948/49 strike, the 1953 state of disturbance due to the Kabaka's exile and the 1959 trade boycott of non-African shops and goods we never united with the Baganda to do anything as such because we do not trust them. Their acts are always very rash and unestimated. Just as the Baganda cannot change their mind to owe their allegiance to Rukirabasaija Agutamba, the Omukama of Bunyoro-Kitara at the expense of their own Kabaka so shall the Banyoro never betray their own Kingdom. Our loyalty is still vested, as it were, in Rukirabasaija Agutamba Omukama of Bunyoro-Kitara to the very end of time.

Representation in the National Assembly

From the creation of Uganda's Legislature up to 1961 we were not represented on that Council until there were direct elections last year, and the people in the Lost Counties elected 4 representatives.

Now we feel greatly perturbed to see that we are still forced to remain under Buganda whose constitution allows a possibility of indirect elections to the National Assembly through the Buganda Lukiiko. Such undemocratic elections automaticaly deprive us of our right to elect representatives of our own choice, as the rest of Uganda will do. The government of Buganda has proved to be extremely unastable and there is not, as there has never been, any justification for further stay in Buganda. Hence our strong demand for the restoration of our land to Bunyoro Kingdom where we are sure to exercise our democratic rights without fear.

Disturbed Areas in the Lost Counties

It has already been stated in Government reports that the Lost Counties' issue has grown to the extent of causing considerable acts of violence and intimidation in the disputed areas. What is surprising is that instead of expediting the removal of the root cause of the said violence, Government chose to send large Police forces in the areas concerned. We would like the Commission to know that Buganda rule in the Lost Counties has been enforced only by the Protecting power. Once that protection is removed, so would the Buganda administration, automatically and without any question. The Banyoro have never accepted the loss of our legitimate rights, and we shall use all possible means to regain those basic rights.

Resolution and Declaration
of the Bunyoro, Rukurato (*Legislative Assembly*)

In October, 1961, shortly after the London Constitutional Conference, the Rukurato of Bunyoro-Kitara passed a declaration that the Lost Counties had reverted to Bunyoro as from mid-night on the day of October 18, 1961.

We all supported this move, since Her Majesty's Government had failed to effect any decision to settle our claims. Later in November, another measure was decided that Bunyoro should take the necessary steps to appoint Banyoro Chiefs to rule the Lost Counties with powers to collect the 1962 taxes. As a matter of fact we are only waiting for the appointment of those Chiefs to whom we shall pay our taxes of this year 1962. We are not prepared to pay our taxes to Buganda this year.

Self-Government and Independence for Uganda

Uganda is moving steadily towards selfgovernment and complete Independence. In our new Constitution every tribe is given an opportunity to run its own Government and to preserve all its traditions. We are sure that Your Lordships will appreciate the view that the Lost Counties should be no exception in this matter.

We ought to be given the same rights, the same privileges, and the same duties under our natural Ruler, the Omukama of Bunyoro-Kitara. What would happen if self-government and independence found us under Buganda rule is everyone's guess, but beyond our imagination, with the exception of one fact that we would then return to the slave trade age to suffer the greatest of cruelties in our history. Lastly, however, we still hope in British justice, freedom, peace, and democracy.

For a brief account of our endless suffering and struggle to free ourselves from the foreign rule of Anglo-Baganda Colonialism in the Lost Counties, we refer Your Lordships to Appendices A and B to this memorandum.

APPENDIX 1A

The following is a summary of the written history of the Banyoro's long struggle for peace and freedom in the lost counties since they were incorporated into Buganda:

1. Preliminary correspondence between the Mubende Banyoro Committee and the Resident, Buganda, early in the 1920's. Subsequent memoranda were issued by our Organisation to the British Government as listed below:
2. To H.E. the Governor of Uganda, dated 31st December, 1931.
3. To H.E. the Governor, dated 10th April, 1944.
4. To the Colonial Secretary, dated 25th April, 1951.
5. To the Colonial Secretary, dated 11th May, 1951.
6. To H.E. the Governor, dated 1st October, 1951.
7. To the Colonial Secretary, dated 1st November, 1951.
8. To H.E. the Governor, dated 16th January, 1952.
9. To H.E. the Governor, dated 26th May, 1952.
10. To H.E. the Governor, dated 12th September, 1952.
11. To H.E. the Governor, dated 18th March, 1953.
12. To the Colonial Secretary dated 23rd October, 1953.
13. To the Colonial Secretary, dated 21st June, 1954.
14. To the Colonial Secretary, dated August, 1954.
15. Telegram/Cable to Colonial Secretary, 1954.
16. To the Colonial Secretary, dated 5th August, 1955.
17. To the Colonial Secretary, dated 14th October, 1957.
18. Telegram to H.E. the Governor with a copy to the Colonial Secretary, dated 11th-September, 1959.
19. Evidence to Wild Constitutional Committee of 26.10.59.
20. Memorandum to H.M. The Queen dated 26th October, 1959.
21. To H.E. the Governor, dated July, 1960.
22. To H.E. the Governor (Ref. Byengonzi) dated 26.10.59.
23. To the Katikiros Conference copied to H.E. the Governor, dated September, 1960.
24. Delegation's address to Colonial Secretary dated 21st September, 1960.
25. To the Colonial Secretary, dated 28th October, 1960.
26. To the Colonial Secretary, dated 10th January, 1961.
27. To the Relationships Commission, dated 15 Jan., 1961.

Many more correspondence and oral evidence have been submitted to the British Government from the beginning of our enslavement to this very day, yet, unfortunately, our legitimate demands have not been met.

APPENDIX 1B

A SUMMARY FOR SOME OF THE INNUMERABLE INSTANCES OF MALTREATMENT, MISGOVERNMENT, AND VICTIMISATION

1. The earliest Baganda Chiefs, namely, Noli Njagi, Mabanga, Semeo Ssenkatuka, Sepria Mutagwanya, Titi Kawesi and many other used the most inhuman measures of beating, making us carry very heavy stones, tying us to trees like goats, and many other forms of torture so as to enforce their rule in these counties. They took away our animals, people, and property by force and made us work like slaves.

2. Saza Chiefs like Auguste Kibuka of Buyaga, (1933), Yonna Yakuza, Buyaga also, (1940's), and S. Kiruruta of Bugangaizi, (1960) issued orders prohibiting the use of Runyoro language at all official and religious places.

3. Messrs Bonifansi Kasaija, Raphael Gahwerra, Peter Tibamwenda, Temuteo Kasambura, and many other have been falsely prosecuted and imprisoned just because they opposed Buganda rule and supported the views of our Committee: the restoration of the lost counties.

4. Three Buyaga Representatives were expelled from the Buganda Lukiiko late in 1956 just because they aired or upheld the Banyoro's demands in the lost lands.

5. In 1958, the Saza Chief of Bugangaizi, Mr. S. Kiruruta, and the Chief of Buyaga, Mr. I. Ndawula, decided to prevent all our members, e.g. M/s. Kosea Rwebembera, Joseph Kazairwe; James Mukas, Andrea Lubega, and very many others from standing for election to the Lukiiko, just because they were Banyoro.

6. An old Munyoro woman, Byengonzi w/o Isingoma, who failed to speak Luganda in a Buganda Court at Malweyo, Bugangaizi, was imprisoned at once for fortnight and later fined Shs. 75/- by a Muganda Magistrate, Mr. C. Kawooya, on 16th June, 1960.

7. In September, 1960, a Buyaga representative, Mr. J. Kazairwe was manhandled by a gang of lawless Baganda traditionalists who invaded the Bulange at Mengo to eject only the members who opposed Mengo Government and told him that he was being ejected because he was a supporter of restoring the lost counties to Bunyoro.

8. Saza Chief Kyambalango of Buyaga, Mr. Kayemba, told a Gombolola Council in his own county that he had bought firearms and ammunition for shooting all the Banyoro who oppose Buganda rule. This happened when that county was a disturbed area towards the end of 1960.

9. A Headmaster of Kikoma Junior Secondary School, in Buwekula County, Mr. Sajjabi—Ssemouuze, just recently proved that for three years he has blocked the way of his own pupils to higher Schools. His own pupils have discovered that their application forms to other Secondary and Training Colleges were destroyed by him. And in his term of office as headmaster, hardly any pupils have been admitted to higher schools.

10. When R. A. the Omukama of Bunyoro travelled through Mubende District last year, many Banyoro people gathered on the roads with an ardent desire to pay our homage to the Omukama, our natural Ruler, from whom we have been separated by the Protectorate Government for over sixty years. Our acts of loyalty greatly disappointed the Baganda Chiefs, because we did what we have never done for the Kabaka of Buganda 1900. Consequently, the Kabaka's Government, in co-operation with the Protectorate Government Officers arrested some of the Banyoro who gathered to greet the Omukama, prosecuted them and sent them to prison for periods of 6 months and one year each as shown hereunder:

(i)   Kosea Rwebembera of Kakumiro, Bugangaizi, sentenced to 6 months' imprisonment at the Magistrate's Court of the Kabaka's Government.

(ii)   Andred Kafero of Muhorro, Gombolola of Sabaddu, Buyaga, sentenced to 12 months' imprisonment.

(iii) John Bagwa of Muhorro, Gombolola of Sabaddu, Buyaga, sentenced to 12 months' imprisonment.

Whereas the last mentioned was released by the Judicial Advisers, the first has already served his sentence while the second is still in prison at the Kabaka's Government Central Prison, Kigo, near Kampala.

APPENDIX 2

UGANDA CONSTITUTIONAL CONFERENCE 1961
RESTORATION OF BUNYORO'S LOST COUNTIES

Memorandum by the Katikiro of Bunyoro Kingdom
Mr. Z. H. Kwebiha

This paper is submitted for consideration by the Uganda Constitutional Conference, since it raises one of the important issues contained in the *Munster Report, Chapter 12: Boundary Disputes.*

Introduction

The term "lost counties" refers to Bunyoro's six counties comprising an area of over 6,000 sq. miles of Bunyoro territory which was given away to Buganda by the then British Commissioner, Mr. E. J. L. Berkeley, on November 19, 1896. Reference: Appendix I the Queen, Page 36. In this connection, it is worth recording the fact that Mr. Berkeley gave away these counties after Unyoro (Bunyoro Kingdom) had already been declared by the Foreign Office of Her Majesty's Government a British Protectorate on 30th June 1896 and was published in the London Gazette of 3rd July 1896. This declaration reads as follows:

"The territory of Unyoro, together with that part of the British sphere of influence lying to the west of Uganda and Unyoro which has not hitherto been included in the Uganda Protectorate, is placed within the limits of the Protectorate, which includes also Usoga and the other territories to the east under the administration of Her Majesty's Commissioner and Consul-General for the Protectorate".

It is also worth to note that the Agreement which conferred British Protection on Buganda in 1893 was confirmed by a notification in the London Gazette of 19th June 1894. It reads as follows:

"It is hereby notified for public information that under and by virtue of the Agreement concluded on 29th May, 1893, between the late Sir G. Portal and Mwanga, King of Uganda, the country of that ruler is placed under the protectorate of Her Majesty the Queen.

This Protectorate comprises the territory known as Uganda Proper, bounded by the territories known as Usoga, Unyoro, Ankole and Koki".

Previous to the signing of the Buganda Agreement on 29th May, 1893, two other Agreements which had been entered into by King Mwanga of Buganda and the British Imperial East African Company in 1890 and 1892 were not honoured by that Kabaka. As will be seen later on the 1893 (1894) Agreement was also dishonoured by him.

It is necessary to record here briefly that on 4th *December, 1893.* the British declared war on Bunyoro and an invasion of the country was launched by a British force accompanied by Buganda spearmen. The confusion and unsettled conditions in Buganda at the time mainly caused by Mwanga's attitude made it necessary for the British to instruct Kabaka Mwanga to order a general mobilisation of the Baganda so as to avoid further fighting amongst the rival factions in Buganda itself, while the invasion of Bunyoro was on.

It is worth recording here that the last battle between Bunyoro and Buganda was fought in 1886 when a large Baganda army under Kangso [sic] was utterly defeated at Rwengali and the Muganda General himself killed.

The preceding paragraph is just to enable the reader to understand that it was not Buganda which declared war on Bunyoro but that Baganda only assisted the British invading force in just the same way as East Africans (Kenya Africans, Uganda Africans and Tanganyika Africans) took part in the 1914 and 1939–1945 wars against Germany. Buganda was the scene of religious and civil wars until Kabaka Mwanga himself fled the country into Tanganyika. In 1897 he escaped from German territory, passed through Buddu after fighting a battle and then escaped to join King Kabarega in Lango District. King Mwanga had with him a Baganda army when he joined Kabarega. The two Kings were captured on 9th April, 1899 and deported to the Seychelles Island in the Indian Ocean. King Kabarega was kept in exile for 24 years (i.e. until 1923).

Sir Harry Johnston after two months stay in the country concluded the 1900 Agreement with the Regents of Buganda on 10th March. The main signatory to this Agreement was Sir Apolo Kagwa, the Katikiro.

Concerning some of the counties claimed by Bunyoro, Sir Apolo Kagwa has this to say in his book "Basekabaka ba Buganda" (King of Buganda):

"*Buyaga*: From old times this country belonged to the King of Bunyoro, but after Mwanga's return in 1896, it was given to the Baganda. There was then established the country of Kyambalango.

Bululi: (This includes a large part of North Singo now claimed by Bunyoro).

"For all times that country belonged to the King of Bunyoro who had the following chiefs in charge of the area: Banda, Kabagambe, Kadoma (Chief of North Singo), Kadyebo, Mutengesa (Chief of North Singo) and Princess Nyangoma. But in the year 1896 the country was given to the Baganda . . . . "

Bugerere (Bunyara) "This country also belonged to the King of Bunyoro who had his Chief Nyamuyojo in charge of the area. On 24th May, 1895, Semei Kakengulu after deserting the Kimbugreship, went and settled in that area until 1899 when he left and went to Bukedi. On 10th March, 1900, the area was made into a county . . . . "

In a book called "Amanya Amaganda nenono zaago" written by Mr. N. Simli more or less the same things are confirmed regarding the counties of Buruli, Bugangaizi, Buyaga and Bugerere (See page 88 and 89).

Note: Buwekula

Under Bunyoro rule, this territory no doubt formed part of the Kingdom of Bunyoro, generally known as Bugangaizi. In Buwekula are situated the royal sacred hills of *Mubende* and *Buuru* where all ceremonial coronation functions took place throughout our history, down to King Kabalega's reign. The traditional caretaker of these sacred sites, NYAKAHUMA, remained in charge of our ceremonial grounds on Mubende Hill (i.e. the present District Headquarters) until she was removed by the British Officials in the year 1907. The Uganda Agreement 1900 was no more than one made to settle the land problem in Buganda because of the difficulty of spheres of influences of rival religous factions. As indicated above, well over 6,000 square miles of Banyoro land (half the area of the entire Kingdom) were incorporated in Buganda and the indigenous people the Banyoro thus became tenants of the Baganda who had entered the Country six years previously (out of this total area approximately 2,000 square miles were given to Baganda Land Lords as freehold title).

Discrimination:

(a) As a result of the transfer of Banyoro territory to the Baganda, the indigenous people became tenants and had to rent to the Baganda to occupy their own land. A few Banyoro have had to purchase freehold land from the Baganda.

(b) The language of the people (Runyoro) was banned in Churches, offices, Courts, schools and other official places.

(c) The entire clan system of the people became disorganised and Birth Registers at Gombololas have been a means of annihilating the identity and custom of the Banyoro in their own country.

(d) The indigenous people (the Banyoro) have been regarded as serfs and sabordinate to their rulers. Not a single person in the entire 6 Lost Counties have ever been made a Saza Chief during the past sixty years. There are only a few Banyoro Gombolola Chiefs and even these are transferred to predominantly Baganda areas and they must identify themselves as Baganda. Nearly all Miruka and Batongolo Chiefs are Baganda.

(c) Scholarships awarded to Banyoro children are very few if any and one must declare that he is a Muganda. In fact a certain School in Bugangaizi bursary forms submitted by Banyoro pupils were each year locked or concealed by the Muganda Headmaster with the result that for many years no bursories were awarded to those children at all until the parents had to take action against the teacher. For the past sixty years, only five natives of the lost counties have received overseas scholarships from the Buganda Government.

The above are only a few examples.

Campaign to restore the Counties back to Bunyoro

(a) In 1907 there was an uprising in Bunyoro known as Ekyanyangire whose aim was to force the Baganda Chiefs out of the country since more than half the area of the Kingdom had been given to Buganda. Many prominent Chiefs were deported to Kenya and some were fined heavily.

(b) In 1921 the people in the lost counties started an association or a political party known as the Banyoro Committee to campaign for the restoration to Bunyoro of the counties. It is probably the first political party to be started in the whole of Uganda.

(c) The abdication of Omukama Yosiya Kitehimbwe had in the main to do with a move for the return of the 'Lost Counties!

(d) All successive Governors of Uganga have on all their visits to Bunyoro been petitioned for the return of the counties. There are Volumes of files in the Secretariat at Entebbe and no doubt at the Colonial Office.

(e) On 7th May, 1931, the demand for the return of the 'lost counties' was first discussed at the Colonial Office when Prince Yosiya Labwoni who was on the Uganda delegation on Closer Union for East Africa made representations. The Hon. S. W. Kulubya, the leader of that delegation was present and he also spoke about the matter. He urged that the matter should be referred back to the Governor in Uganda.

(f) At the signing of the Bunyoro Agreement on 23rd October, 1933, R. A. Omukama raised the matter in his speech. (About 1930, there was a move to hand back these areas to Bunyoro but for unknown reasons it did not materialise. Professor Ingham also mentions this in his book, *Making of Modern Uganda*.

Bunyoro's Constitutional approach to settle the problem

(a) In January 1955 the return of the counties was raised with H.E. Governor, Sir Andrew Cohen, where discussing the new Bunyoro Agreement 1955.

(b) While discussing the Buganda Agreement 1955 in London, the Bunyoro Rukurato sent a telegram to the Colonial Secretary (Mr. Littleton) asking for participation to discuss the boundary between Buganda and Bunyoro. The people in the 'Lost Counties' also asked that their areas should not be included in a new Buganda Agreement (1955). The reply from the Government was that the question of boundaries was not to be discussed.

(c) On 5th October, 1955 a Bunyoro delegation led by Dr. Muganwa, Chief Judge of Bunyoro, met the Governor at Entebbe to discuss the matter. The Governor stated that the matter could not be re-opened.

(d) On 22nd August, 1956, a twelve-man delegation went to Mengo and met the Kabaka's Minister to discuss a problem which affected the Kingdoms. The Conference proved a complete failure as the Kabaka's Ministers, despite the Katikiro of Buganda's letter agreeing to hold talks, refused to discuss the matter. My speech at Mengo and the Statement issued to the press are attached to this paper.

Petitions

(a) Ever since its inception in 1921, the Banyoro Committee has sent numerous letters and telegrams both to the Governor and the Secretary of State demanding that they be restored to their mother Kingdom, Bunyoro. In fact there are volumes of files on the subject in Entebbe.

(b) On 8th March, 1948, R. A. Omukama of Bunyoro submitted to the Secretary of State a memorandum in the form of a booklet entitled "The Bunyoro's Claim of their Lost Lands". The booklet has 46 pages.

Petition to the Privy Council

In 1957 a Bunyoro delegation visited London and obtained Legal Opinion on the matter by Leading Counsel, Mr. R. W. O. Wilberforce (he is now a judge of the High Court of England). This opinion was made available to the Governor of Uganda and as a result the Colonial Office Legal Advisor (Sir Keneth Robert Wray). After studying the document, he produced an opinion and in his Note to his own opinion doubted the legal validity of the transfer of the lands to Buganda by Britain.

In March/April, 1958, another two-man delegation from Bunyoro visited London and met the then Secretary of State for the Colonies, Mr. Lennox Boyd, who promised that the British Government would use justice when the Omukama's petition was presented.

On 27th November, 1958, the Omukama's Patition to the Privy Council was received by Her Majesty The Queen at Buckingham Palace. In a letter acknowledging receipt of the Petition, Her Majesty's Secretary stated that the Petition would be forwarded to the Secretary of State for the Colonies as he was the Minister responsible for advising The Queen on this subject.

There was then a long period to get a reply as to what was being done with the Petition.

On 23rd November, 1959, a six-man Bunyoro delegation led by myself met H.E. the Governor and his Senior Advisers at Entebbe. A lengthy discussion ensued when it was pointed out that the matter was still being studied as it had legal complexities. The Governor stated that he had written to the Colonial Secretary on 18th November, 1959, urging him to take action in the matter.

On 12th December, 1959, R. A. Omukama and his advisers met the Secretary of State at Entebbe to discuss the matter.

Other Meetings

13th August, 1960, at Entebbe, Acting Governor met Omukama of Bunyoro with his advisers.

20th September, 1960, Secretary of State for the Colonies met R. A. Omukama and his advisers, including a London lawyer to discuss the subject of leave to submit the Petition to the Privy Council.

On 9th February, 1961, a Bunyoro delegation met the Governor at Entebbe and I quote from a record of the meeting made:

"In answer to a question by Mr. Magezi, His Excellency said that it would be possible for alterations to the Buganda and Bunyoro agreements to be negotiated to provide for any change in boundaries which might be agreed upon as a result of the Constitutional Conference in London."

15th July, 1961, H.E. the Governor, met R. A. Omukama and his advisers to discuss the 'Lost Counties' issue and the Petition submitted in 1958.

Privy Council

In spite of the exhaustive ways taken by Bunyoro to have the matter settled which has involved the Bunyoro Government in considerable expenditure, the British Government have, hitherto, refused to refer the Omukama's Petition to the Privy Council. No official reply from the British Government has been given so far.

Asked to give the legal reasons for not referring the Petition to the Privy Council, the Colonial Secretary and his advisers on 10th August, 1961, stated that the Colonial Office was not bound to give reasons. This took place in London when R. A. Omukama and his advisers met the Secretary of State for the Colonies to discuss the Petition at the latter's invitation (vide his letter of 30th June this year).

At one stage, in 1960, the British Government directed that the Kabaka should be provided with a copy of the Petition as the Kabaka's Government was directly involved in the case.

The Kabaka's reply and comment on the Petition is given in his letter 420/B dated the 18th June, 1960, addressed to H.E. the Governor. In this letter His Highness opposes the Petition being referred to the Privy Council. Yet, the Kabaka admitted the possibility of alteration of the Bunyoro-Buganda boundaries in the following words:

> "If it were decided, largely on historical grounds, to alter boundaries, boundaries which have remained unchanged for more than sixty years, it would be inequitable that revision should be confined to the Territories referred to in the Petition. My Government might well decide to put forward claims to any or all of the lands which formed part of the ancient Kingdom of Buganda."

The Munster Report recommendation

The first sentence in paragraph 247 of the report reads:
"*We emphasise that we have no desire to suggest the ratification of boundaries for purely historical reasons.*"

Contrary to the above, the last sentence in paragraph 250 the Commission has this to say, "*On the other hand we must remember Buganda's services to the Protectorate in its early years.*"

Presumably, Buganda's early services include such things as the Baganda themselves fighting against their own Kabaka in Buganda and the Baganda's participation in the battles against the Sudanese in the mutiny at Lubwa's. If that is the case then there can be no justification in using Banyoro lands and sovereignty as rewards for such services.

With regard to the Census, it should be remembered that this was carried out in 1959 a year after Bunyoro had lodged her petition for the return of the Counties. It is admitted in the report that the figures given in paragraph 251 of the report are disputed by Bunyoro. These figures reveal unbelievable discrepancies as will be shown down below when the 1948 Census figures for Mubende and parts of North Singo are compared.

In the Census of 1948 published by the East African Statistical Department 1950 (Geographical and tribal studies), the population of Mubende District is composed as follows:

> Banyoro   70% (See page 17)
> Baganda   21%

According to the 1959 Census, the percentage of Banyoro in Mubende has dropped to about 54% and that of Baganda has risen to 28% in a period of 11 years!

Other figures of interest are given here below:

Gombolola	Tribe	1948 %	1959 %
Mutuba II Singo	Banyoro	55	12
	Baganda	39	63
Munyoke Bugargazzi	Banyoro	89	88
	Baganda	9	9
Sabadu ,,	Banyoro	81	39 ?
	Baganda	14	53 ?
Sabagabo ,,	Banyoro	90	79
	Baganda	6	12
Sabawali ,,	Banyoro	85	84
	Baganda	11	12
Musale ,,	Banyoro	87	86
	Baganda	9	8
Munyoke Buwekula	Banyoro	25	14
	Baganda	61	61
Sabadu ,,	Banyoro	27	2 ?
	Baganda	68	91 ?
Sabagabo ,,	Banyoro	45	14 ?
	Baganda	26	37
Sabawali ,,	Banyoro	42	7 ?
	Baganda	46	76 ?
Musale ,,	Banyoro	46	25
	Baganda	$46\frac{1}{2}$	59

Resolution of Katikiro's and Secretaries General Conference

Two resolutions have recently been passed by the Conference of the Katikiro's and Secretaries-General of Uganda, which sat at Jinja in August last. The last resolution passed is quoted herebelow:

"Whereas it is now clear that Her Majesty's Government has evaded to give a decision on the Lost Caunties issue before going to the Uganda Constitutional Conference in London;

"And whereas it is the view of this Conference that it is likely there shall be serious trouble if Uganda attains independence before this matter is settled;

"And whereas this Conference has understood the historical mistake made by Her Majesty's Government in handing over the Lost Counties to Buganda;

"And whereas this Conference is greatly concerned about political tension going on within the Lost Counties."

Now, therefore be it resolved:

That this Conference urges Her Majesty's Government to rectify the mistake before the country attains her independence.

That this Conference is strongly of the opinion that proposals for settling the matter such as recommended by the Munster Commission must be discussed at the forthcoming London Conference by all those taking part in the Conference.

Uganda Press and 'Buganda's Position'

The issue of the Lost Counties has been the subject of numerous articles in the Uganda newspapers both English and Vernacular for many years.

In the booklet 'Buganda's Position' published by the Katikiro of Buganda recently and in a document 'Buganda's Independence' which was signed by all Lukiiko Members, the 1900 Agreement is denounced and disowned and only the 1894 Agreement is recognised. This is a very important point as regards the boundary between Bunyoro and Buganda. Bunyoro agrees fully with the 1894 Buganda Agreement in so far as boundaries between the two Kingdoms are concerned.

Historically and factually there can therefore be no conquest by Buganda of the six Counties.

Disturbed Area:

This aspect of the matter is covered by the report of the Munster Commission. The position even today is that a large police force has had to be sent to some of the areas of the Lost Counties and more Police sub-stations have been established and roads patrolled by motorised units of the Police who are equiped with radio transmitters.

Conclusion

A new Constitution for Buganda and Uganda is being negotiated now. The new Buganda Agreement is designed to replace the Buganda Agreements of 1894, 1900 and 1955. This new Agreement will then become not only the Constitution of Buganda but part of the Constitution of the whole of Uganda and will be binding for all times.

The new Buganda Agreement must exclude Bunyoro's six Counties. There is no justification whatsoever to keep these Counties again within the boundaries of Buganda. After all Buganda's interest in the area is freehold land and under the principles of a bill of Human rights these rights will have to be respected by Bunyoro.

The Constitutional Conference is here to work a Constitution to enable the country to move forward smoothly and in peace. Britain is withdrawing her Colonial rule and Baganda Colonial rule in Bunyoro's Counties should not be allowed to continue. The Counties should be returned now.

APPENDIX 2A

Appendices to document U.C.C. (61)19 by Mr. Z. H. Kwebiha, Katikiro of Bunyoro on the "Lost Counties".
Extract from paragraphs 25 and 27 of "Enquiry into Land Tenure and the Kibanja System in Bunyoro, 1931". (Published by Uganda Government)

"Para. 25.
Although for some years the scene of much disturbance, Baganda Chiefs gradually established and consolidated interests in these occupied counties and it was generally understood that they were, or were to be, added to Buganda as a reward for its loyalty and assistance. This area within which many of the earlier Bunyoro Kings had maintained their headquarters and had been buried, was of course inhabited by Bunyoro tribesmen, for the most part of servile agricultural clans, and many of these thus became tenants of Baganda Landlords".

"Para. 27.
Finally, on 10th March, 1900, Sir Harry Johnston entered into the Uganda Agreement. By this agreement the boundaries of Uganda were formally advanced to the Kafu-Nkusi Rivers, and the final dismemberment of Bunyoro, which was thus confirmed in its present dimensions, was complete". Bunyoro's claims to suzerainty on the western side of Lake Albert still remained but were finally ceded to the Belgians as a result of the Anglo-Congolese Boundary Commission of 1906/08.

APPENDIX 2B

The Speech of the Owekitinisa Katikiro of Bunyoro-Kitara at Mengo on the 22nd of August, 1956, at the opening of the negotiations with Buganda Government about Bunyoro's counties ceded to Buganda

The Owekitibwa Katikiro of Buganda, Abebitibwa the Ministers and Members of the Buganda and Bunyoro Delegations. The 22nd day of August, 1956 will be recorded as an important and memorable day in the history of Uganda. Important, in that it is first occasion when two African Governments of Uganda have sat at a round table to discuss a problem which greatly affects them.

I am convinced that it is the bounden duty of Buganda and Bunyoro to do everything that within our power lies to foster the progress and development of Uganda. Indeed the whole of Uganda should see to it that all causes of mistrust, misunderstandings and grievances are amicably settled.

That His Highness the Kabaka permitted his Government to negotiate with R. A. Omukama's Government about Bunyoro's Counties wrongfully ceded to Buganda is gratifying.

The Counties under discussion today are clearly known to have been part and parcel of the Kingdom of Bunyoro, and in saying this I have history to support me. The following are the Counties in question: Buhekura, Buyaga, Bugangaizi, Rugonjo (North Ssingo), Buruli and Bunyara (Bugerere). These Counties have immeasurable importance and significance attached to them in our traditions, indeed they are the very heart and care of the Bunyoro Kingdom.

I suggest, and I confidently trust, that we will all approach this problem in a responsible, sincere and fair minded spirit, which alone will put an end to mistakes and misunderstandings which have for a long time existed between us; in so doing we shall be pursuing the correct way towards greater development of Uganda.

The importance of these discussions cannot be over-emphasised for the whole of Uganda, and in fact, all the Countries interested in the welfare and progress of Uganda are keenly waiting to hear of the results of these negotiations. I therefore sincerely hope that these talks will lead us to a successful settlement of the problem.

APPENDIX 2C

Statement made by Katikiro of Bunyoro on Buganda—Bunyoro meeting held at Mengo on Tuesday 22nd August, 1956— re-Bunyoro's Counties ceded to Buganda

After receiving a letter from Owekitibwa Katikiro of Buganda permitting the Bunyoro delegation to come and "CONFER" with the Buganda Government Ministers on the question of the ceded counties of Bunyoro wrongfully included in Buganda, the Bunyoro delegation met Ministers of Buganda in the Katikiro's Office at Mengo this morning at 10 a.m.

In a short welcome speech, Owekitibwa Kintu said that "We allowed the Bunyoro delegation to come so as to hear what you have got to tell us. In reply the Owekitinisa Katikiro of Bunyoro said (see Katikiro's speech attached).

The Owekitibwa Kintu said he was sorry he was not prepared to add anything at all to the reply given by Her Majesty's Government about this problem of Bunyoro's ceded counties. It was pointed to him that in his letter No. S.P. 1/4 dated 2nd August, 1956 he said Ministers of the Kabaka's Government will be ready to confer with the Bunyoro delegation on the Mubende counties, he could not agree with this but insisted that besides what he had already said he would add *absolutely nothing*.

Then there followed a discussion in which the Bunyoro delegates tried, in vain, to stress the need for an amicable settlement of all problems and misunderstandings which are interfering with the unity of all the people of Uganda—a unity which is a sine quo non for the attainment of Self-Government for Uganda. The Owekitibwa Katikiro of Buganda, however, said that since Buganda had already made an agreement with H.M. Government in Britain, the ministers were out and out to preserve in its entirety ((BUTIRIBIRI) that agreement. Anybody who failed in that would be failing in his duty towards his country in particular and towards Uganda in general, said Mr. Kintu. The Bunyoro delegation were however of the opinion that agreements are made and amended whenever it is considered necessary, and that an agreement was a means and not an end in itself, and therefore should not be allowed to interfere with our main object of achieving Self-Government for Uganda.

After seeing that there was no development made about this crucial point, the Owekitinisa Katikiro of Buganda asked the Owekitibwa Kintu whether he would be prepared to issue to the press a joint statement on what had happened. But Owekitibwa Kintu could not agree to this joint statement and instead preferred to instruct the Information Officer, Buganda to publish a statement on behalf of H.M. Government.

APPENDIX 2D

Copy of H.H. Kabaka's letter No. 420/B dated 18th June, 1960 to H.E. Governor of Uganda.

Your Excellency,

I refer to the Resident's letters; No. C.54/13/01 of 27th April and 27th May, regarding the petition of the Omukama of Bunyoro to Her Majesty the Queen. My comments are as follows:

1. It is proposed that the questions raised in the petition shall be referred to the Privy Council "for consideration and determination". It is not clear what form of reference is contemplated. If what is intended is a special reference to the Judicial Committee of the Privy Council under Section 4 of the Act of 1833, it seems to me that this course would be wholly inappropriate. The purpose of a special reference is to obtain the opinion of their Lordships of the Judicial Committee on a question of Law."

    The issues raised by this petition are essentially historical and political rather than legal. Moreover, the allegations of misgovernment involve questions of fact which could certainly not be determined on a special reference.

2. If, however, the reference is not to the Judicial Committee and is to include questions of policy as well as Law. I would observe that the inclusion of the six counties in the Kingdom of Buganda was clearly recognised in the Uganda Agreement 1900 which now forms part of the Buganda Agreements 1900 to 1955. I am advised that so long as these Agreements remain in force, they are binding on both parties and connot be unilaterally varied. I have always understood that this view was shared by Her Majesty's Government, and in this connection I would refer to the speech made in the Legislative Council by the Chief Secretary on the 15th November, 1955. I cannot therefore see what purpose the proposed reference would serve, since Her Majesty's Government could not give effect to any recommendations favourable to the petitioner without a breach of their treaty obligations.

3. If it were decided, largely on historical grounds, to alter boundaries which have remained unchanged for more than sixty years, it would be inequitable that revision should be confined to the Territories referred to in the Petition. My Government might well decide to put forward claims to any or all of the lands which formed part of the ancient Kingdom of Buganda.

4. Paragraphs 34–57 of the petition set out a number of complaints some of which are of a minor—one might almost say trivial—description. I would point out that such grievances can be raised at any time in the Great Lukiiko by the eighteen members who represent the Territories in question.

APPENDIX 3

MINUTES OF THE SEVENTH CONFERENCE OF THE
KATIKIROS AND SECRETARIES-GENERAL OF
UGANDA AND THEIR ADVISERS, HELD AT JINJA
FROM 15th TO 17th AUGUST, 1961

PRESENT:

Busoga
Mr. Y. K. Mulondo, Chairman.
Mr. J. B. Lubandi, Adviser.
Mr. Y. B. Walukamba, M.B.E.,
  Adviser.
Mr. W. B. Mwangu, Adviser.
Mr. W. B. Mwangu, Adviser.

Acholi
Mr. W. O. Lutara, Secretary-
  General.

Ankole
Mr. K. K. Nganwa, Enganzi.
Mr. P. K. Kanyamunyu, Adviser.
Mr. E. L. Kyoya, Adviser.

Bukedi
Mr. Y. M. Kirya, Secretary-
  General.
Mr. Y. F. Wafula, Adviser.
Mr. J. P. Otimu, Adviser.

Bugisu
Mr. J. G. Wanyoto, Secretary-
  General.
Mr. G. W. N. Bwayo, Adviser.

Bunyoro
Mr. Z. H. Kwebina, Katikiro.
Dr. I. K. Majugo, Adviser.
Mr. E. R. Muchwa, Adviser.

Mr. J. C. Rujumba, Secretary to
  delegates.

Kigezi
Mr. K. M. S. Kikira, Secretary-
  General.
Mr. H. Kakuyo, Adviser.
Mr. S. Mukombe—Mpambara,
  Adviser.

Karamoja
Mr. E. L. Athiyo, Secretary-
  General

Lango
Mr. Y. L. Otimu Ag. Secretary-
  General.
Mr. Akena Adoko, Legal Adviser.
Mr. J. M. Okae, Adviser.

Madi
Mr. David Luga, Secretary
  General.
Mr. P. A. Labite, Adviser.
Mr. C. E. Lou, Adviser.

Teso
Mr. S. E. Egweu, Secretary-
  General.
Mr. G. E. Takau, Adviser.
Mr. P. E. Esabu, Adviser.

Toro
Mr. M.B. Gafabusa, Adviser.
Mr. D. R. Boguma, Adviser.

KSG/16/61 COMMUNICATION FROM THE CHAIR

When he addressed the conference, Mr. Y. K. Mulondo, the Secretary General of Busoga and Chairman of Conference, again welcomed all the delegates to Busoga and hoped they would enjoy their stay in Jinja. He said that he had little to say since it was a continuation of the previous conference.

He announced that His Excellence the Governor had agreed to address the conference on the following day and would arrive at 10.30 a.m. after following day. He then advised the delegates to prepare questions which would be put before His Excellency the Governor after his speech.

KSG/17/61 CONFIRMATION OF THE PREVIOUS MINUTES

(a) *Gulu Conference*

The Conference rejected the minutes on the ground that there were omissions and discrepancies e.g. the summary at the end of the meeting. It was then unanimously agreed that the minutes should be rewritten and they should include all the missing points, before they are confirmed.

(b) *Jinja Conference*

After amending the word "landy" page 13, first line in the last paragraph, to read "lady" the minutes, having been circulated and read, were confirmed and signed by the Chairman as correct record.

KSG/18/61 MATTERS ARISING FROM JINJA CONFERENCE:

1. *KSG/7/61: The London Conference*

In view of their previous resolution that THREE delegates should be sent from each District to the London Conference, the delegates considered the representation of ONE delegate from each District to be totally inadequate; and they unanimously agreed after a long debate to take up the matter with His Excellency the Governor during question time.

11.00–11.20 a.m. BREAK.

Later (16/8/1961), the Conference authorised the Chairman to write to His Excellency, informing him that the Conference still sticks to its previous resolution that THREE delegates should represent each District at the London Conference.

2. *KSG/12/61: The Chief Minister's Address*

It was agreed that the question raised by Mr. Kwebiha that the Chief Minister should be asked to make his views and the views of his party on the Munster Report known to the general public before the London Conference should be shelved and discussed in any other business. Later (17/8/1961 it was unanimously dropped.

KSG/19/61: THE QUESTIONS PREPARED FOR HIS EXCELLENCY

(a) During the course of the business, the conference prepared and approved: the following questions for His Excellency the Governor to answer:

1. To ask him how many delegates will represent Buganda at the London Conference; to be asked by Dr. Majugo.
2. To ask the Governor how indirect election of Buganda representatives to the National Assembly would work democratically—to be asked by Mr. Egweu.
3. To ask the Governor the reason for not voting at the London Conference, to be asked by Mr. Akena.
4. To ask the Governor the reason for holding the Conference in London—to be asked by Mr. Kirya.
5. To ask the Governor what he thinks of the preliminary talks before proceeding to London—to be asked by Mr. D. Luga.
6. To ask the Governor about Bunyoro's burning question of the lost counties (Conference's resolution, page 12 of Jinja Minutes para. 4) to be asked by Mr. Okae.
7. To ask the Governor why the default powers exclude Buganda (page 180); to be asked by Mr. Lubandi.
8. To ask the Governor if there will be a new agreement for Buganda in case the London Conference fails; to be asked by Mr. Nganwa.
9. Mr. Kwebiha to ask the Governor as resolved in Minute KSG/11/61 page 7, 1(a) (Buganda's relationship to the Central Government)
10. Mr. Okae to ask the Governor about the misuse of power by the Central Government (by making their political tours semi-Officials and making officers of the Local Governments their agents).
11. To ask the Governor to give the status of the delegates to the London Conference—to be asked by Mr. Wanyoto.
12. Mr. Esabu to raise the question of the special Court for Buganda
13. Mr. Lutara to ask for the draft copies of the work of the Commissioner on Special Duties.

KSG/20/61 MR. JOMO KENYATTA

The Conference unanimously decided to send the following telegram to Mr. Jomo Kenyatta:

"CONFERENCE OF KATIKIROS AND SECRETARIES GENERAL OF UGANDA ASSEMBLED AT JINJA OFFER YOU AND PEOPLE OF KENYA WARM CONGRATULATIONS ON YOUR RELEASE FROM LONG IMPRISONMENT AND SUBSEQUENT RESTRICTIONS AND FOR YOUR FIGHT FOR AFRICAN FREEDOM."

The meeting adjourned at 1.15 p.m.

The meeting on the 16th August, 1961 at 9. a.m.
The meeting opened with prayer.

KSG/21/61 ADMISSION OF THE PRESS

It was unanimously agreed THAT the Press and Information should be present during His Excellency the Governor's speech and question time.

KSG/22/61: THE MUNSTER REPORT

(a) *The Legal System (Report page 170–172)*

Mr. Kwebiha, Bunyoro said that the clause, "In future the Principal Court should have jurisdiction over all races" was not clear to him and wondered if it would be applicable to all Districts or Buganda alone. He went on to say that each District should have customary laws written down. The Chairman made it clear that steps will be taken by the Central Gov't regarding the proper framing of the customary Ordinance.

Mr. Okae then wanted to know what was happening in other districts with regard to legal representation. It had been resolved in Lango that advocates should start forthwith to represent the accused. He was informed by the chairman that since most of our Magistrates are not well versed in law, it would be inopportune to back the system at this juncture; however it will be very useful after the present arrangement of training the magistrates at Nsamizi.

After some discussion, it was agreed THAT the question "why Buganda should have special Courts" should be taken up by Mr. Esabu with His Excellency the Governor.

10.15–10.30 BREAK.

KSG/23/61 THE GOVERNOR'S ADDRESS

At 10.35 His Excellency the Governor escorted by Mr. Badenoch and the Hon. Bataringaya the Minister of Local Government arrived.

He was welcomed by Mr. Y. K. Mulondo who asked him to address the conference on the Munster Report, East African Common Services Organisation and to answer questions at the end of his address.

Mr. Mulondo went on to say that he had hoped a copy of the white paper on the E.A. Common Services Organisation would have been issued by that time and he hoped that His Excellency would be able to supply a copy that morning.

In reply to the introduction, His Excellency intimated that he had read the minutes of the previous conference with great interest and congratulated the members on a very good and careful way in which the minutes had been prepared.

He continued that a white paper on the common services organisation was issued by Her Majesty's Government and it has received full publicity in the press at the time of its publication. He was surprised that the Secretaries General had not had a copy and he would certainly see that they received a copy when he got back to Entebbe.

His Excellency then proceeded on to read his speech a copy of which is attached to the minutes as appendix "A".

KSG/24/61 QUESTION TIME

1. Dr. Majugo asked how many representatives Buganda would have at the London Conference. To which His Excellence answered that the proposal is that Buganda should have the same number of representatives as each province i.e. 4 or 5. The figure had been based on population.

Mr. Kwebiha then asked if His Excellency was certain that Buganda would attend the London Conference. His Excellency answered that he was hopeful that they would and felt it would be wise for them to attend.

In reply to a question from Mr. Akena about the number, His Excellency said that it would be the Secretary of State who would decide the number of representatives.

His Excellency then went on to state that it was the Secretary of State's Conference and it is he who would issue invitations. Apart from the expense, there are indications of the limitation of space and that practice at such conferences is not to run them on voting basis. The whole purpose is to enable the Secretary of State to hear the views of the various representatives and then to try to reach generally agreed decisions.

Replying to a question from Mr. Baguma, Toro entreating His Excellency to take the question of the number of representatives seriously, His Excellency defined that by population he meant the whole population block size of Buganda as compared with the block size of other provinces.

2. Mr. Egweu, Teso, entreated His Excellency to inform the Conference if the Uganda Government supports the recommendations in the Report which grants the Lukiiko option to send indirectly elected representatives to the future National Assembly which shall be a directly elected body.

His Excellency answered that that was a matter still to be decided but the option offered to Buganda by the Report, in view of the recent past history, has neither been finalised by the Lukiiko nor by anyone else.

Mr. Kwebiha asked His Excellency to disclose what had been discussed at the preliminary conference with Buganda, to which His Excellency answered that it was within the general ambit of the Munster Report.

3. Question 3 about voting was pre-answered by His Excellency when answering question one in the penultimate paragraph.

4. Mr. Kirya asked why the London Conference should not be held in Uganda instead, to which His Excellency answered that the Secretary of State could not possibly spare the time to come to Uganda due to the pressure of work he has in his office.

5. Giving his opinion about the preliminary talks in Uganda, His Excellency said that he did not see any point in having preliminary talks in Uganda.

Mr. Akena then asked how the Secretary of State would assess the general feeling of the Conference since voting was not to take place. His Excellency adivised him to wait until he saw the Secretary of State in the Chair at work. He is very experienced at this kind of Conference and would be quite able to sense the general feeling and would give a very sound and fair deal.

From the chairman, a supplementary question was raised if the Secretary of State would sum up at the end of every session.

His Excellency answered that he could but if time made it impossible, the Secretariat would deal out by the following morning, draft minutes of the previous days proceedings.

6. Answering Mr. Okae's question about Bunyoro's petition on the lost counties, His Excellency said that he was not in a position to answer the question before the press and preferred to leave the matter until the Omukama reported on the recent discussions with the Secretary of State on the question of the Petition. But he said with certainty that the solution proposed by the Report would be carefully considered in London.

Mr. Kwebiha asked if the question would be discussed in or outside the London Conference, to which His Excellency answered that since it was not a matter for the plenary Conference, he thought the Secretary of State would wish to discuss it outside the Conference.

In answering the question of forwarding the lost counties issue to the Privy Council, His Excellency said that appeals could only be taken to the Privy Council on what was called justifiable issues.

7. Mr. Lubandi, Busoga asked if there would be close supervision in connection with the grants given to Buganda and if more funds would be made available to Local Governments.

His Excellency answered that there would be no distinction in the supervision, Buganda would be treated in the same way as the rest of the Protectorate but regarding the misuse of grants, a commission of enquiry would take up the matter and report accordingly.

He went on to say that as the Government has run into considerable deficit it was unlikely that there would be substantial increases in grants to Local Governments. At the same time, the Government realised that Local Governments would not be prepared to accept less than their present grants. In view of these difficulties, the Government set up a working party which was examining the issue.

8. Mr. Nganwa Ankole, asked if the recent talks with Buganda had bearing on the national assets on Buganda soil and whether Government would enter into another agreement with Buganda if the London Conference failed.

His Excellency replied that Buganda's attitude to the national assets in Buganda was a generous and realistic one and that there was no intention on the part of the Buganda to deprive the rest of the country of their use of the national assets.

Regarding the failure of the London Conference, he said that neither His Excellency nor the Secretary of State contemplated its failing. He believed it would succeed. The Secretary of State would hold the Conference whether people decide to boycott it. "We are equipped to go forward to our independence" he asserted. He stressed that the London Conference was a very genuine and sincere attempt to unite Uganda so that it can go forward to independence peacefully.

9. Question No. 9 was pre-answered in the first answer to question No. 8.

10. Mr. Okae asked about the misuse of powers by the Central Government Ministers who make their political tours semi-official thereby making civil servants their agents; and that the recent decision with regard to Kigezi was broadcast long before the Kigezi District Council knew about it whereas the political parties were aware of it.

His Excellency replied that there was no discourtesy intended in the case of Kigezi and that the Chief Minister found it necessary to make the decision known as soon as possible thus the statement was issued by wireless and in the press that day.

He undertook to inform the Chief Minister about the misuse of powers as explained by the chairman.

His Excellency informed the conference that the Governor should no longer be regarded as a Court of Appeal on the decisions of official Ministers but all the complaints about the Local Government should be directed to the Minister of Local Government who would report it to his colleagues and if necessary, he would bring it to the Cabinet. He continued that there was no use showering him with telegrams, he was no more almighty.

11. Mr. Wanyoto, Bugisu; asked His Excellency to give the status of the delegates going to London. To this His Excellency answered that it was not his conference but had no doubt the Colonial Secretary would spend the first day agreeing on the procedure and that the final decision at that stage of the constitutional development rest with Her Majesty's Government. It would therefore help the Colonial Secretary if the representatives were not inhabited in their views, but spoke freely so that the decisions taken had general measure of support throughout Uganda.

12. Mr. Esabu raised the question of a special court for a special Sector of people, to which His Excellency answered that it was proposed to have a uniform judicial system for the whole country gradually intergrating the African Courts and the Protectorate Courts—to be achieved in stages and that the first draft of it has been included in the basic paper and would be considered at the conference though it did not comply with the recommendation exactly. He continued that it was not intended that Buganda should have a particular type of court system whilst the rest of the Country has another, he intimated that not even the Baganda people themselves would like it.

13. Mr. Lutara asked if the basic papers for the London Conference could be distributed before the delegates left for the Conference. His Excellency answered that though he very much liked the delegates to study them before going to London, he could not say precisely when they would be ready for ditribution because of the long process of preparing them.

KSG/25/61 DISTRICTS BEING
REPRESENTED BY 3 DELEGATES

The Chairman said that as requested in his short address, the conference wanted to discuss the issue of 3 delegates from each district with His Excellency.

Both Messrs: Kwebiha and Mpambara put emphasis on the in-
adequacy of representation especially in the case of the delegates
falling sick.

His Excellency replied that the Chief purpose of the conference was
using the recommendations of the Report to evolve a constitution for
Uganda as a whole that would see the country safely through the next
constitutional stage to independence as the country hoped. He continued that it was most unlikely that the Secretary of State could meet
the demand of THREE or TWO representatives. Giving his opinion,
His Excellency thought the Secretary of State had gone a long way in
having a district representation at all.

KSG/26/61 VOTE OF THANKS

The Chairman called upon Mr. Lutara, Acholi to move a vote of
thanks to His Excellency.

(a) *Mr. Lutara Acholi*, thanked His Excellency the Governor
for his patience in answering so many question and for gracing
the conference with his presence. He hoped that the Governor's
name would go down in history as the last Governor of Uganda
who had governed the country so well and ably.

(b) *His Excellency* replied that he was very much touched by
what Mr. Lutara had said. He could see very many friends around
the conference table and he valued that friendship which continued
to this day.

They were doing all they could, His Excellency continued to bring
Uganda as quickly as they could to its independence.

They might have different points of view, but they all have one
common aim in view. Uganda was the best equipped to go forward
to independence, and it was his earnest wish that it would do so
peacefully and swiftly.

His Excellency left the Conference at 12.30 p.m.

KSG/27/61 DRAFT PAPERS ON THE MUNSTER REPORT

After some discussion about the issue, the conference passed the
following resolution:

THAT this conference urges the Governor of Uganda to send
to the various districts and members of this conference as soon as
possible the draft papers on the Munster Report which have been
prepared by the Commissioner on Special Duty as a basis for discussion at the London Conference so as to enable the people of
the said districts and members of the said conference to brief their
delegates to the said conference.

The Conference adjourned at 1.30 p.m.
The Conference resumed on the 17th August, 1961 at 9 a.m.
The meeting opened with prayer.

KSG/22/61 The Munster Report Continued)
   (b) *land Tennure* (page 172)
After some discussion, it was agreed that the recommendations
on land Tenure (i) Crown Land (ii) Land Boards (iii) Land in Towns
be accepted but regarding recommendation (iv) The smaller towns
should be administered by the District Councils until they grew to
municipality status, (v) Racial policy, (iv) Citizenship (vii) Expiring
Leases and (viii) Compulsory Acquisition were all accepted.

All land tenure proposals were accepted by the Conference.
   (c) *Human Rights (page 187).*
The Conference accepted the principles of this Appendix.
   (d) *Devolution of Powers:* It was agreed that it should be deleted
from the Agenda since the members did not wish to discuss it.

KSG/28/61 POSTMORTEM OF HIS EXCELLENCY'S ADDRESS
(A) *Misuse of papers by the Central Govt. Ministers*
When many delegates upon the issue and after a resolution proposed
by Mr. Akena and seconded by Mr. Kwebiha had been amended
several times, the following resolutions were passed:
1. Be it resolved:
       That this conference views with grave concern the recent
    events which have taken place as a result of inconsistent Govern-
    ment under similar circumstances in Local Government matters
    and these have created a sense of instability and insecurity in
    Local Government authorities.
   The following are instances of this:
    (a) When the Acholi District Council was unable to function
    because the quoram could not be formed because some members
    boycotted the meetings of the council the Government resolved
    the problem by reducing the quoram.
    (b) And yet when a similar situation arose in Bukedi, the Acholi
    precedent was not followed, but instead the Government
    dissolved the council
    (c) Furthermore, although the Kigezi District Council was
    properly constituted and functioning well inspite of the boycott
    by some members, yet the Government decided to dissolve
    the Council.
    (d) The Conference is also perturbed by the decision to elect

another Enganzi of Ankole after the expiration of only eight months of the 4 years appointment of the present Enganzi.

2. THAT this conference urges His Excellency the Governor to look into the question of misuse of powers by the Protectorate Government Ministers as put before him when he addressed the conference in Jinja.

(B) *The Lost Counties issue*

After a long discussion, the following resolution drafted by Dr. Majugo, was unanimously passed by the Conference after some amendments.

1.00–2.30 Interval.

Whereas it is now clear that Her Majesty's Government has evaded to give a decision on the Last Counties issue before going to the Uganda constitutional Conference in London: And whereas it is the view of this conference that it is likely there shall be serious trouble if Uganda attains independence before this matter is settled:

And whereas this conference has understood the historical mistake made by Her Majesty's Government in handing over the lost counties to Buganda.

And whereas this conference is greatly concerned about political tension going on within the Last Counties.

Now, therefore be it resolved:

That this conference urges Her Majesty's Gov't to rectify the mistake before the country attains her independence.

That this conference is strongly of the opinion that proposals for settling the matter such as recomended by the Munster Commission must be discussed at the forthcoming London Conference by all these taking part in the conference.

KSG/29/61 ANY OTHER BUSINESS

1. *Absence without apology*

It was unanimously resolved:

That in future, copies of the minutes of the Katikiros and Secretaries General Conference should not be sent to absent members without apology.

2. *Constitutional Safe Guard*

Mr. Mukambo Mpambara, Kigezi moved a motion that the Katikiros and Secretaries General Conference should be safeguarded in the future constitution.

It was agreed that the issue should be shelved until the next conference.

3. *Place and Date of Next Conference*

By 16 votes against 6 it was agreed that the next Conference should be held at Masindi during the period October/November, 1961 after the London Conference.

KSG/30/61 VOTE OF THANKS

(a) *Mr. Nganwa Enganzi of Ankole*, moved a vote of thanks to the chairman and all concerned for the manner in which the Conference had been conducted. He asked the chairman to convey the thanks of all members to those responsible for the use of the Hall accommodation etc, and to both Secretaries who had sat throughout the Conference.

(b) *The Chairman Mr. Y. K. Mulondo*

Secretary General of Busoga replied that he would pass on the kind remarks and thanks of all members to those concerned and said how pleased he had been. He would welcome them back at any future date.

APPENDIX 4

THE 18 POINTS GIVEN BY THE UGANDA ARMY
UNDER MAJOR GENERAL AMIN IN JUSTIFICATION
FOR TAKING OVER POWERS OF GOVERNMENT
ON 25th JANUARY 1971*

1. The unwarranted detention without trial and for long periods of a large number of people, many of whom are totally innocent of any charges.

2. The continuation of a state of emergency over the whole country for an indefinite period which is meaningless to everybody.

3. The lack of freedom in the airing of different views on political and social matters.

4. The frequent loss of life and property arising from almost daily cases of robbery with violence and kondoism without strong measures being taken to stop them. The people feel totally insecure, and yet Kondoism increases everyday.

5. The proposals for National Service which will take every able bodied person from his home to work in a camp for two years, could only lead to more robbery, and general crime when homes are abandoned.

6. Widespread corruption in high places, especially among Ministers and top civil servants has left the people with very little confidence, if any, in the Government. Most Ministers own fleets of cars or buses, many big Houses, and sometimes even aeroplanes.

7. The failure by the political authorities to organise any election for the last eight years whereby the people's free will could be expressed. It should be noted that the last election within the ruling party were dominated by big fellows with lots of money which they used to bribe their way into "winning" the elections. This bribery, together with threats against the people entirely falsified the results of the socalled elections. Proposed new methods of election requiring a candidate to stand in four constituencies will only favour the rich and the well known.

8. Economic policies have left many people unemployed and even more insecure and lacking in basic needs of life like food, clothing, medicine and shelter.

9. High taxes have left the common man of this country poorer than ever before. Here are some of the taxes which the common man has to bear:

DEVELOPMENT TAX
GRADUATED TAX
SALES TAX
SOCIAL SECURITY FUND TAX

The big men can always escape these taxes or pass them on to common man.

10. The prices which the common man gets for his crops like cotton and coffee have not gone up and sometimes they have gone down whereas the cost of food, education, etc. have always gone up.

11. Tendency to isolate the country from East African Unity, e.g. by sending away workers from Kenya and Tanzania, by preventing the use of Uganda money in Kenya and Tanzania, by discouraging imports from Kenya and Tanzania, by stopping the use in Uganda of Kenya and Tanzania money.

12. The creation of wealthy class of leaders who are always talking of socialism while they grow richer and the common man poorer.

13. In addition, the defence council of which the President is the Chairman, has not met since July 1969 and this has made administration in the Armed Forces very difficult. As a result Armed forces Personnel lack accommodation, vehicles, and equipment. Also general recruitment submitted to the chairman of Defence Council a long time ago has not been put into effect.

14. The Cabinet office, by training large number of people (largely from the Akokoro County in Lango District where Obote and Akena Adoko, the chief General Service Officer come from) in armed warfare has been turned into a second army. Uganda therefore had two armies, one in the Cabinet, the other regular.

15. The Lango development master plan, written in 1967 decided that all key positions in Uganda's Political, Commercial, army and industrial life have to be occupied and controlled by people from Akokoro county, Lango District. Also the same master plan decided that nothing must be done for other districts especially Acholi District. Emphasis was put on developing Akokoro county in Lango District at the expense of other areas of Uganda.

16. Obote on the advice of Akena Adoko has sought to devide the Uganda Armed Forces and the rest of Uganda by picking out his tribesmen and putting them in key positions in the Army and everywhere. Examples: The Chief General Service Officer, the Export and Import Corporation, Uganda Meat Packers, the Public Service Commission, Nyanza Textiles and a Russian Textile Factory to be situated in Lango.

17. From the time Obote took over power, 1962, his greatest and most loyal supporter has been the Army. The Army has always

tried to be an example to the whole of Africa by not taking over the Government and we have always followed this principle. It is therefore now a shock to us to see that Obote wants to divide and downgrade the Army by turning the Cabinet Office into another Army. In doing this, Obote and Akena Adoko have bribed and used some Senior Officers who have turned against their fellow soldiers.

18. We all want only Unity in Uganda and we do not want bloodshed. Everybody in Uganda knows that. The matters mentioned above appear to us to lead to bloodshed only.

For the reasons given above we men of Uganda Armed Forces have this day decided to take over power from Obote and hand it to our fellow soldier Major-General Idi Amin Dada and we hereby entrust him to lead this our beloved country of Uganda to peace and goodwill among all.

We call everybody and Government departments in Uganda to continue with their work in the normal way.

We warn all foreign Governments not to interfere in Uganda's Internal Affairs. Any such interference will be crushed with great force, because we are ready.

We are firm believers in the Unity of East Africa and of Africa in general and we shall cement our friendship with neighbouring and all African countries and the world at large, more than ever before. For the moment a curfew is necessary and will be observed by everybody between 7 p.m. and 6.30 a.m. from now everyday until further notice.

Power is now handed over to our fellow soldier Major-General Idi Amin Dada, and you must await his statement which will come in due course.

WE HAVE DONE THIS FOR GOD AND OUR COUNTRY.

Uganda Argus (Kampala), 26th January 1971.